IRON MAIDEN

THE READING PERFORMANCES

Neil Daniels

IRON MAIDEN

THE READING PERFORMANCES

Neil Daniels

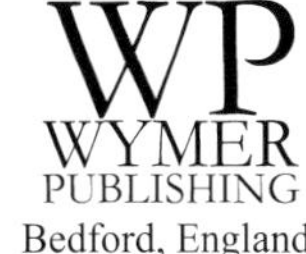

WP
WYMER
PUBLISHING
Bedford, England

First published in Great Britain in 2018
by Wymer Publishing as Iron Maiden At Reading
ISBN: 978-1-908724-92-2 (limited edition hardback in metal flight case with prints)

www.wymerpublishing.co.uk
Wymer Publishing is a trading name of Wymer (UK) Ltd
Tel: 01234 326691

*"I tend not to look back too much; I tend to look forward.
So, I suppose, I know, we've had a fantastic career, so if it ended tomorrow,
it's been amazing, and I can live with that."*
Steve Harris

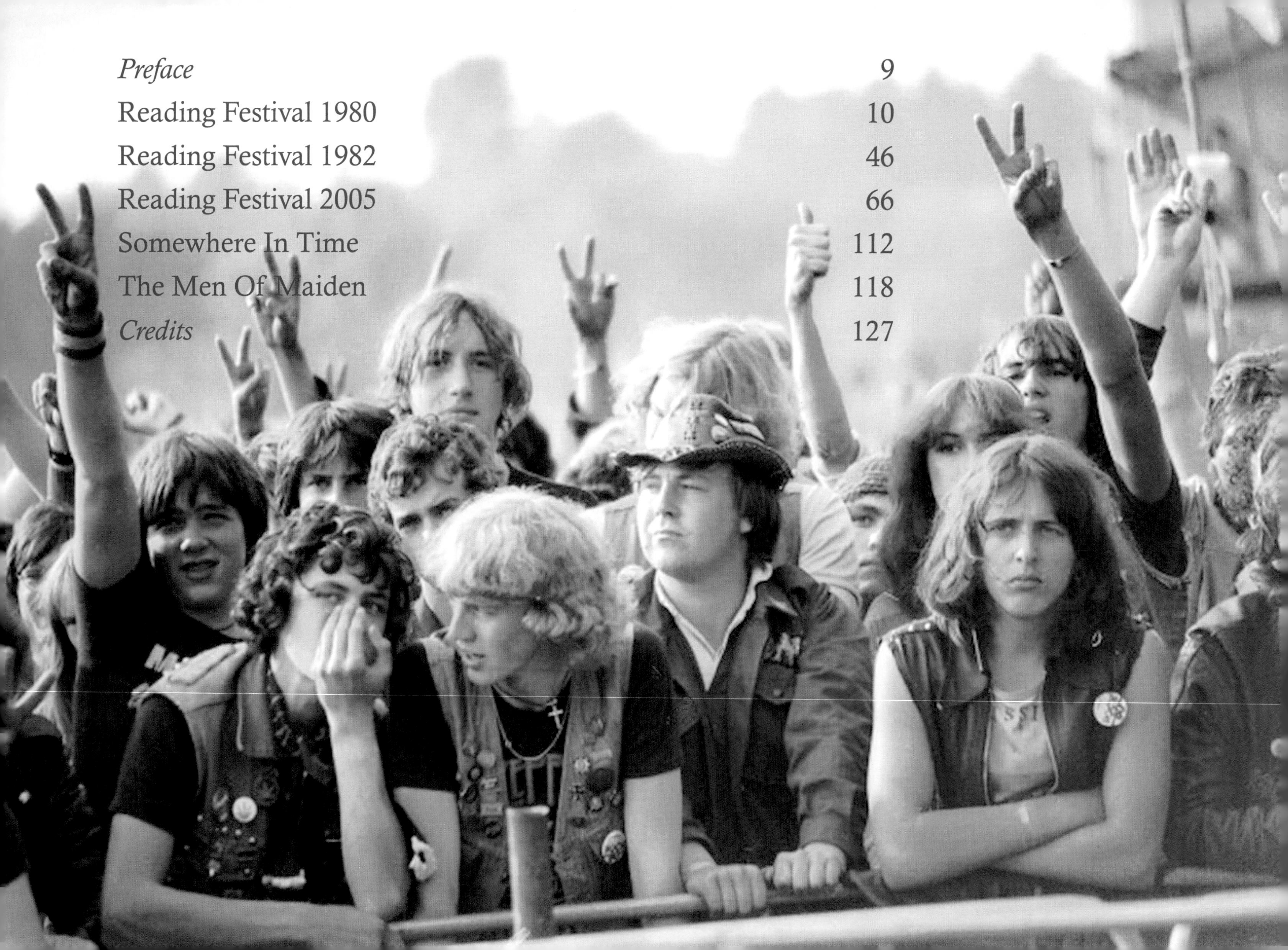

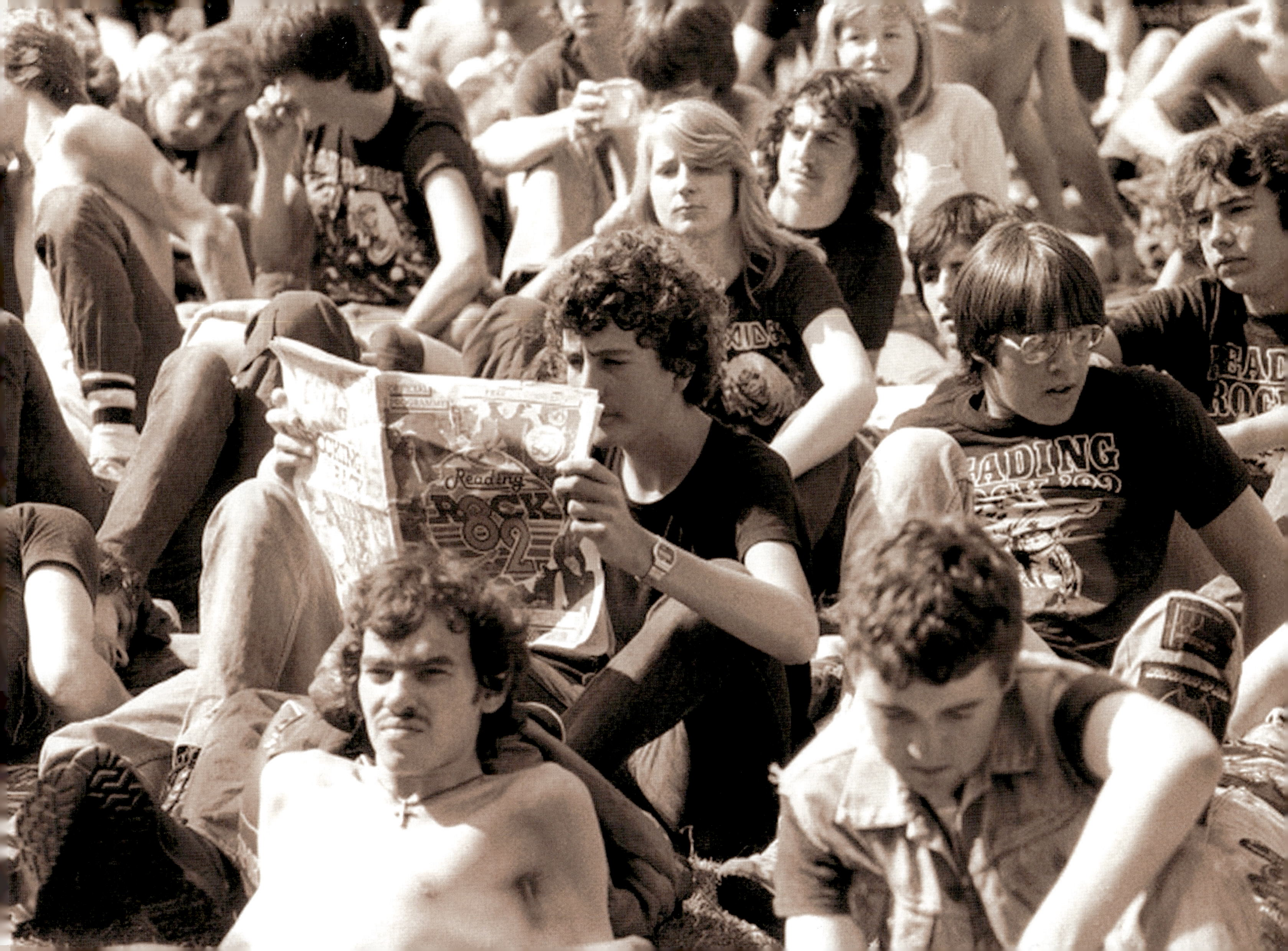

"...the most interesting things that happen in your life tend to be the first things that happen to you."

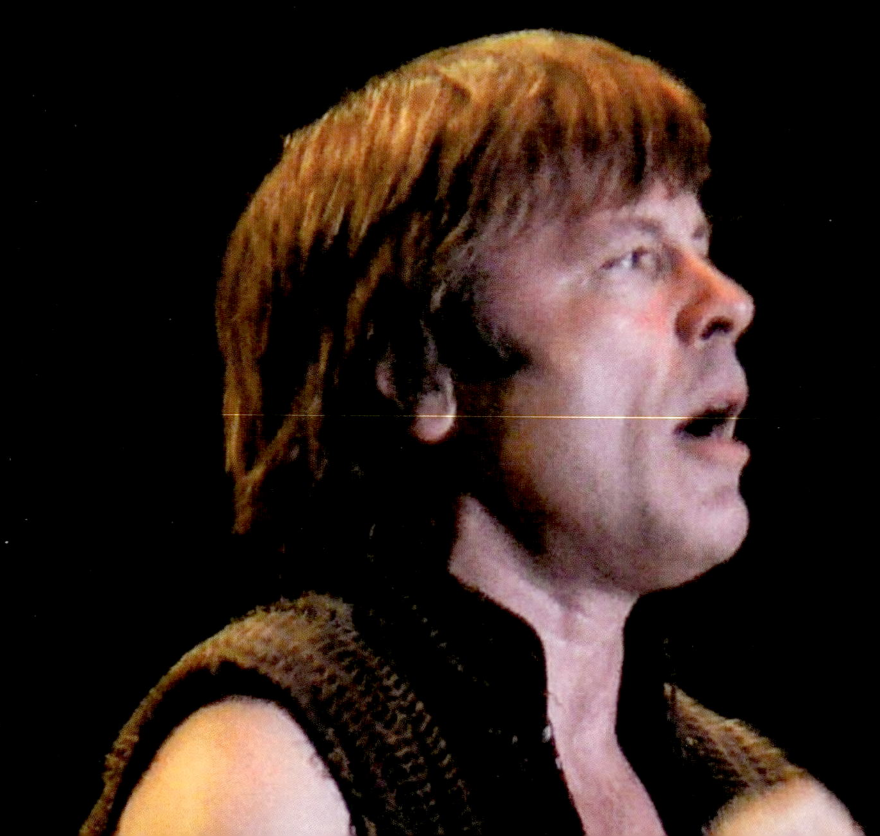

PREFACE

Said legendary Iron Maiden singer and modern day Renaissance Man Bruce Dickinson to the BBC. "So the first time I headlined Reading festival, it was like, 'Wow!' The first time you headline Donington, 'Wow!' I don't know how many times we've headlined Donington now. Quite a few. So when somebody says, 'Oh, you're gonna headline Donington,' you're, 'Oh, cool'."

The all-powerful heavy metal conquerors Iron Maiden formed in London's East End in 1975 but it took several line-up changes before they cemented their status as pioneers of the now legendary New Wave Of British Heavy Metal movement that lasted from around 1979 to about 1981. As with all musical movements the NWOBHM was just a short period of time but it spawned many great (and not-so-great) bands. It's impact on metal cannot be overstated and neither can that of Iron Maiden.

While Maiden's first two albums – *Iron Maiden* and *Killers* – are iconic in their own way it was not until former Samson singer Bruce Dickinson replaced Paul Di'Anno in 1981 that Maiden's flight to success truly took off. And man, would Maiden take the world by its balls.

The iconic trilogy of *The Number Of The Beast* (1982,) *Piece Of Mind* (1983) and *Powerslave* (1984) gave the band worldwide fame and success in North America. The aforementioned albums are often included in 'greatest heavy metal albums' polls and they have lost none of their impact over 30 years later. 1988's *Seventh Son Of A Seventh Son* was also a masterpiece after the somewhat experimental *Somewhere In Time* in 1986.

While the band suffered from a downward slide in the mid nineties after the departure of Bruce Dickinson and the hiring of ex Wolfsbane Blaze Bayley, Maiden steadily made a comeback beginning with 2000's reunion album *Brave New World,* and indeed right up to the end of the decade the band began re-building their career. In 2018, they are quite simply a force to be reckoned with and are arguably Britain's finest metal outfit with the ultimate line-up of Steve Harris, Bruce Dickinson, Dave Murray, Adrian Smith, Nicko McBrain and Janick Gers.

They are not just a masterful recording band but a live band of the utmost professionalism. They represent heavy metal at its most brilliant.

Their three Reading Festival appearances have gone down in the history books for various reasons. Reading appeared to offer the band a number of opportunities that would help them cement their iconic line-up of the 1980s and beyond.

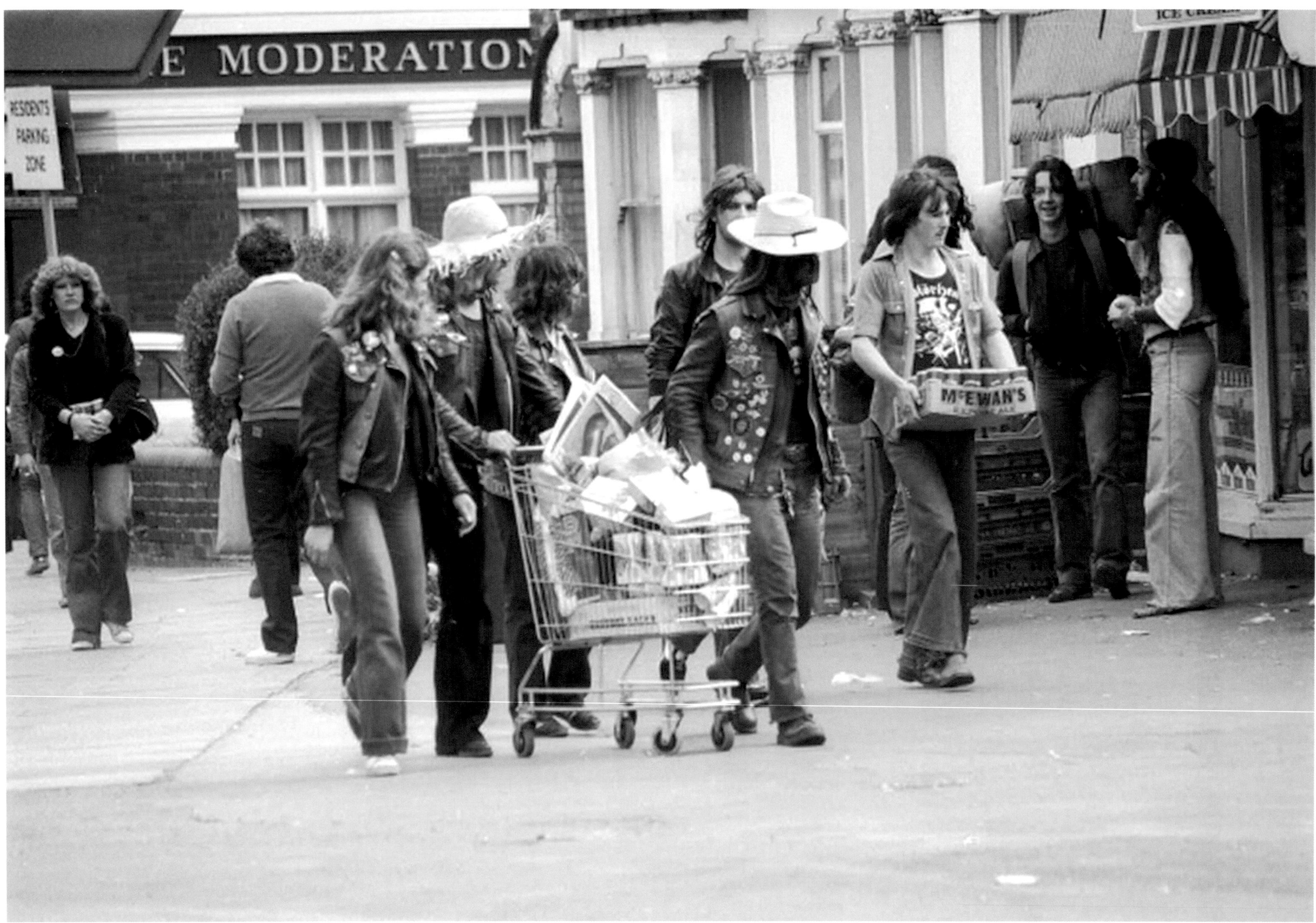
E MODERATION
ICE CREAM
RESIDENTS PARKING ZONE
McEWAN'S

Reading Festival 1980

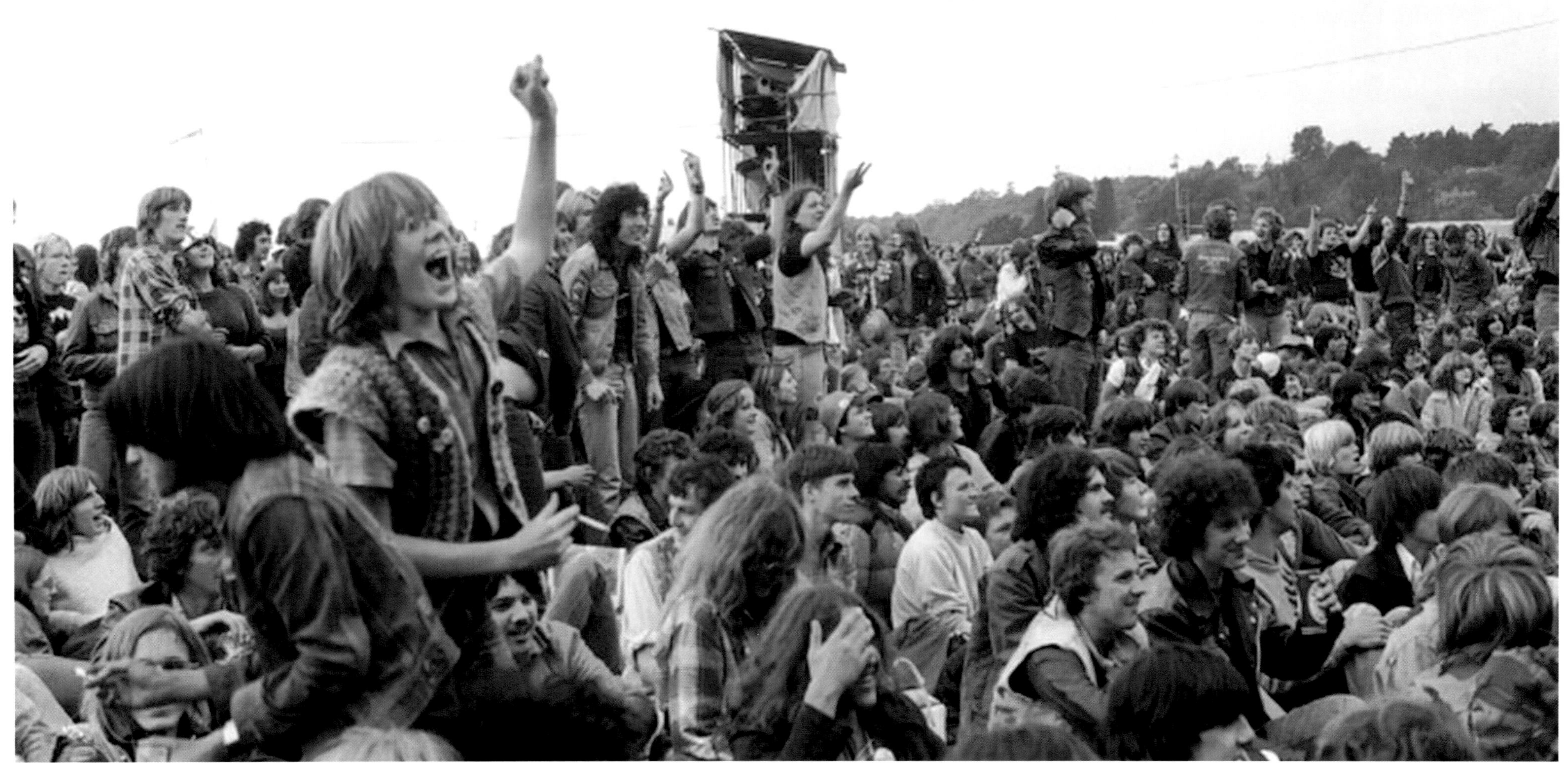

Festivals can make or break a band. They provide the perfect platform for up and coming bands to gain the attention of a new, hungry audience wanting some blood-thirsty rock and roll. They can also be nerve-wracking experiences. Stories of artists being "bottled" and booed off stage have plagued festivals since the early beginnings of live music. But that is part of the game. Reading Festival was an integral part of the early years of Iron Maiden. They showed naysayers exactly what they could do and boy did they woo audiences. But first, a little back story is needed.

The year was 1979 when a particularly hacked-off Satan unleashed hordes of possessed metal musicians to wreck havoc on the popular music scene. Those who are familiar with this notorious period in the annals of rock music are well aware of its true origins and of the effect it would have in the UK and the rest of

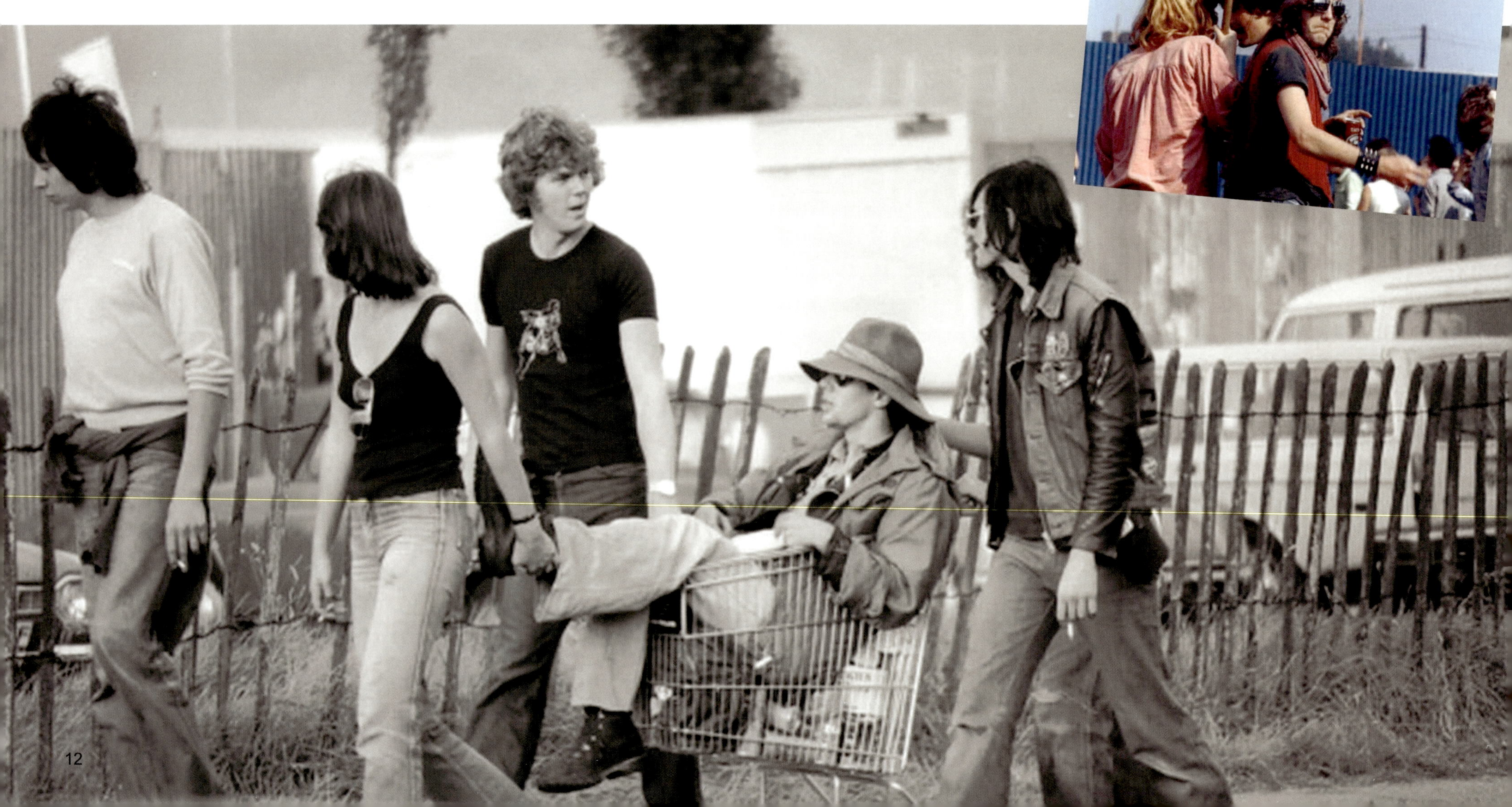

the unassuming world.

This brilliantly conceived tale of bloodthirsty excitement and incredibly loud, fast music spawned most famously, Def Leppard, Saxon, Venom and many more bands from all over the British Isles. Yet it was the East End Londoners, Iron Maiden who became the most popular, commercially successful and world domineering metal act; a power they still possess to this day.

By 1980 Iron Maiden had become the biggest band of the NWOBHM. There wasn't an act like them.

The first leg of the *Iron Maiden* Tour in support of their self-titled debut wound up with a string of dates at the Marquee club in the Big Smoke in mid July. They played three dates, although the band claims seven. However, all narratives of anyone/everyone involved refer to three gigs in a row at the Marquee, though the band lists seven on their tour history.

And then on July 19 they performed in Oulu, Finland at the Kussrock Festival. They were thrilled with the response they got abroad with fans greeting them outside the venues holding banners saying 'Iron Maiden Go Over The Top'. It was evident that word of mouth hand spread to mainland Europe from the UK. The band were not even aware of how popular they were in some European countries. Their couple of trips outside of the UK was a bona-fide success.

Singer Paul Di'Anno continued to struggle with his voice possibly due to the increasing vocal register of the band's live shows. Burr contracted food poisoning before a gig in Edinburgh and it was so bad he wasn't advised to perform but the band's chief driver and roadie Vic Vella dragged him out of bed with some of the other roadies to and got him to the stage. He fainted at the end of the gig. The band's first headlining tour, though, was a roaring success and included their first ever headline performance at the Rainbow on June 20. They'd even appeared on TV for an episode of ITV's *Twentieth Century Box* which focused on "New Wave Metal" that was aired on August 18 and featured clips of Maiden performing at the

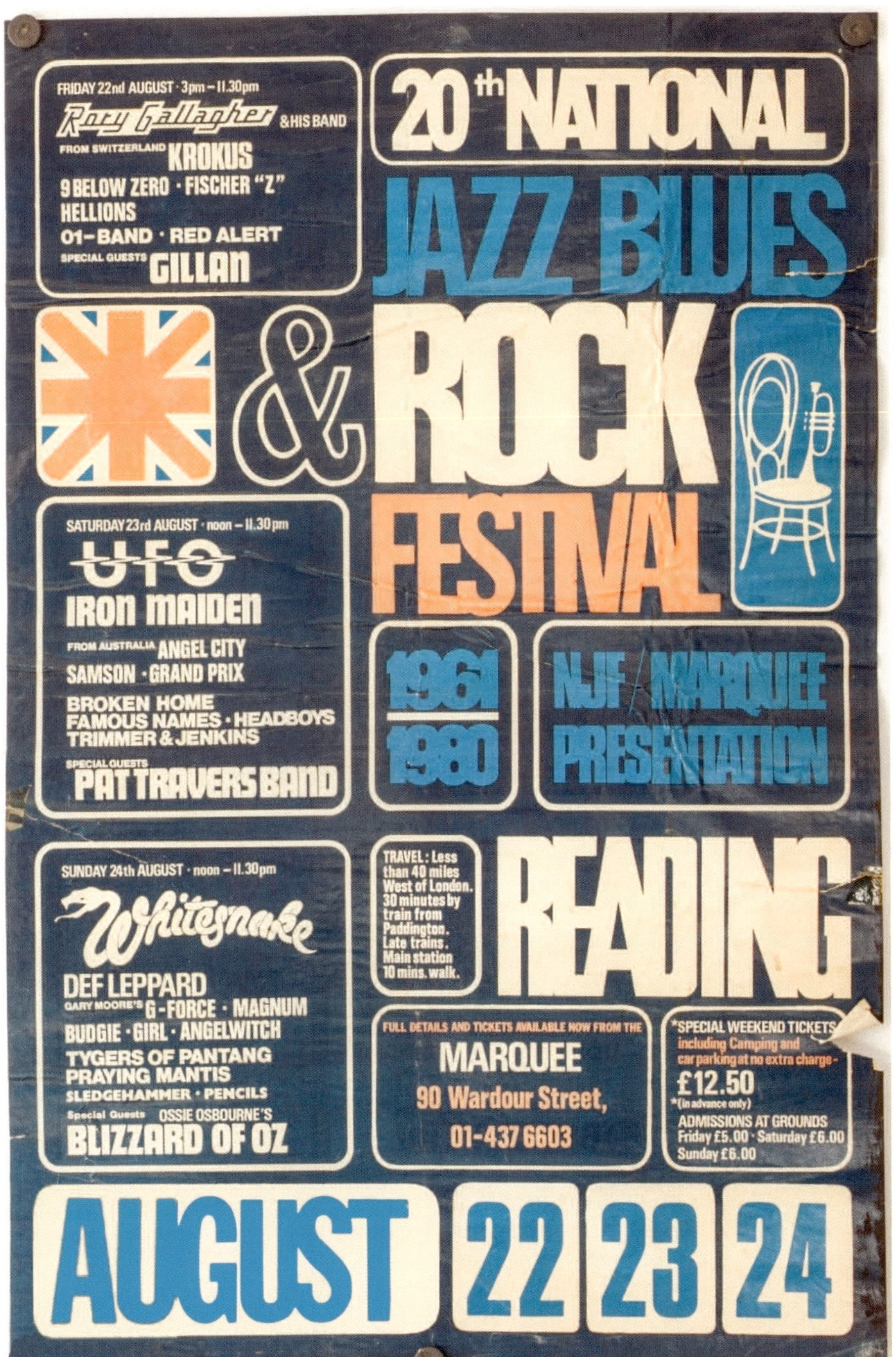

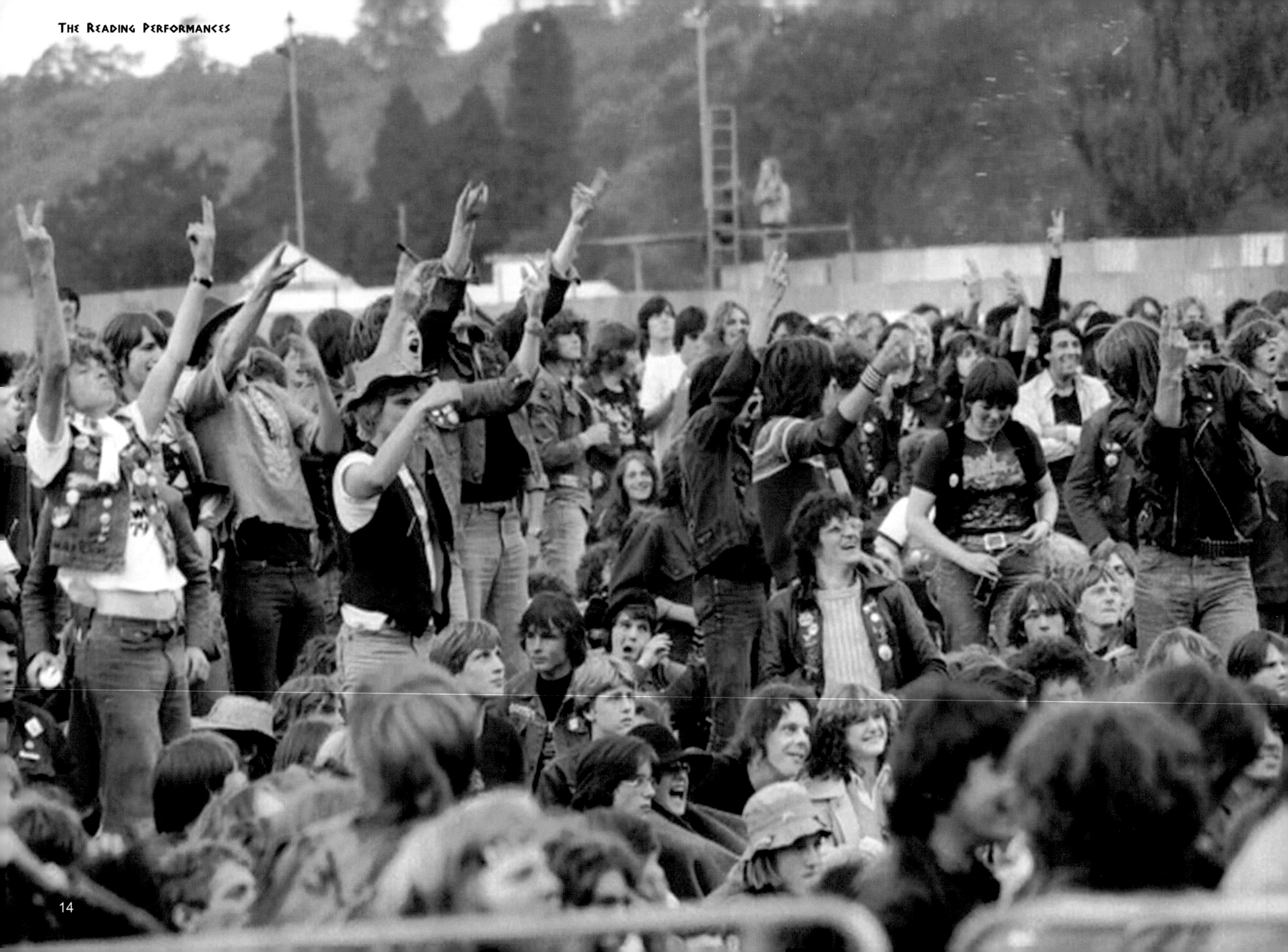

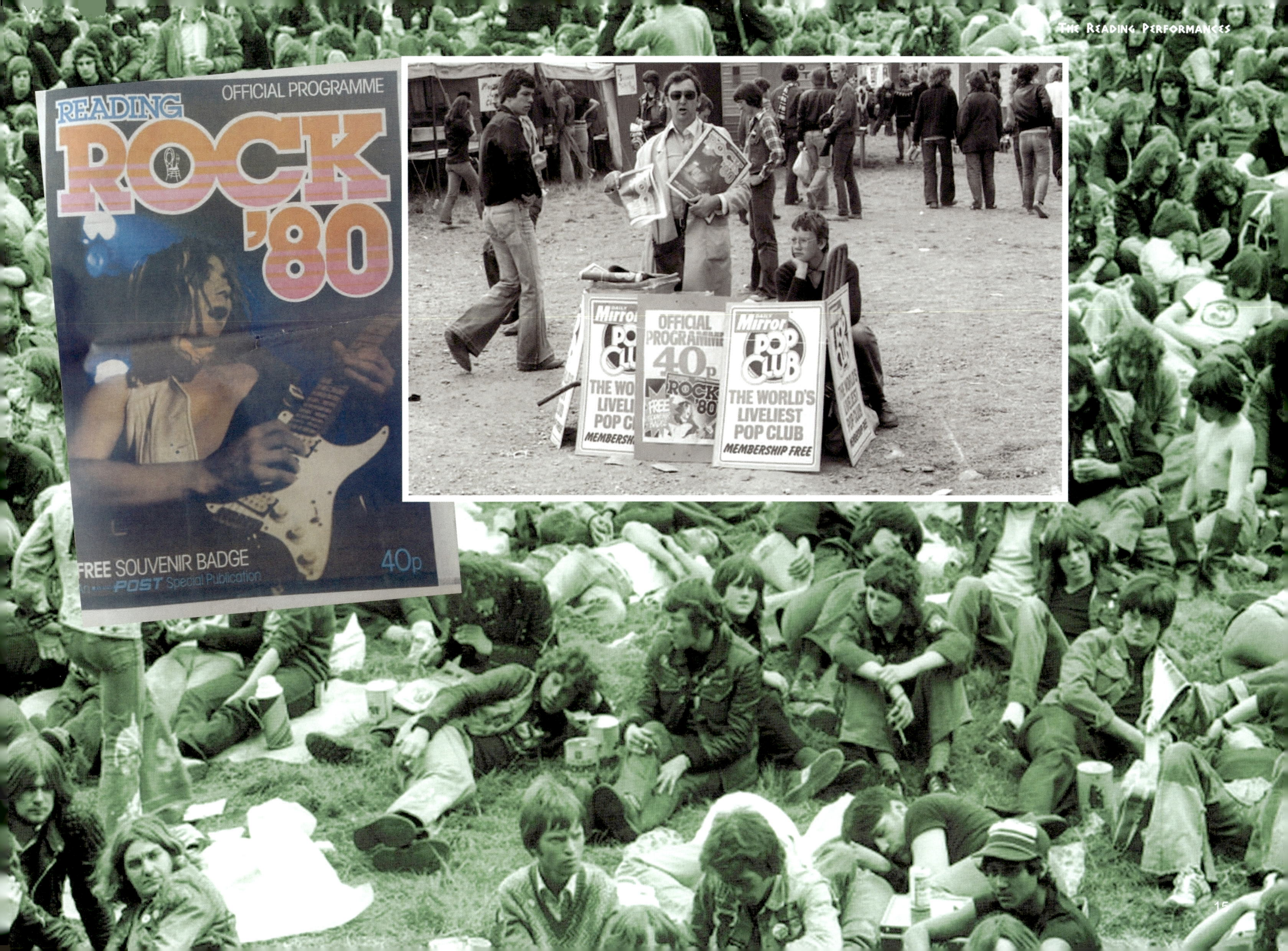

OFFICIAL PROGRAMME
READING ROCK '80
FREE SOUVENIR BADGE
POST Special Publication
40p

DAILY Mirror POP CLUB
OFFICIAL PROGRAMME 40p
ROCK '80
DAILY Mirror POP CLUB
THE WORLD'S LIVELIEST POP CLUB
MEMBERSHIP FREE

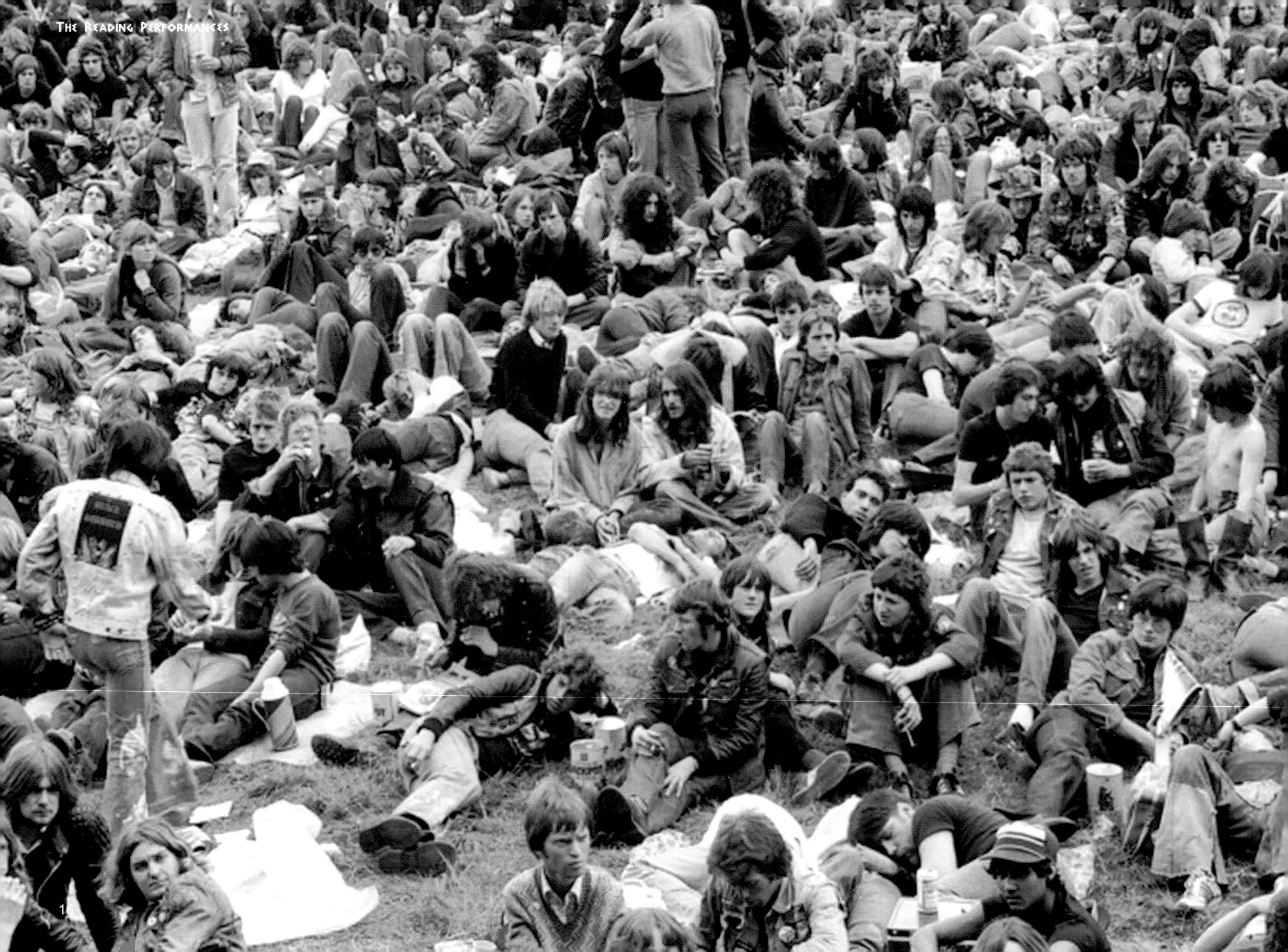

Marquee that had been filmed earlier on in the tour. Maiden played a couple of shows in London and West Runton in mid August before an all-important slot at the Reading Festival on August 23.

The Harris/Di'Anno/Murray/Stratton/Burr line-up journeyed through 'Sanctuary', 'Wrathchild', 'Prowler', 'Remember Tomorrow', 'Killers', 'Running Free', 'Transylvania', 'Phantom Of The Opera', 'Iron Maiden' and 'Drifter'. Christ, did they hit the nail on the head with a truly indelible show. It was as if Maiden had been

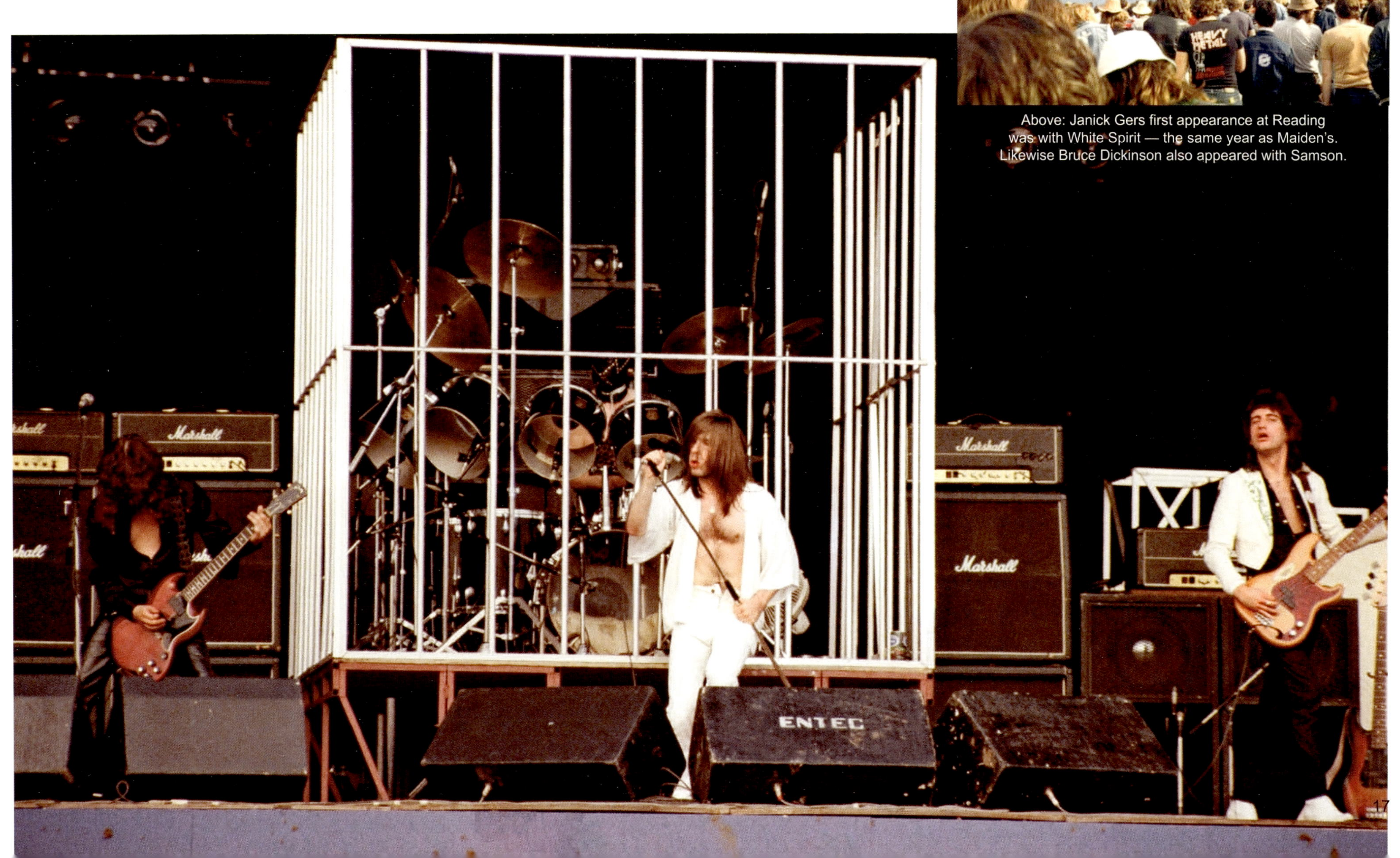

Above: Janick Gers first appearance at Reading was with White Spirit — the same year as Maiden's. Likewise Bruce Dickinson also appeared with Samson.

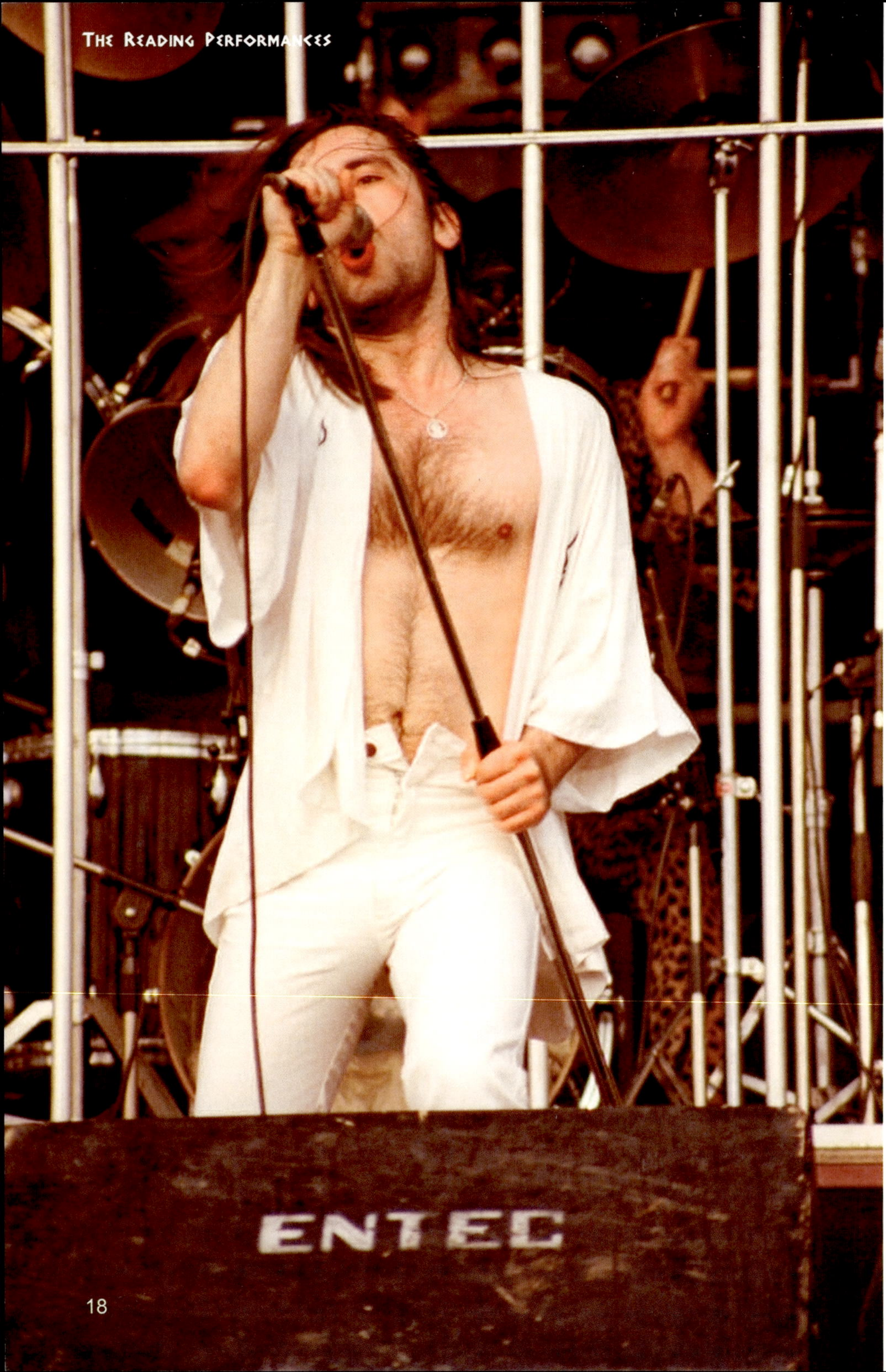

Bruce Dickinson with Samson at Reading the year before he joined Maiden. At the time he referred to himself as Bruce Bruce. Rod Smallwood was not endeared by this and was adamant that it wasn't the way for Maiden.

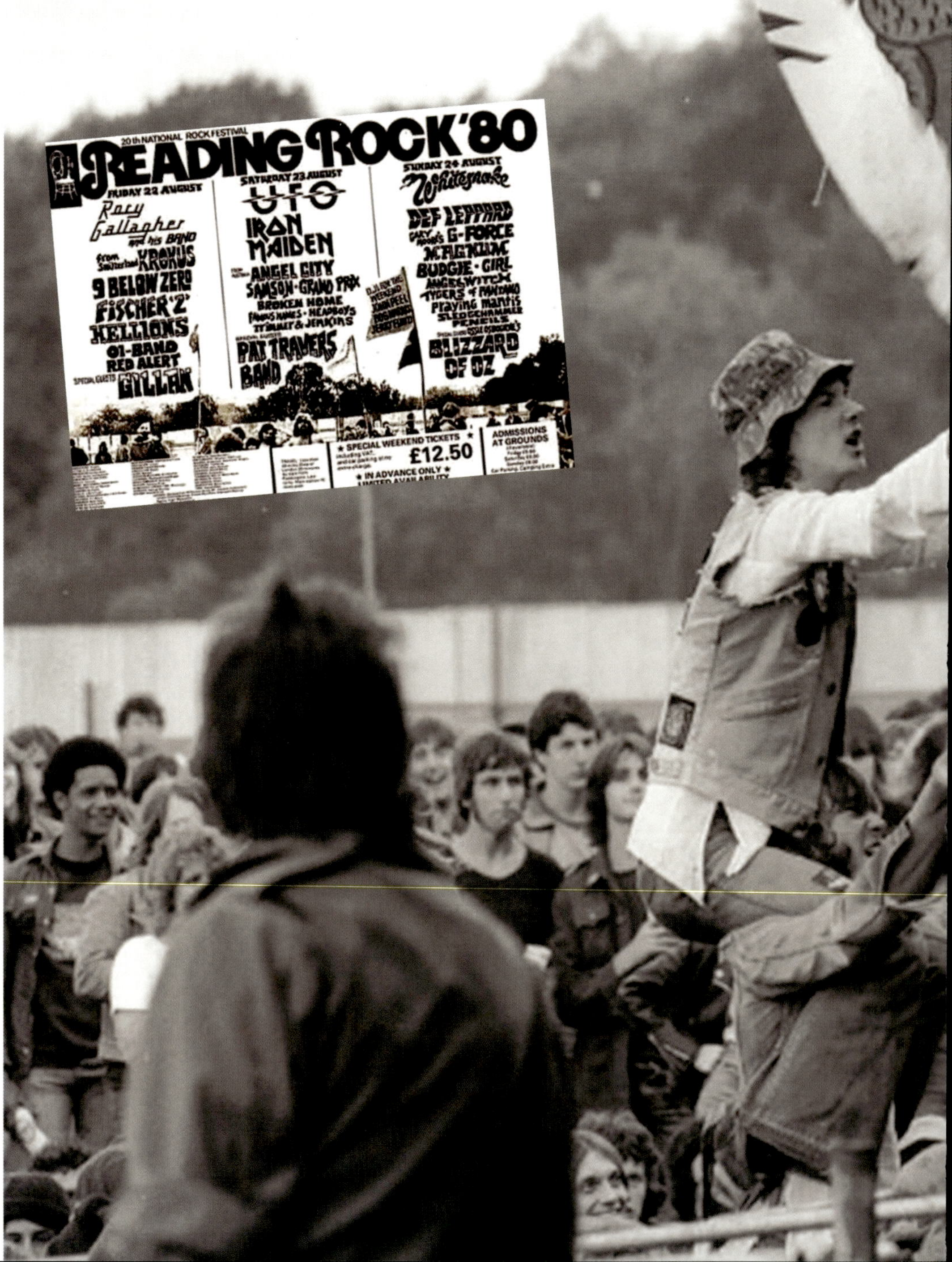

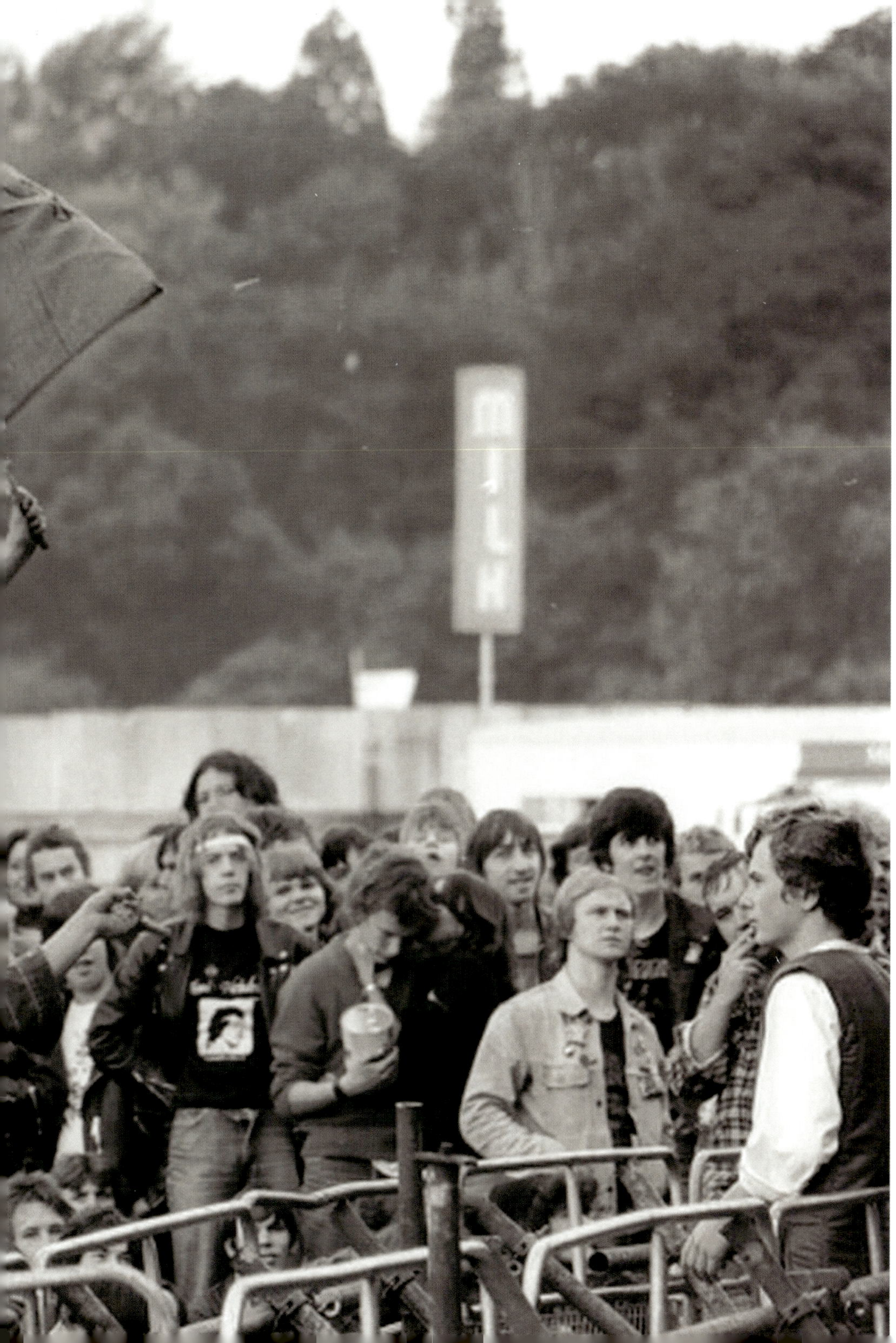

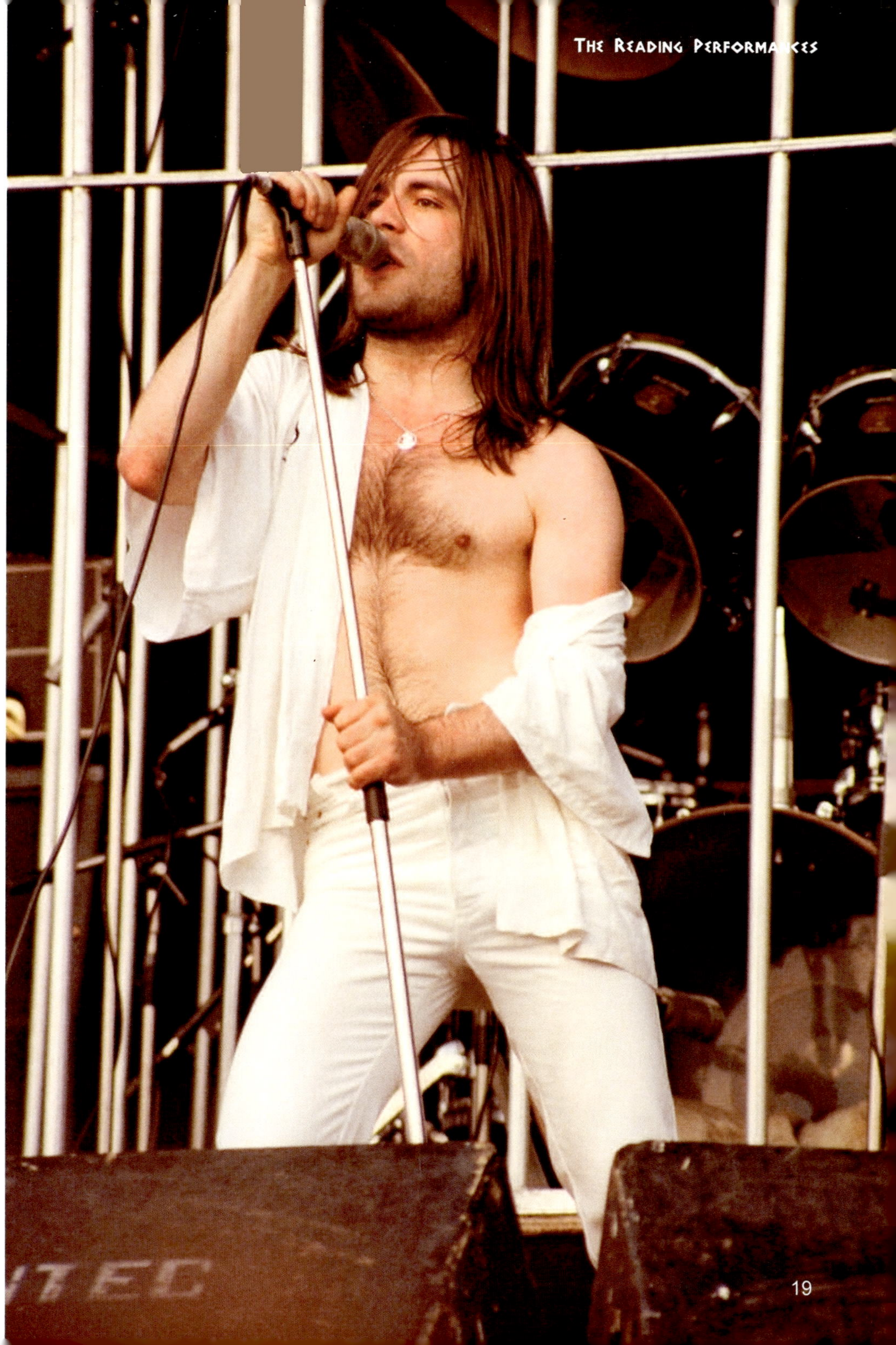

performing for decades.

Originally a Jazz Festival dating back to the 1950s Reading has become one of the UK's — and indeed the world's — most enduring and prestigious festivals. By the 1970s Reading had become the hotbed of the latest progressive rock bands. Progressive in the sense of its innovation as opposed to the movement with bands such as Yes and ELP. Reading was the first festival to fully embrace punk and saw such bands as Sham 69 and The Stranglers perform on its stages. Where else in the UK would you see Status Quo perform on the same bill as New York punk iconic Patti Smith and British New Wave band The Jam in 1978? 1979 then saw German hard rockers Scorpions perform along with upcoming New Wave act The Police. Inevitably the punk and New Wave fans clashed with the heavy metal enthusiasts just as the Mods and Rockers had in the sixties. The fans were passionate. By the early 1980s though, Reading had become the place for the latest hard rock and heavy metal bands to perform. Enter Iron Maiden.

Reading Festival was the place where rock fans could check out the hottest new bands in the pre-internet age and when there wasn't any "metal press" other than the hallowed pages or *Sounds* and *Melody Maker*. Maiden were second on the bill to headliner's UFO. The band featured the same line-up as that on their self-titled opus: bassist Steve Harris, Dave Murray and Dennis Stratton on guitars and Clive Burr on drums.

The performance can be found on the 2002 *BBC Archives* collection and remains a cherished part of any metal fans collection. The festival also featured Friday headliners Rory Gallagher, Saturday headliners UFO and Whitesnake on Sunday 24. Slade, Pat Travers, Krokus and Def Leppard were also on the mouth watering bill though five bands (G-Force, Ozzy Osbourne's new solo band Blizzard Of Oz, Angel

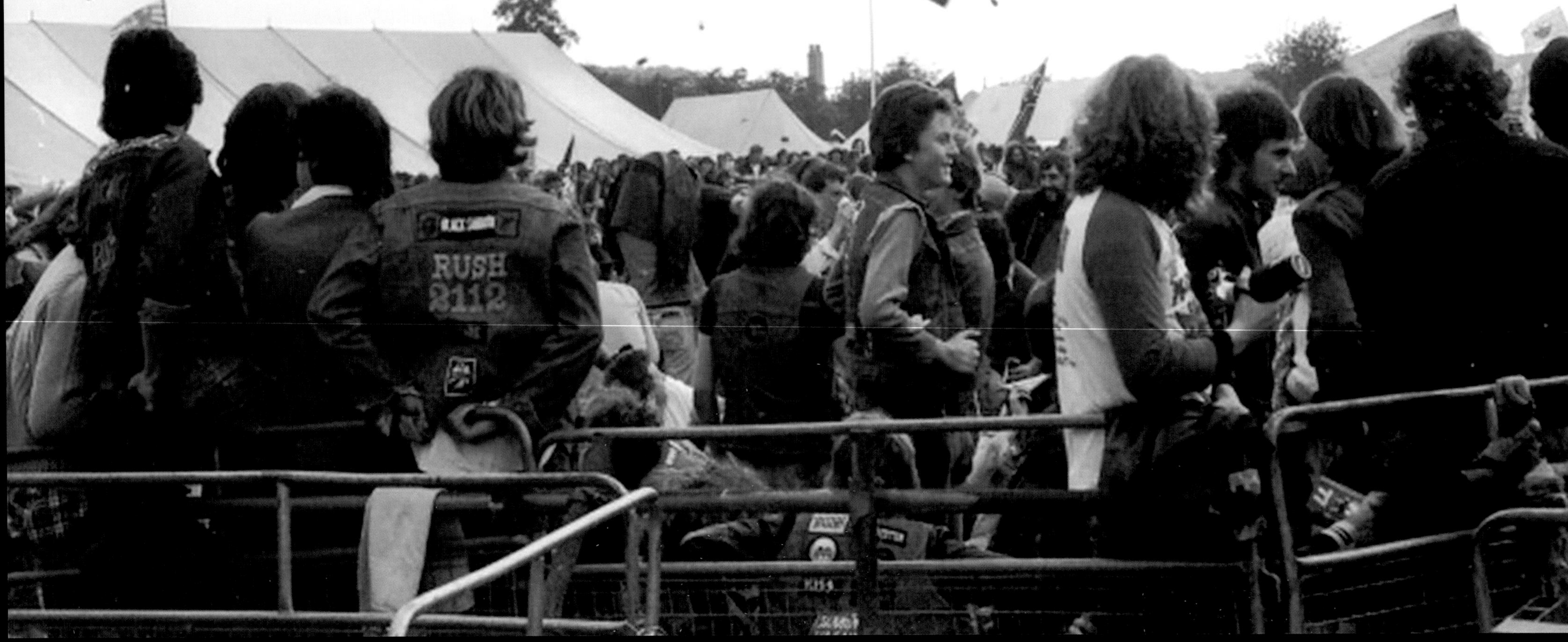

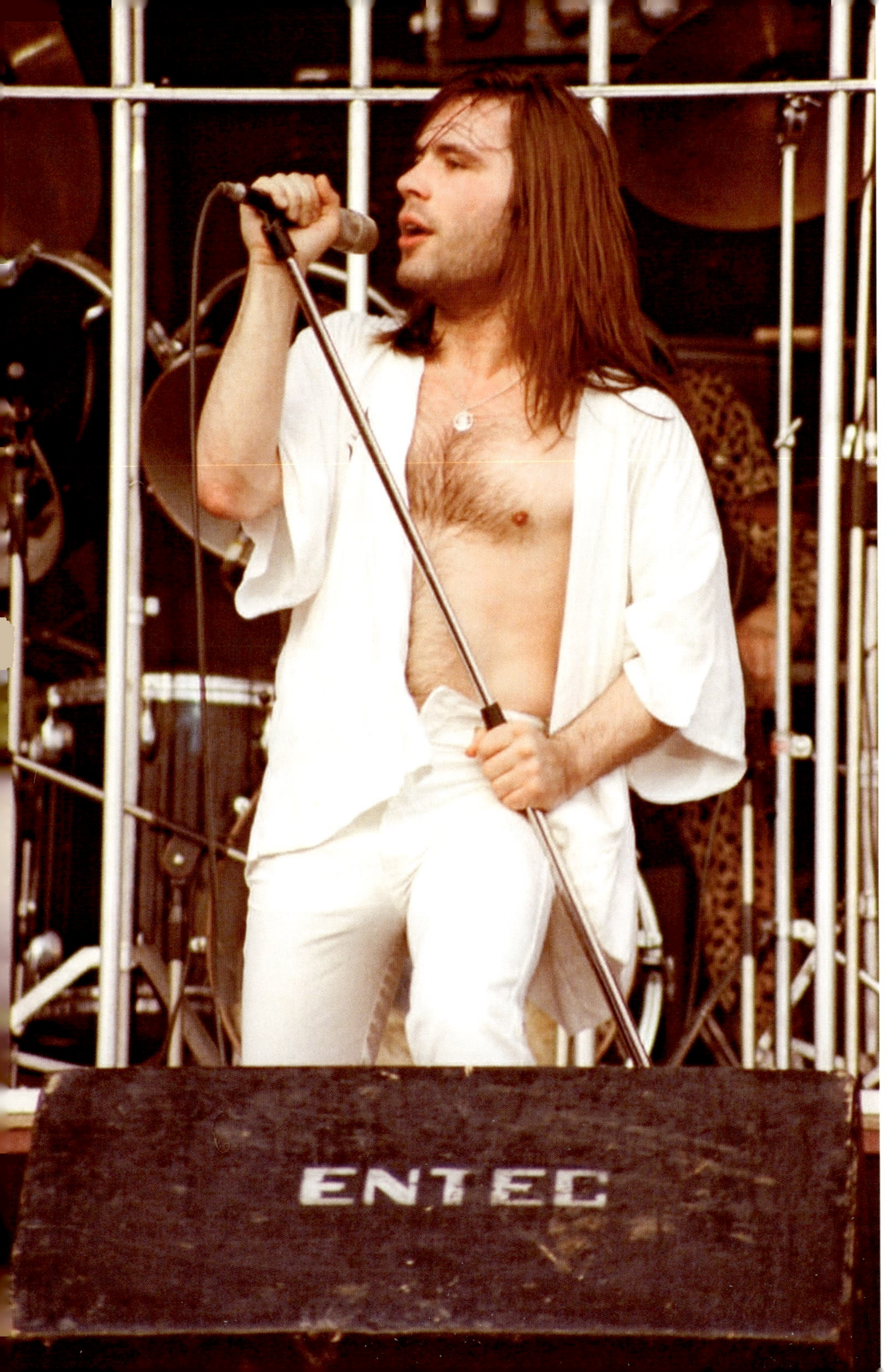

ENTEC

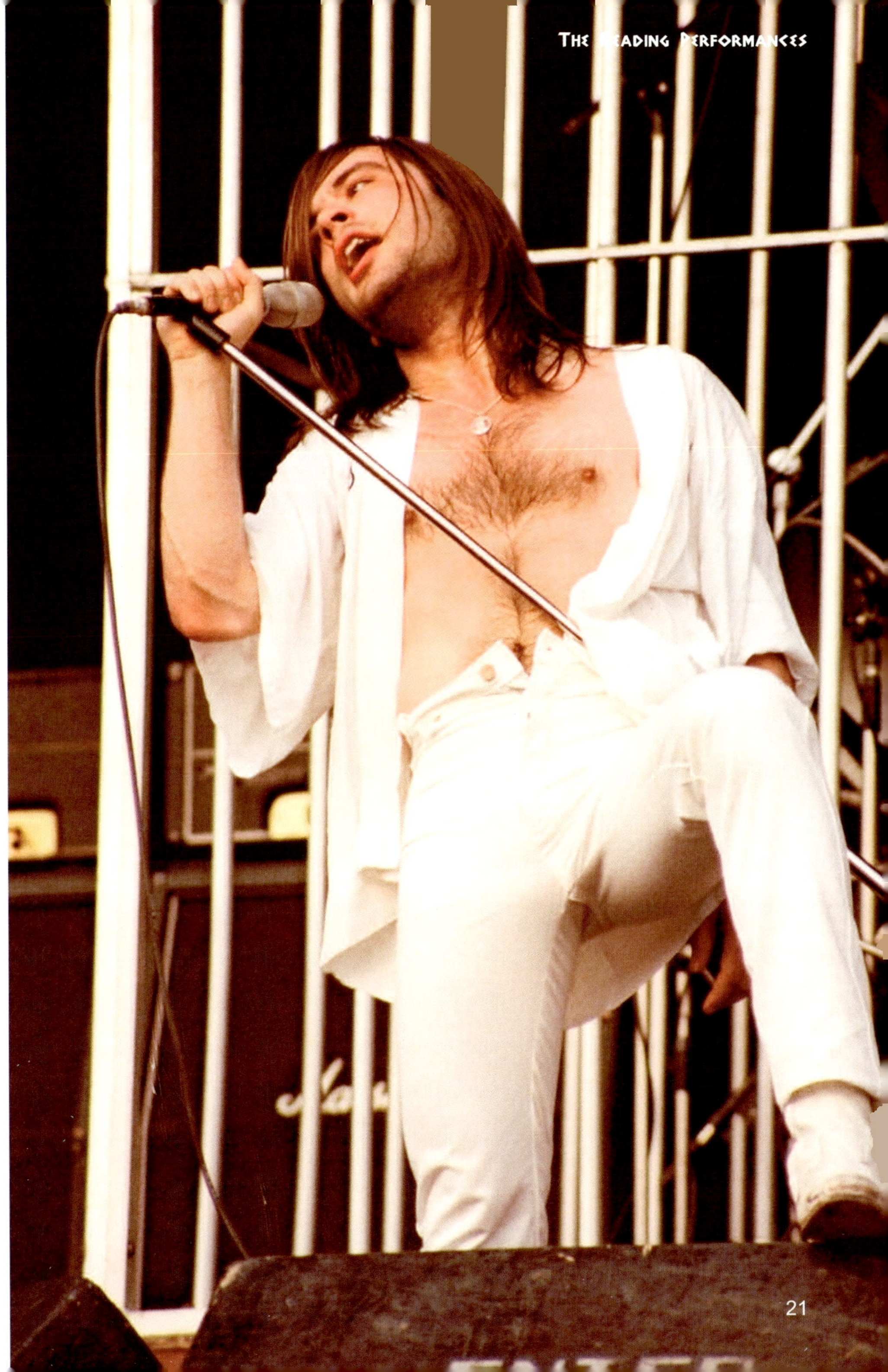

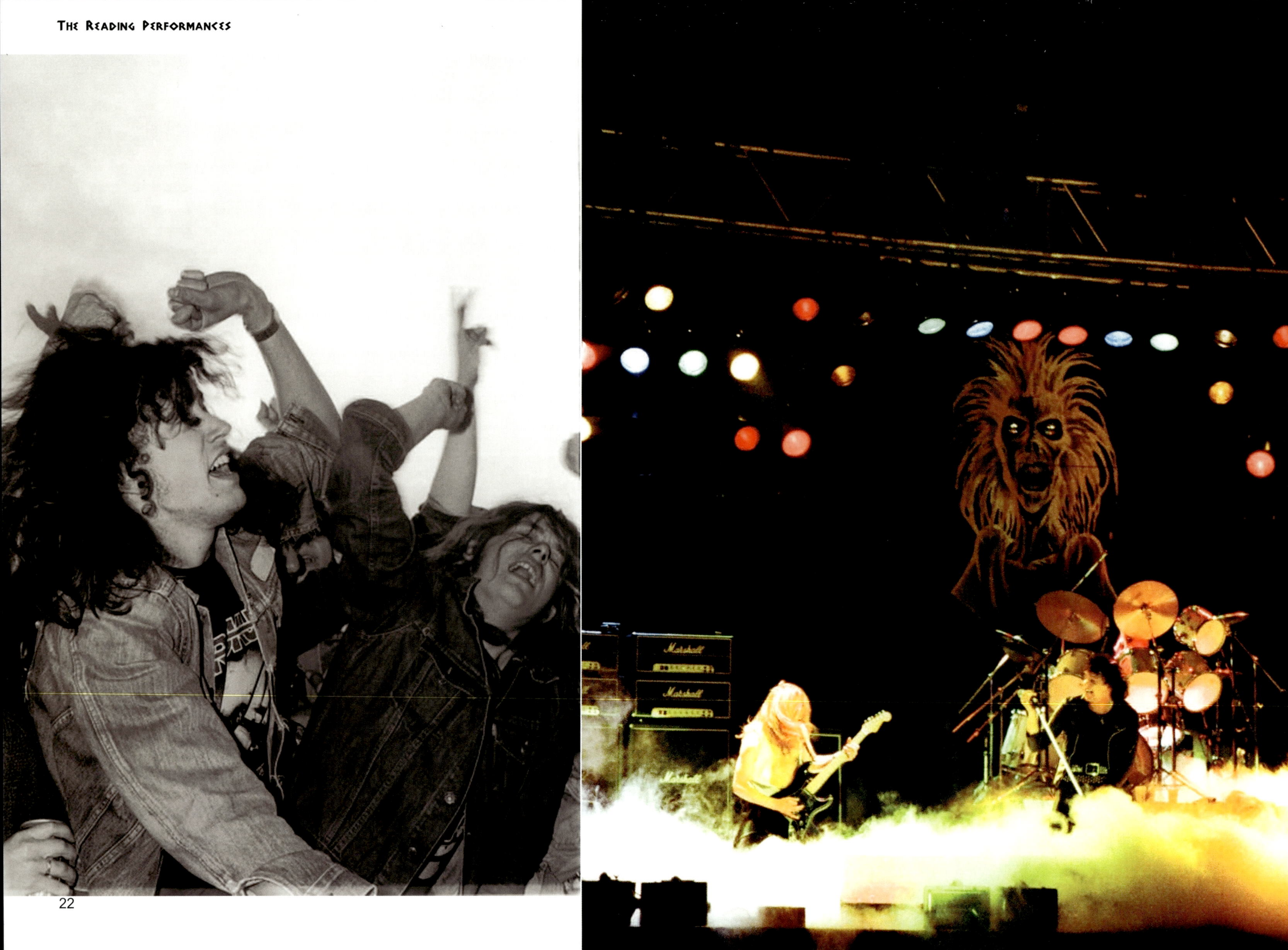

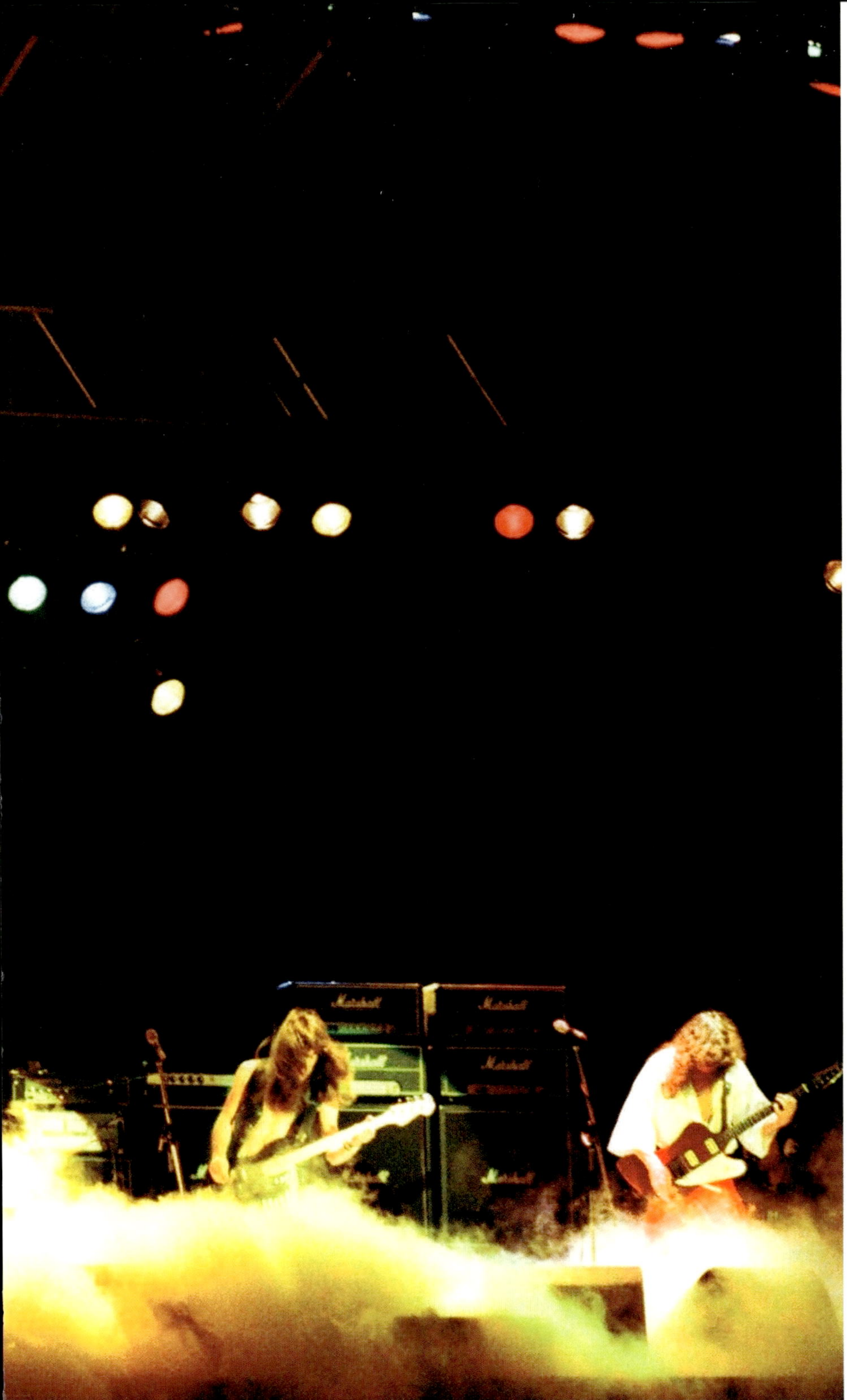

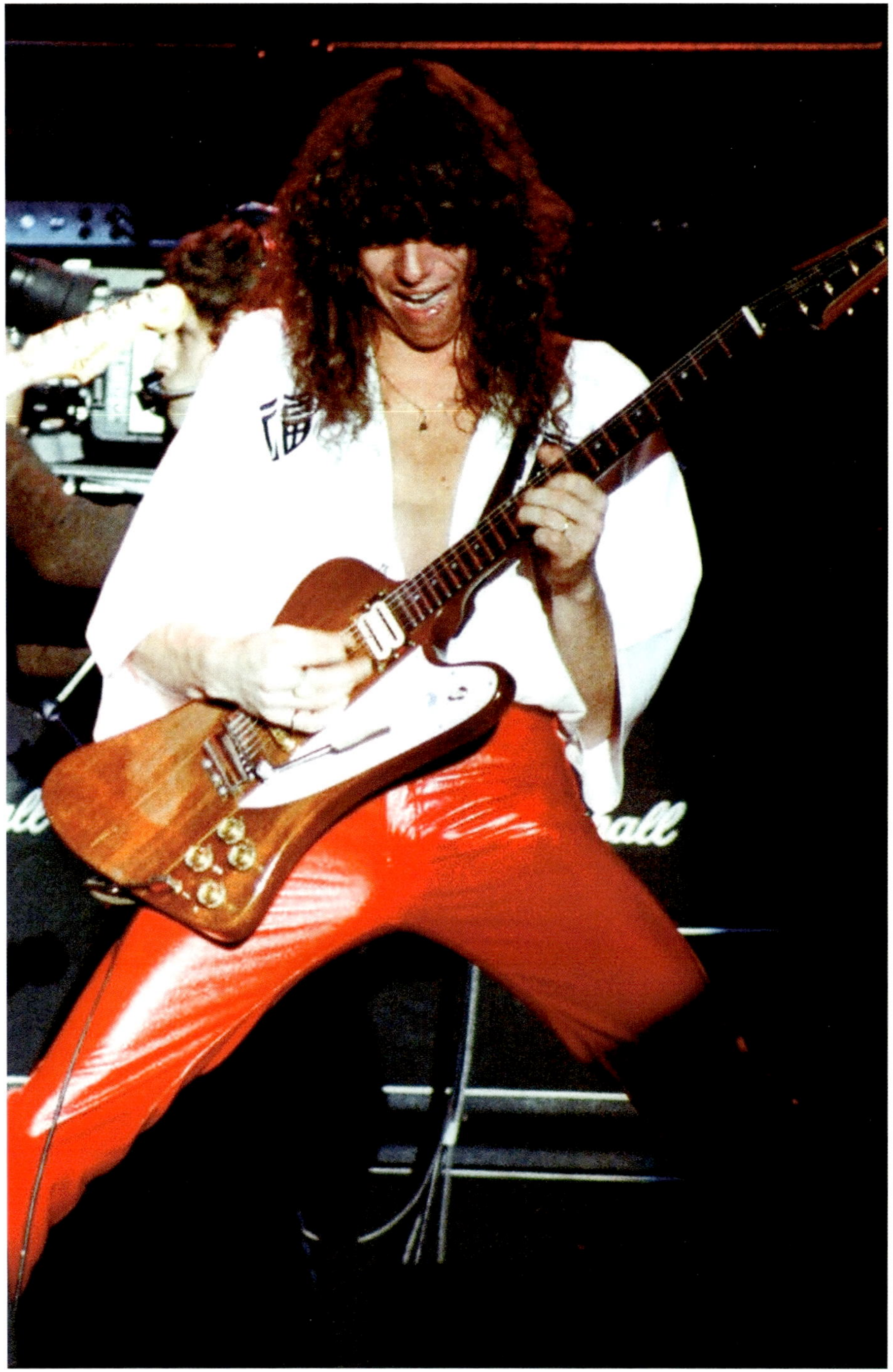

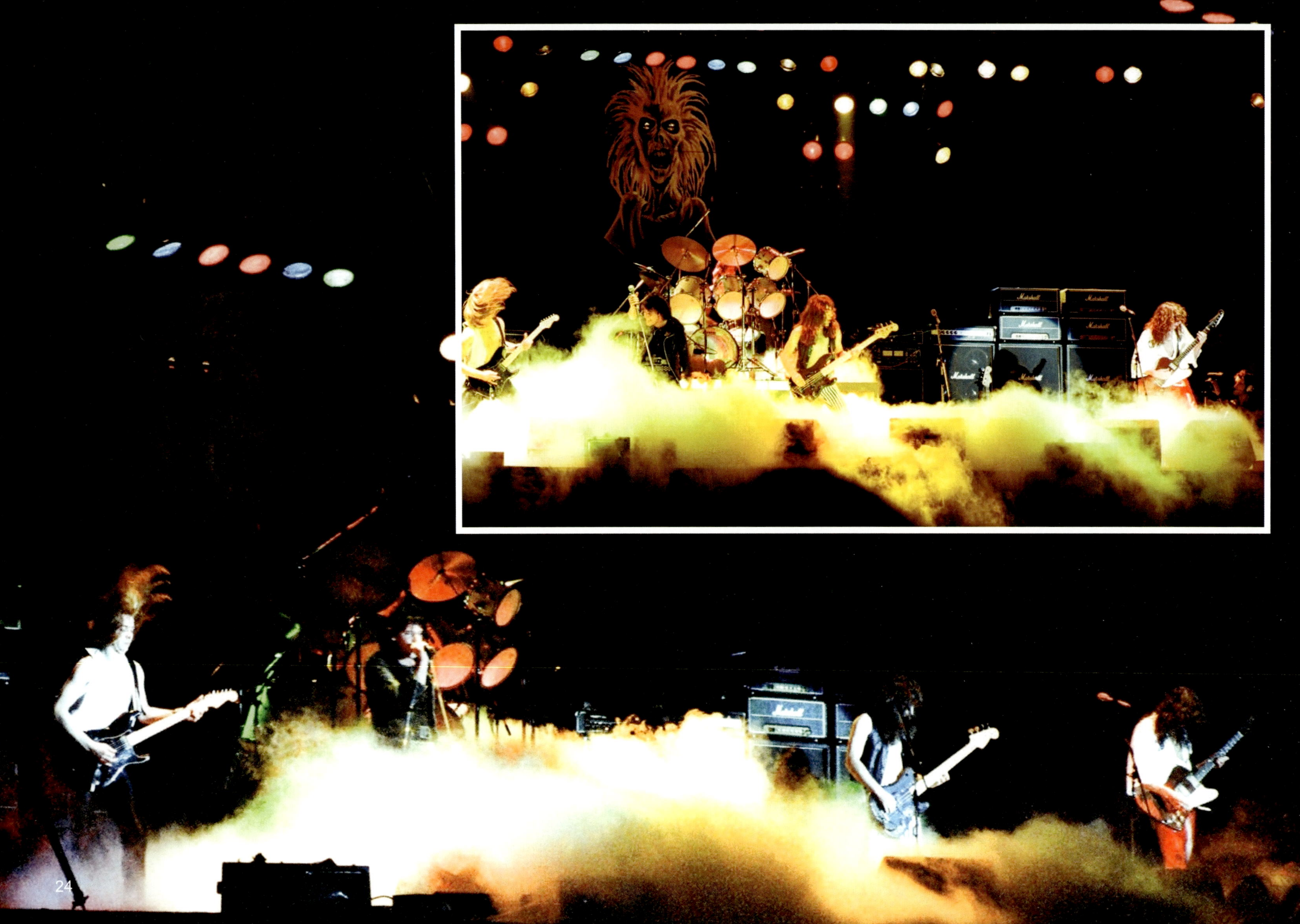

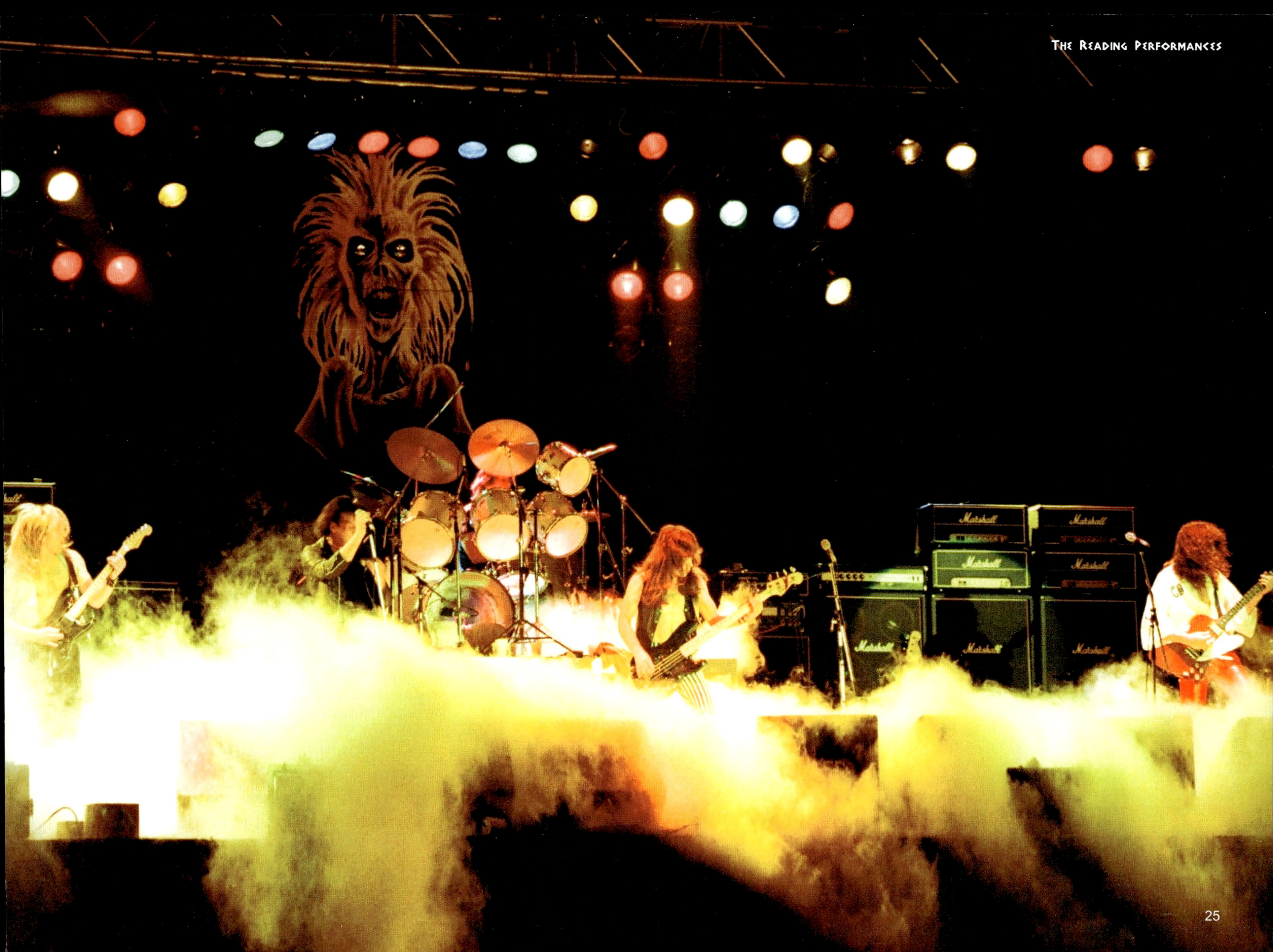

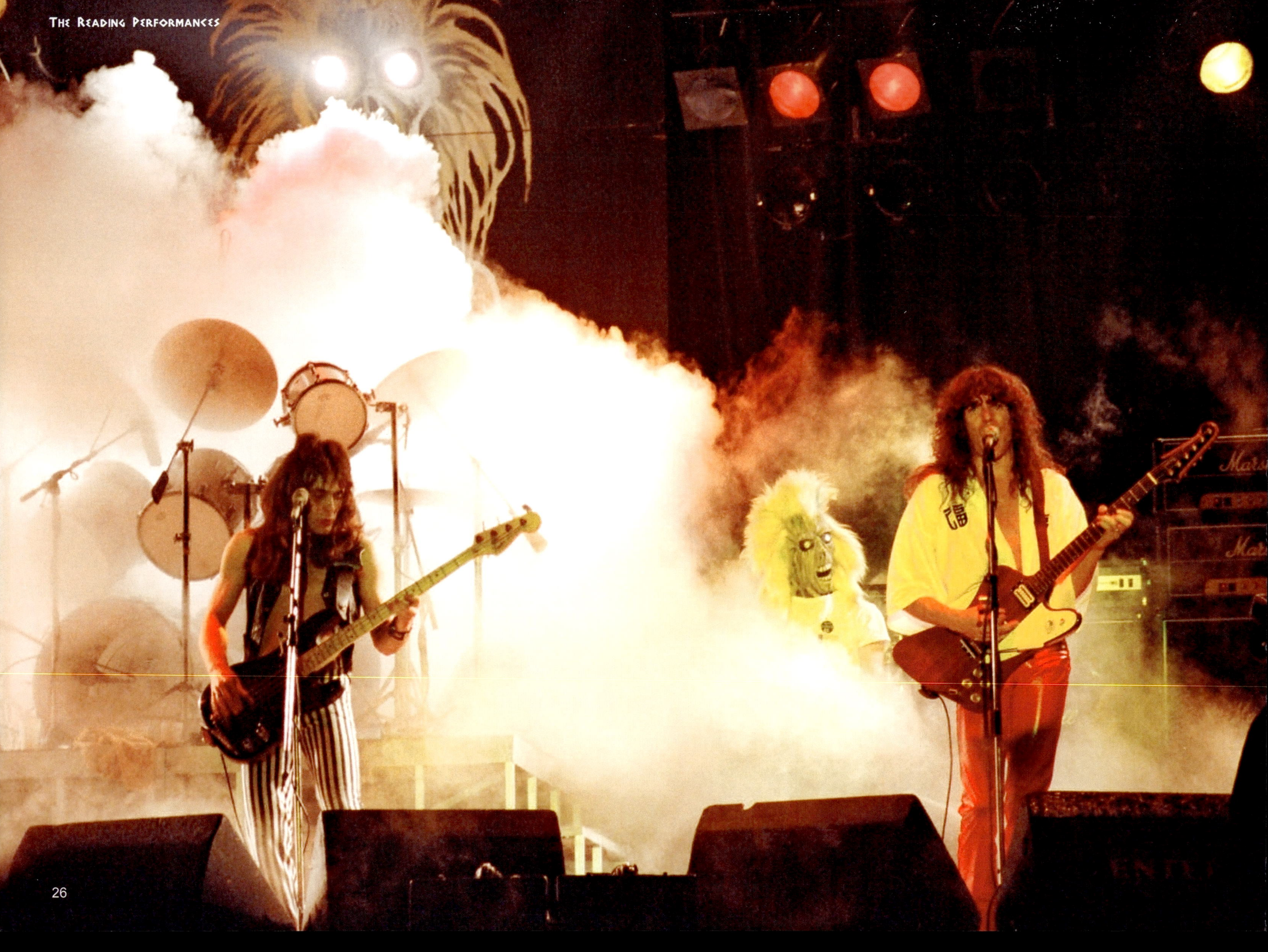

City, Wishbone Ash and The Q-Tips – it was Slade that replaced Ozzy) had to pull out of the pull for various reasons ranging from difficulties with work permits to other commitments. A band called Samson were also on the bill with a certain Bruce Dickinson. Let's not forget White Spirit were also on the bill with guitarist Janick Gers. This was certainly a convenient line-up. The seeds were being sown for what would be the definite Maiden incarnation. And this is why Reading remains important to Maiden's chronology.

Geoff Barton and Robbi Millar wrote of Maiden's performance in *Sounds*: "From here on in it was up, with Iron Maiden putting on a performance of their lives and giving UFO a run for their money. Taking to the giant Reading stage like Wayne Fereday to goalscoring, the Maiden looked more like seasoned festival veterans than East End HM'ers with minimal experience of outdoor events... Towards the end of the set Iron Maiden urged the spotlight operators to turn their beams 'on to the people'. But this was no crass Scorpions style stunt. The band genuinely wanted to see the size of the assemblage out front."

Maiden played a new number called 'Killers' at Reading festival August 23 1980, which featured different lyrics. 'Killers' would become a staple Maiden number to this day. What better place to showcase it than Reading.

"I remember the night at Reading Festival in front of 30,000 people playing 'Remember Tomorrow'," Di'Anno said to *Spotlight Report* in 2010, "and seeing the lighters go up in the air, fuckin' hell mate, talk about shivers. We weren't that big then so we hadn't experienced that kinda stuff, amazing."

It was an important concert and despite a brilliant set from ageing glam rockers Slade over the weekend it was Maiden that walked away champions.

The second leg of *Iron Maiden* support tour actually ended

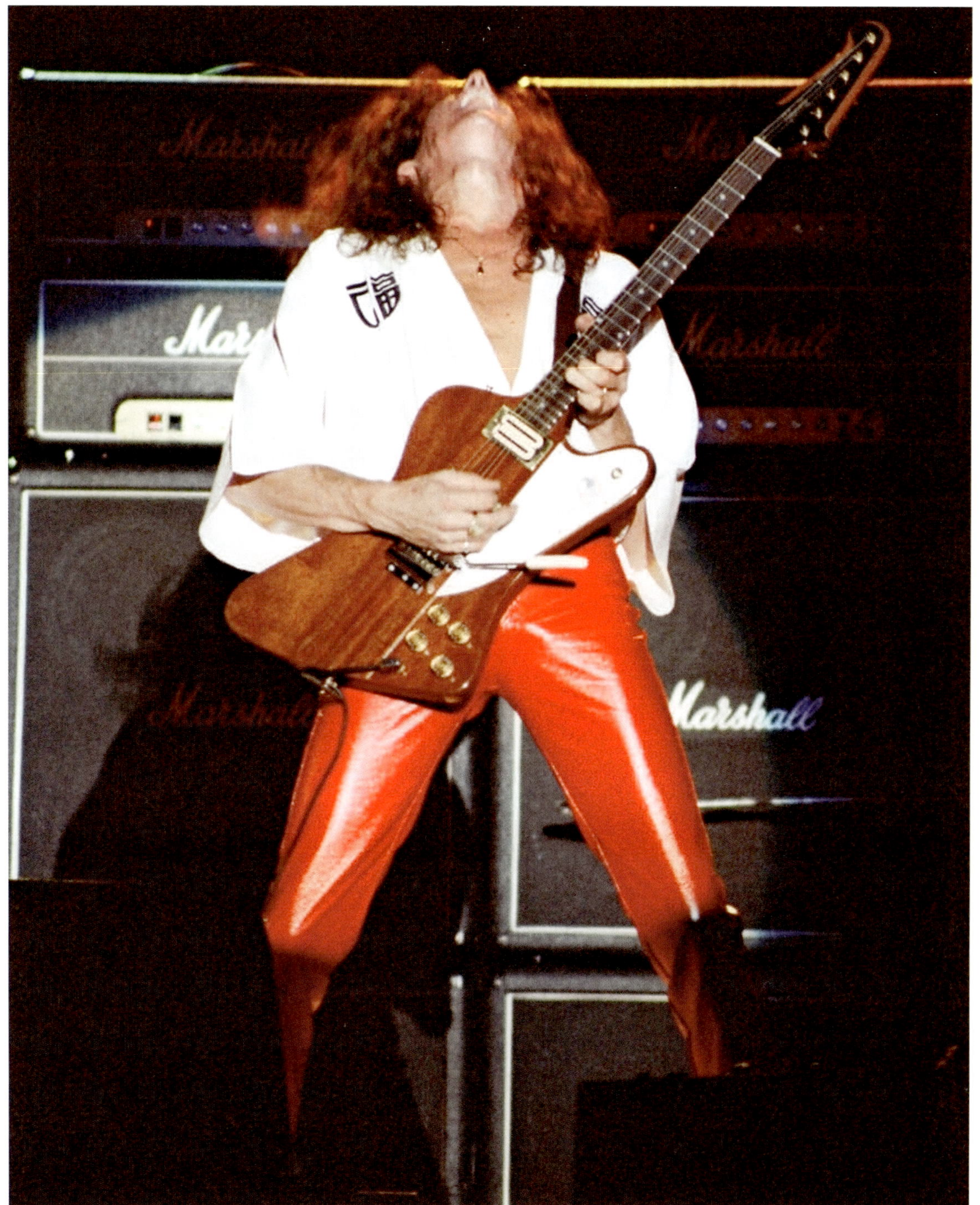

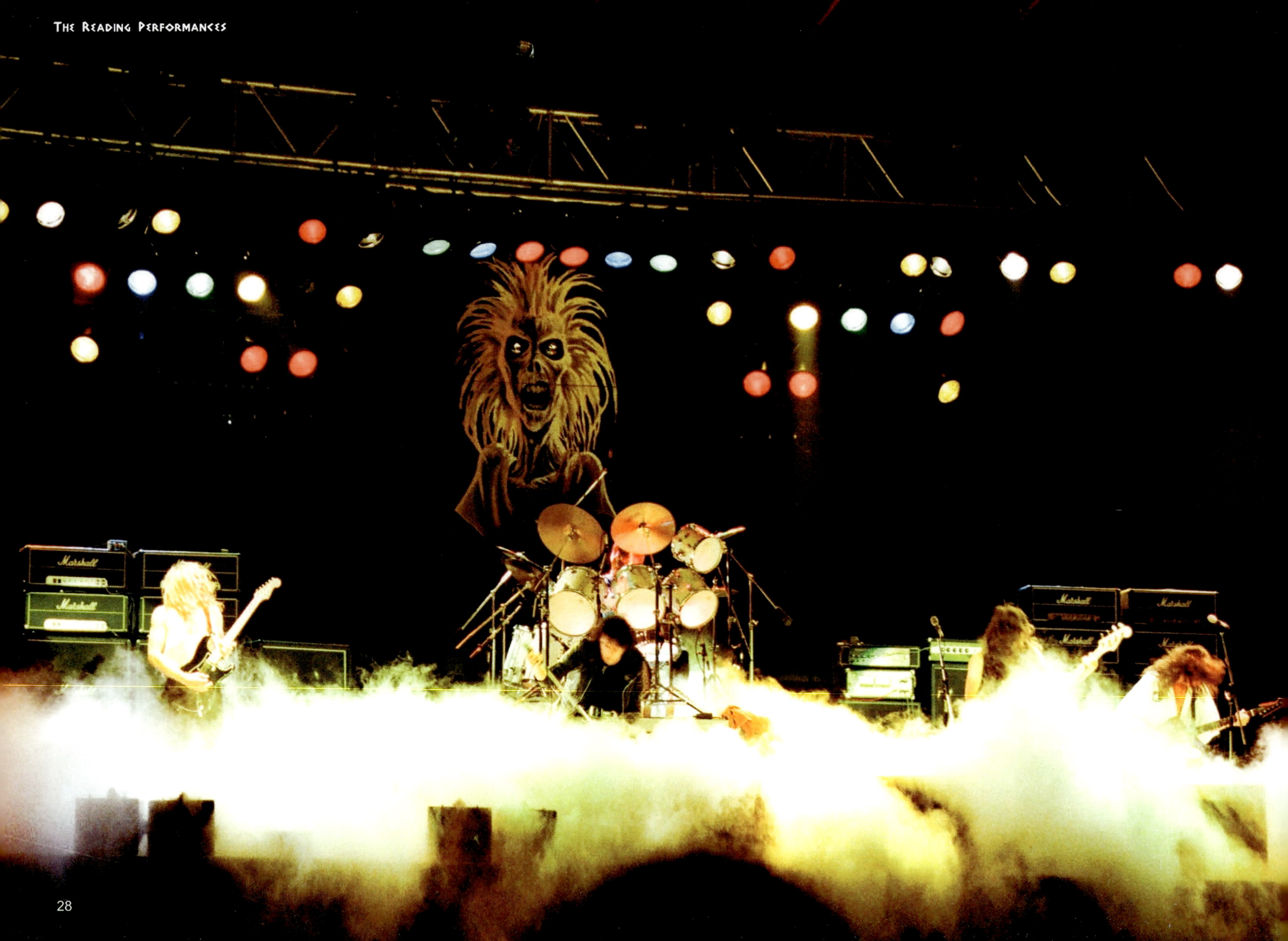

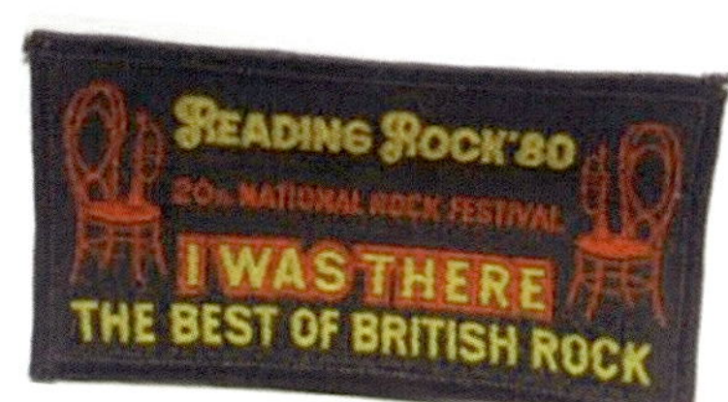

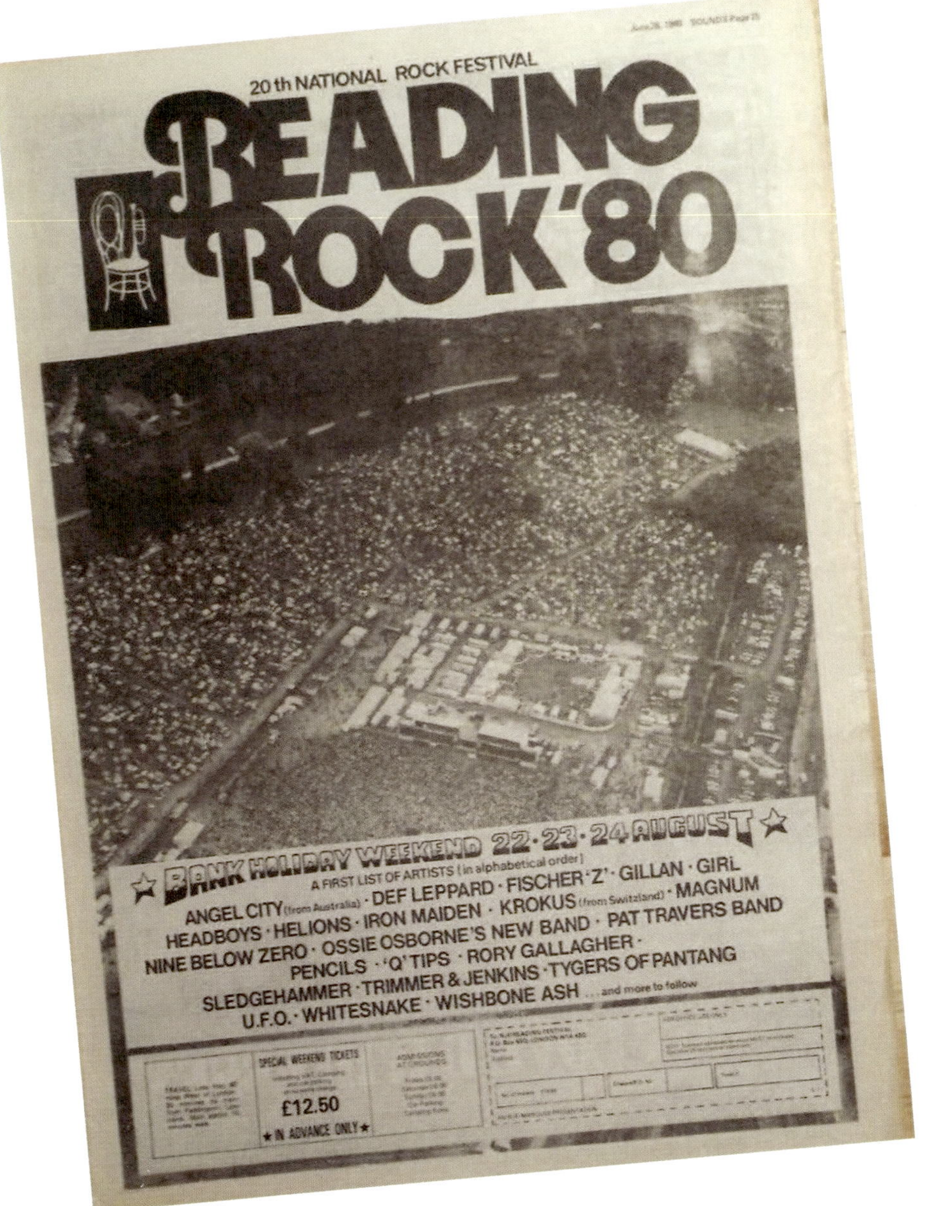

June 28, 1980 SOUNDS Page 25

20th NATIONAL ROCK FESTIVAL

READING ROCK '80

BANK HOLIDAY WEEKEND 22·23·24 AUGUST

A FIRST LIST OF ARTISTS [in alphabetical order]

ANGEL CITY (from Australia) · DEF LEPPARD · FISCHER 'Z' · GILLAN · GIRL
HEADBOYS · HELIONS · IRON MAIDEN · KROKUS (from Switzland) · MAGNUM
NINE BELOW ZERO · OSSIE OSBORNE'S NEW BAND · PAT TRAVERS BAND
PENCILS · 'Q' TIPS · RORY GALLAGHER ·
SLEDGEHAMMER · TRIMMER & JENKINS · TYGERS OF PANTANG
U.F.O. · WHITESNAKE · WISHBONE ASH ... and more to follow

SPECIAL WEEKEND TICKETS
£12.50
★ IN ADVANCE ONLY ★

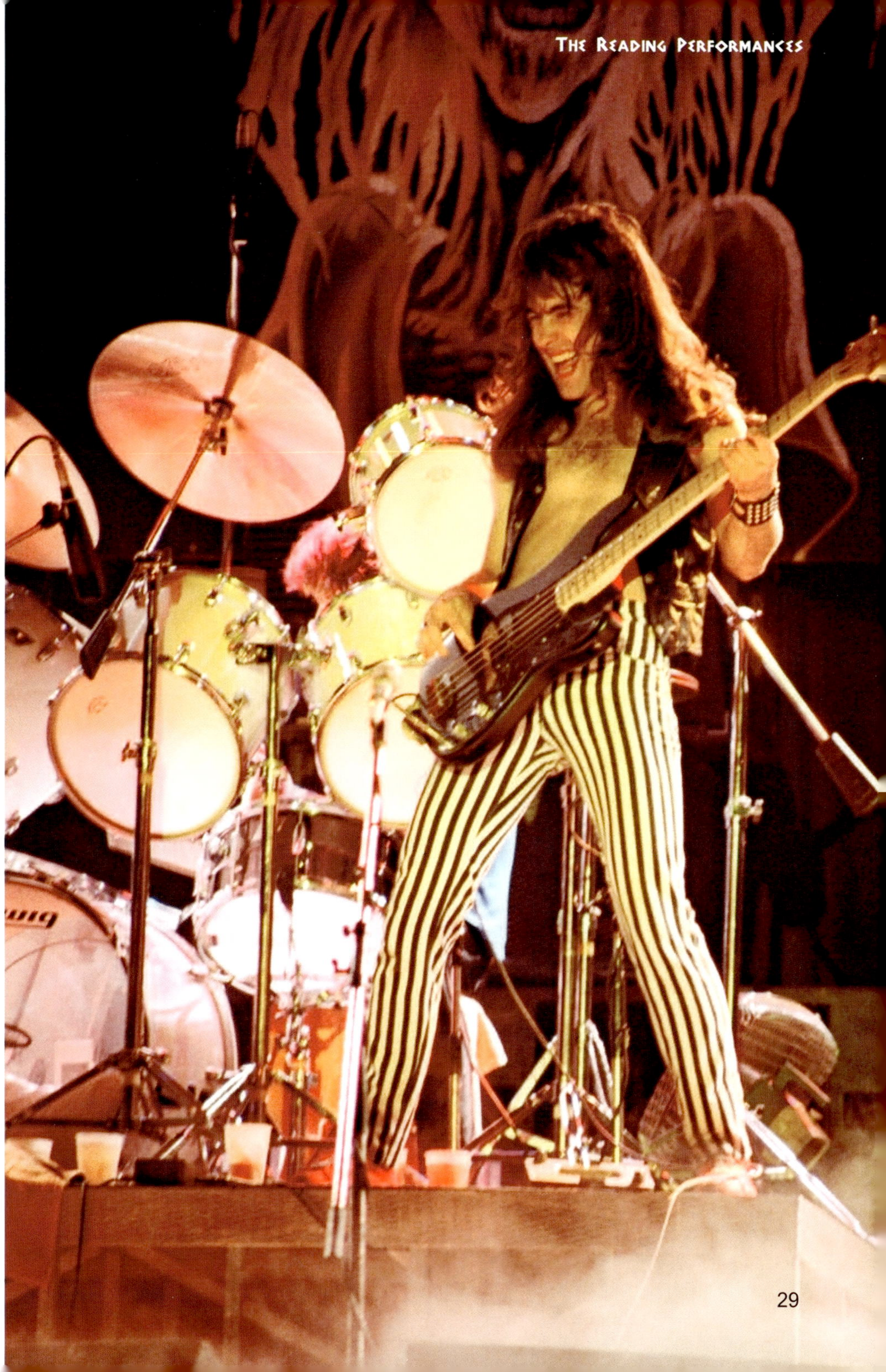

Reading on August 23. The first leg had ended April 10 or 14 (depending on if the April 14 gig really happened) when the band undertook *Metal For Muthas* leg number two.

It is important to put Reading into perspective to understand it's important in Maiden's history. The Reading appearance was followed by a support slot on KISS' European tour in support of their *Unmasked* album from August 29 (some reports, notably from KISS historians, suggest the tour began on August 30 which is likely) to October 13, though, after the initial batch of dates

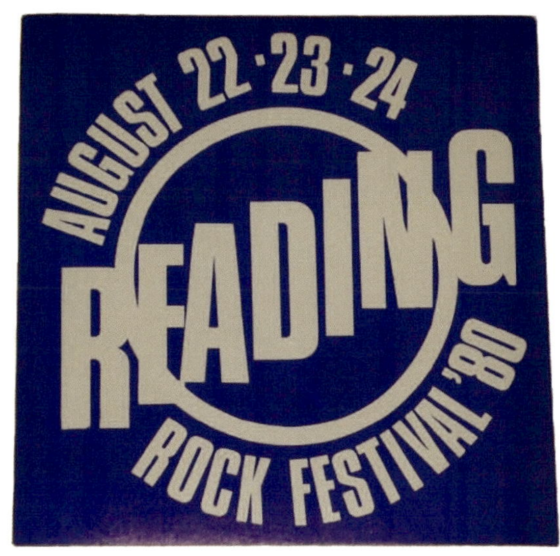

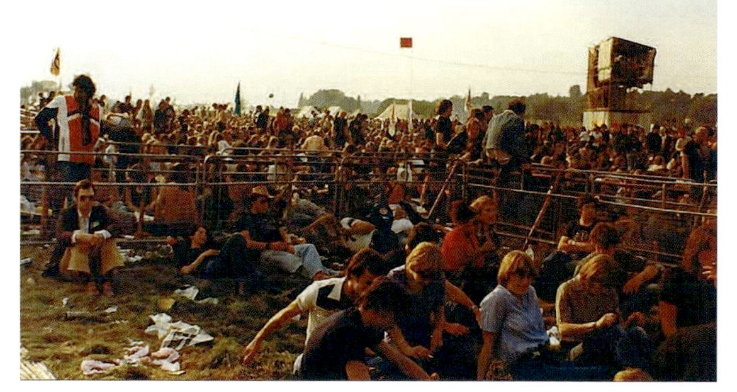

in Italy it has been reported that Maiden played two of their own shows at the Marquee club on September 4 and 5 before Strafford on September 5 and 6 and then London on 8 and 9. They subsequently picked up with KISS again in Nuremberg on the eleventh. These dates obviously contradict each other. KISS performed in Strafford as ticket stubs prove this to be correct. Maiden did, in fact, sit out on the UK leg of the KISS tour and later reconvened with KISS on

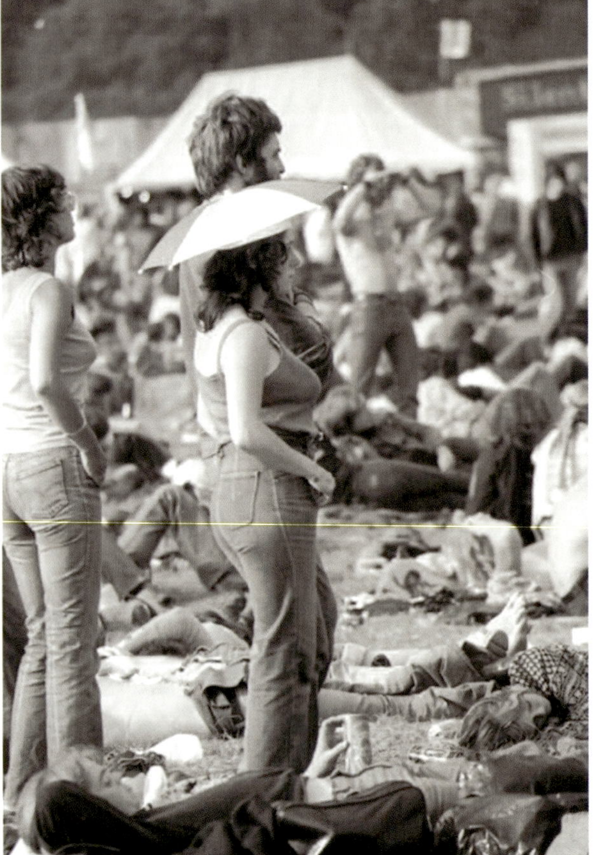

September 11. It is believed that Maiden took a week off for relaxation and sun at the holiday resort of Lido De Jesolo on the Adriatic Coast.

Stratton: "Supporting KISS in 1980 was great. As I'd had experience with Quo around Europe, KISS was great. I got on really well with Paul Stanley and Gene Simmons. They took me out on my birthday in Stockholm. Everything was fine. As you can see if you look on the Internet on Facebook, Wikipedia and websites you'll see photos of me and Gene Simmons and Paul Stanley and I got on very well with them."

The 24 date KISS tour took Maiden through Italy, Germany, Belgium, France, Holland, Sweden, Denmark and Norway and saw them play to a staggering 350,000 screaming rockers.

"Yeah, he [Gene Simmons] was fantastic, he was really good," Di'Anno enthused to Nando Machado and Daniel Dystyler of *Wikimetal* in 2012. "The guys really gave us a lot of help. It was our first ever European tour, as well. Yeah, it was really nice, the guys were fantastic and I think even on Steve's birthday as well they came on stage and they did this custard pie thing in the face. Everybody got messy and KISS had to delay the show for about an hour or something,

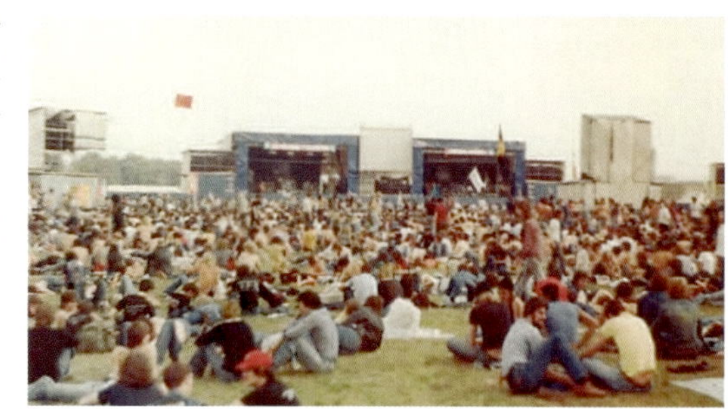

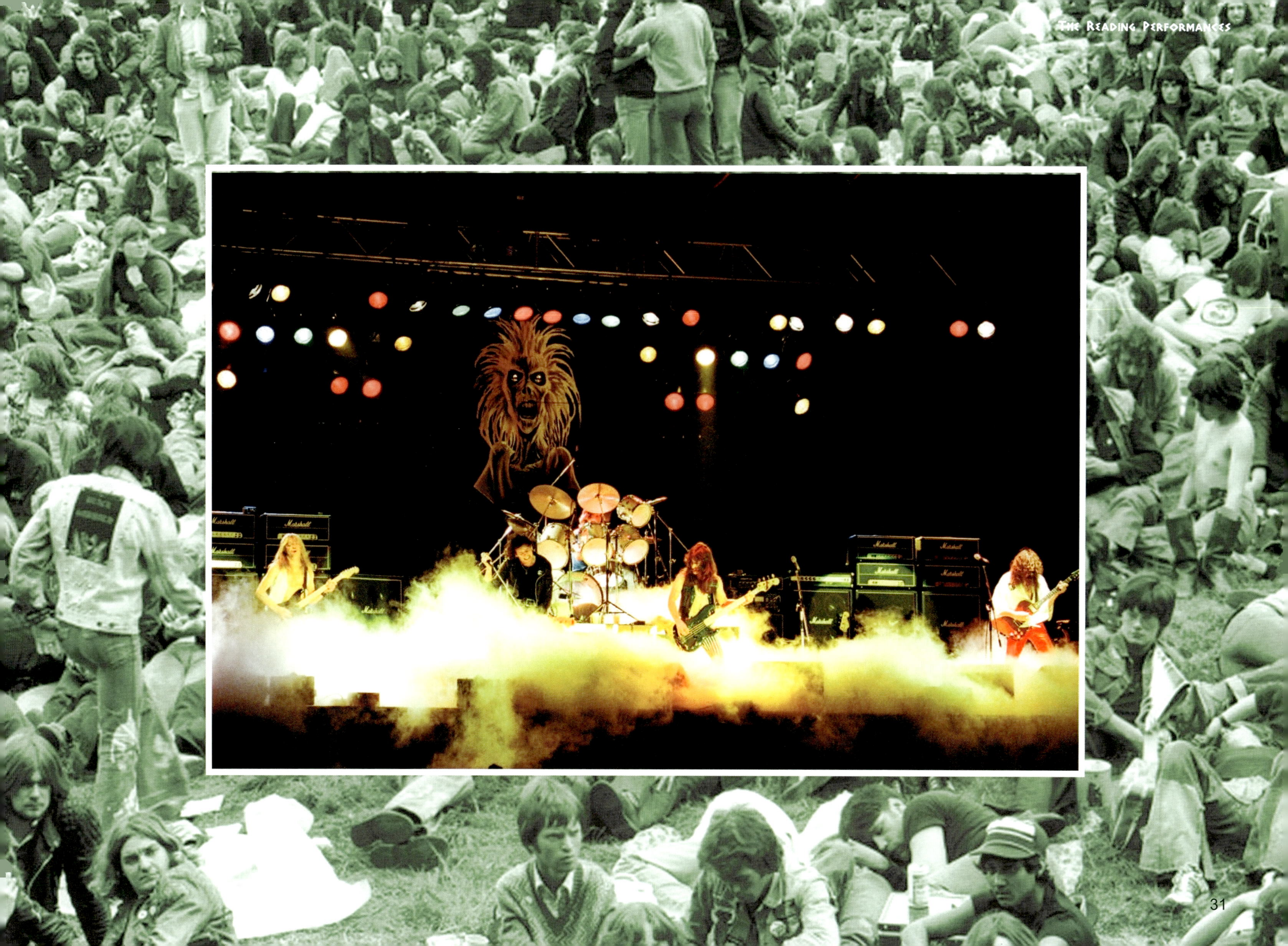

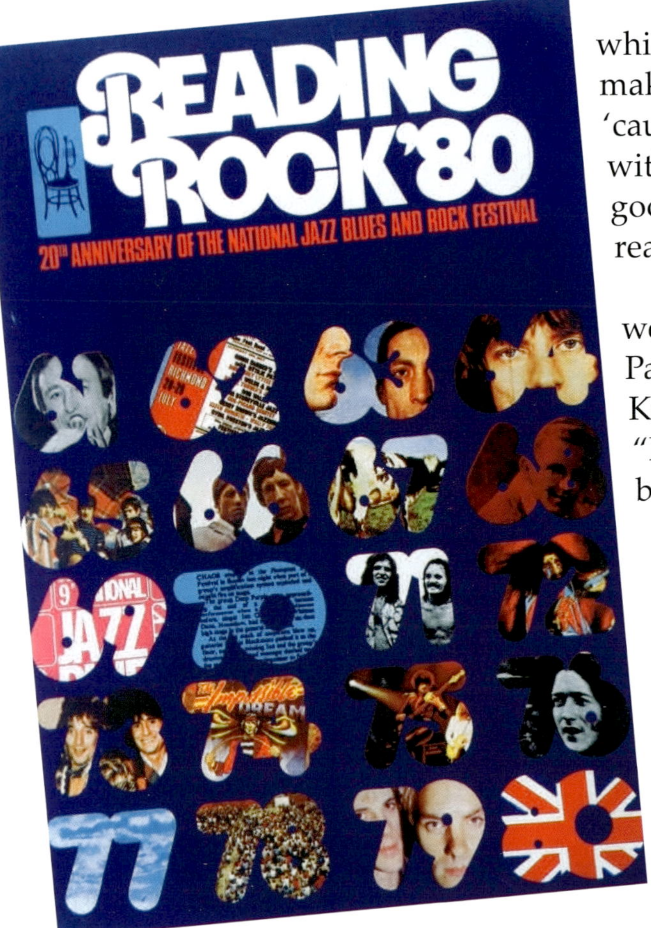

while they changed all their make-up and everything 'cause we made a lot of mess with them, as well. And good, good fun, it was a really fantastic tour."

"...when the band were touring with KISS in Paris," early fan club runner Keith Wilfort remembers, "Paul Di'Anno fancied a beautiful girl at the bar in a club, he spent most of the evening chatting her up. The local promoter tried to warn him off, but he wouldn't have it, it turned out later that he'd spent the evening trying to make out with a transvestite. Fortunately it was discovered before he went back to 'her' place... but he got endless stick from the rest of the band and crew for a while."

The road jaunt gave Maiden some major exposure outside of the British Isles. However, in October after the end of the tour Dennis Stratton left over perceived musical differences with the band and manager Rod Smallwood. Stratton's last show with the band was in Drammen, Norway on the final night of the KISS tour.

The band felt that it would be beneficial to play some shows with Stratton prior to working on their upcoming second album. Metal fans could not wait for a new album after witnessing the band at Reading.

The entire *Iron Maiden* Tour lasted for over seventy shows and saw the band's fanbase grow dramatically. Maiden's gig at the Rainbow on December 21 was filmed and released in May the following year as *Live At The Rainbow* featuring the songs 'The Ides Of March', 'Wrathchild', 'Killers', 'Remember Tomorrow', 'Transylvania', 'Phantom Of The Opera' and 'Iron Maiden'.

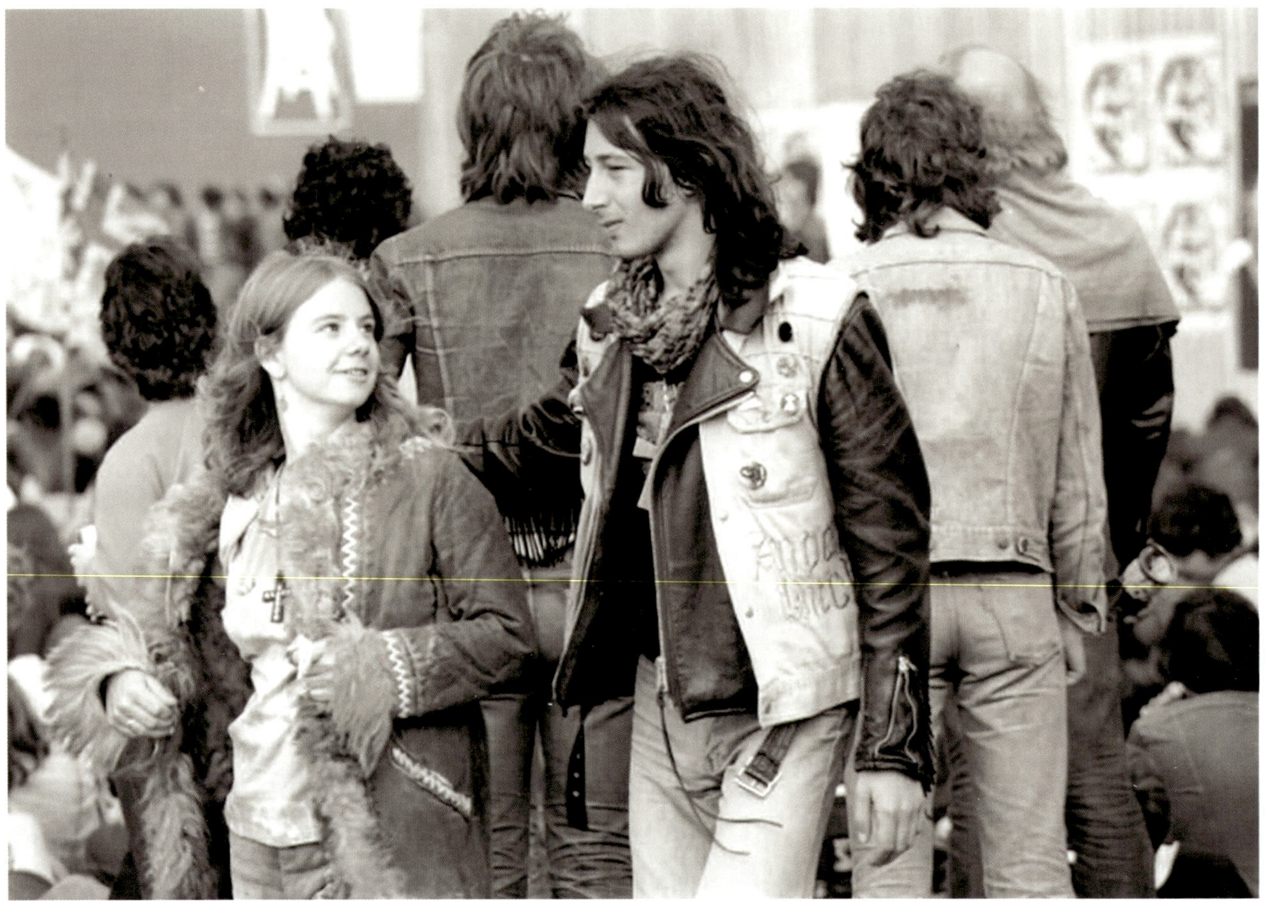

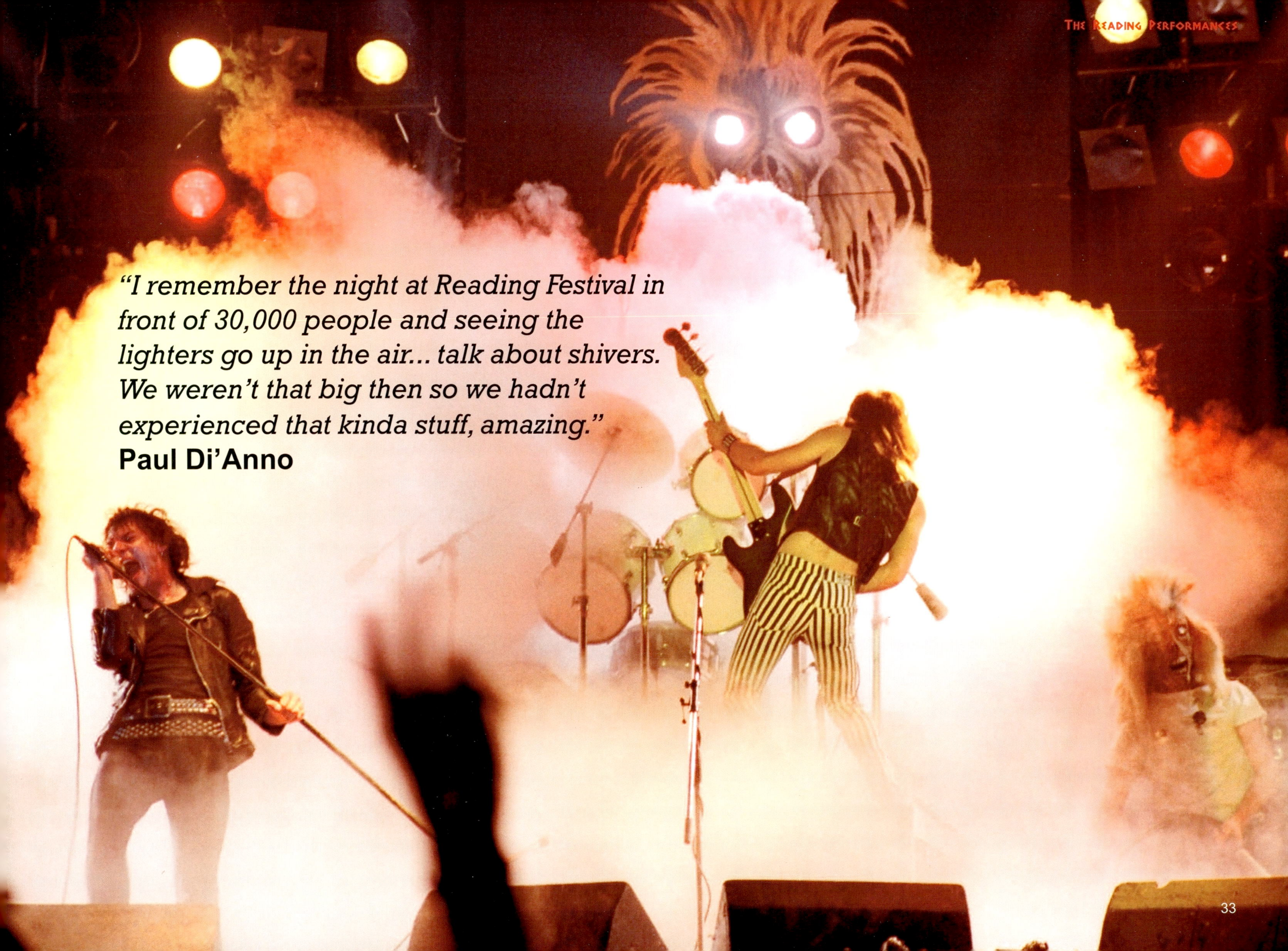

"I remember the night at Reading Festival in front of 30,000 people and seeing the lighters go up in the air... talk about shivers. We weren't that big then so we hadn't experienced that kinda stuff, amazing."
Paul Di'Anno

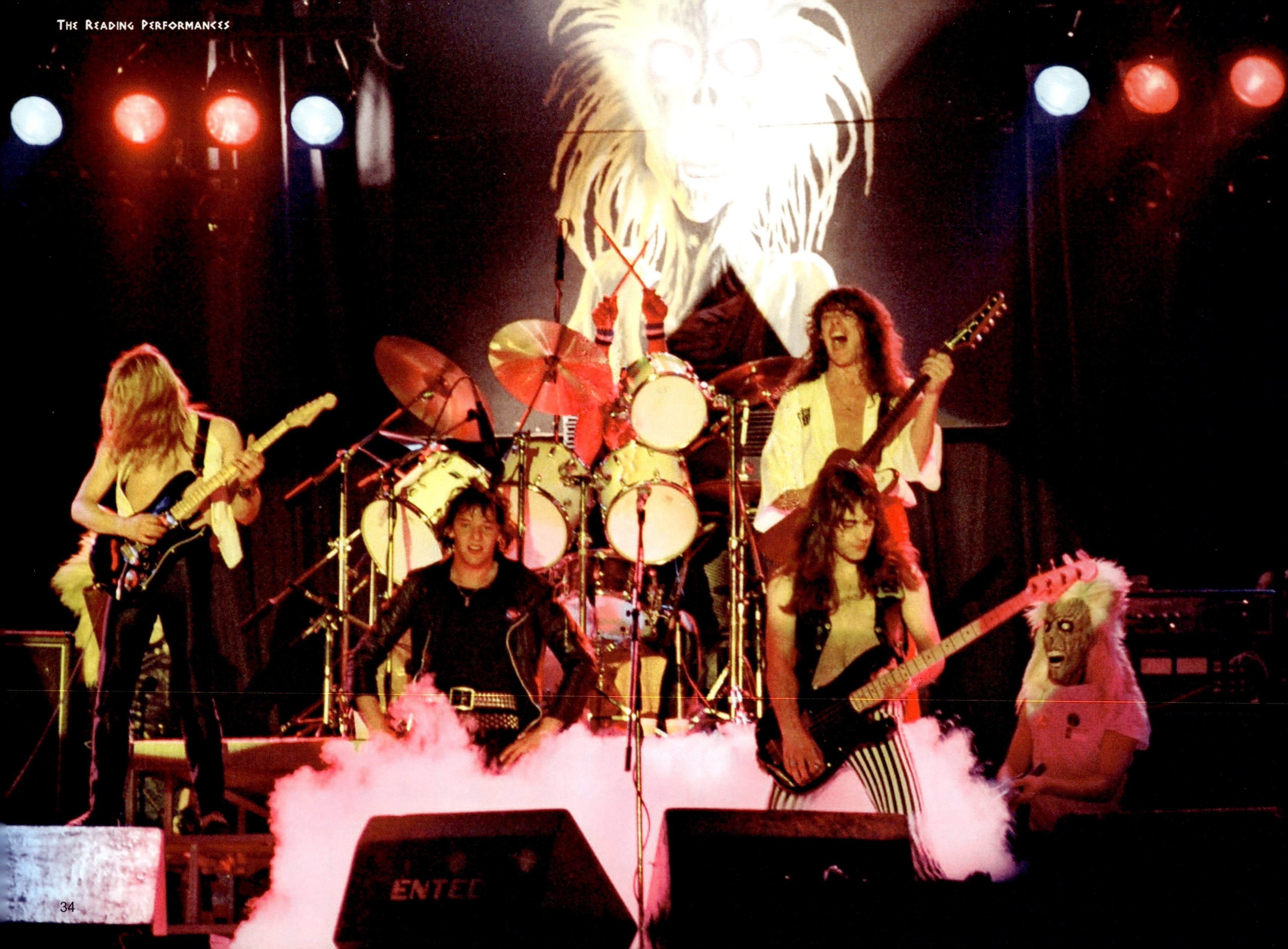

ENTEC

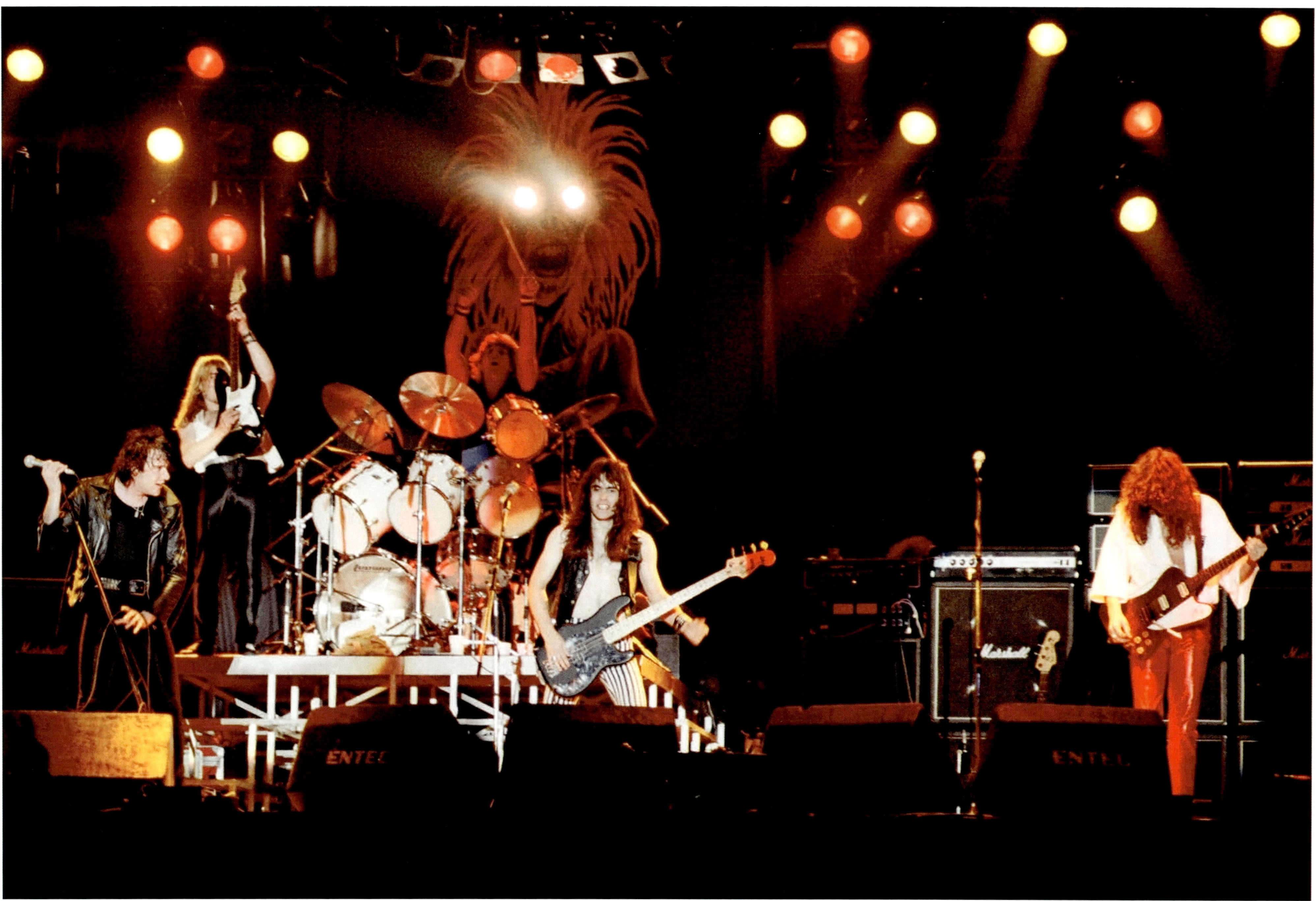

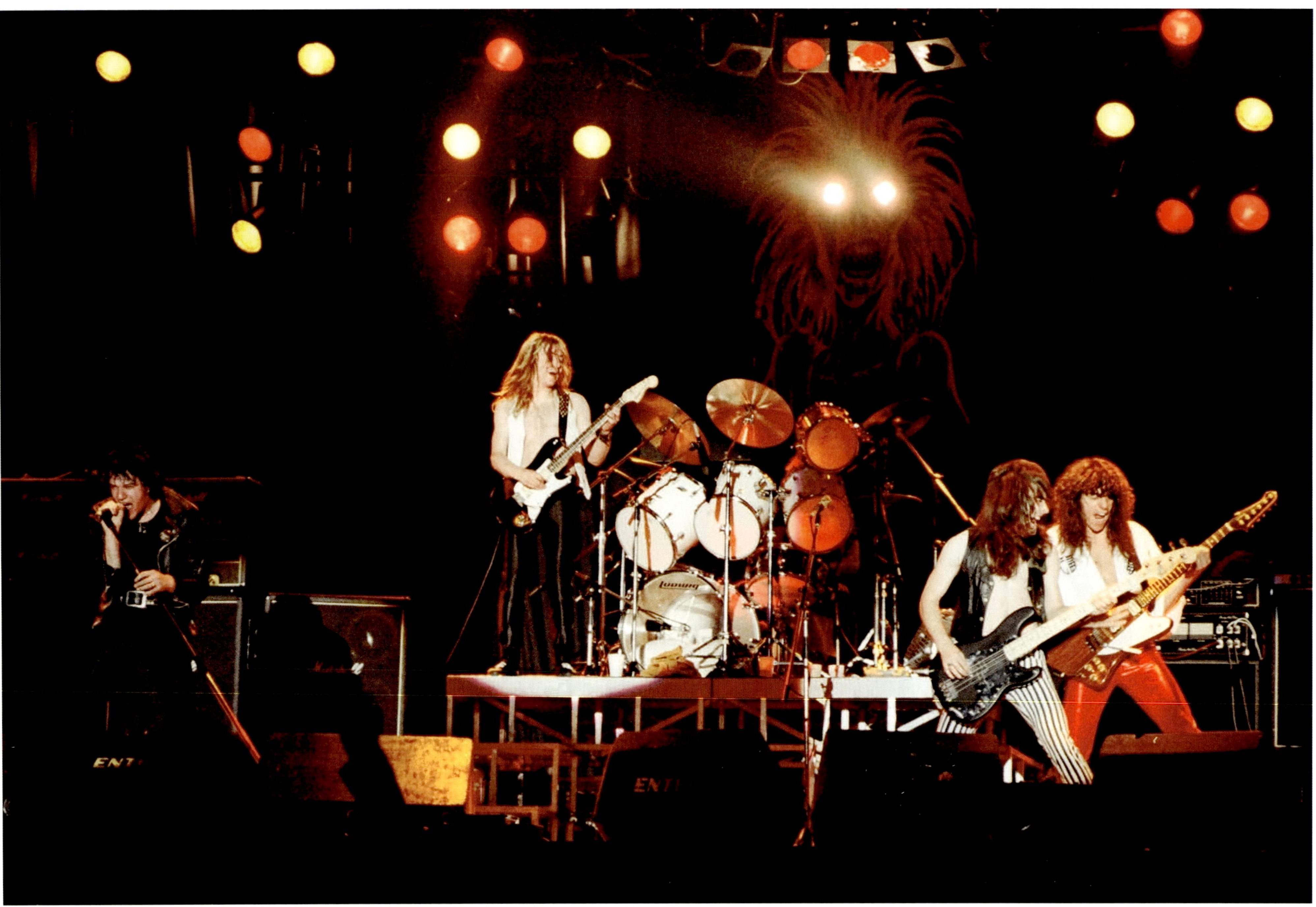

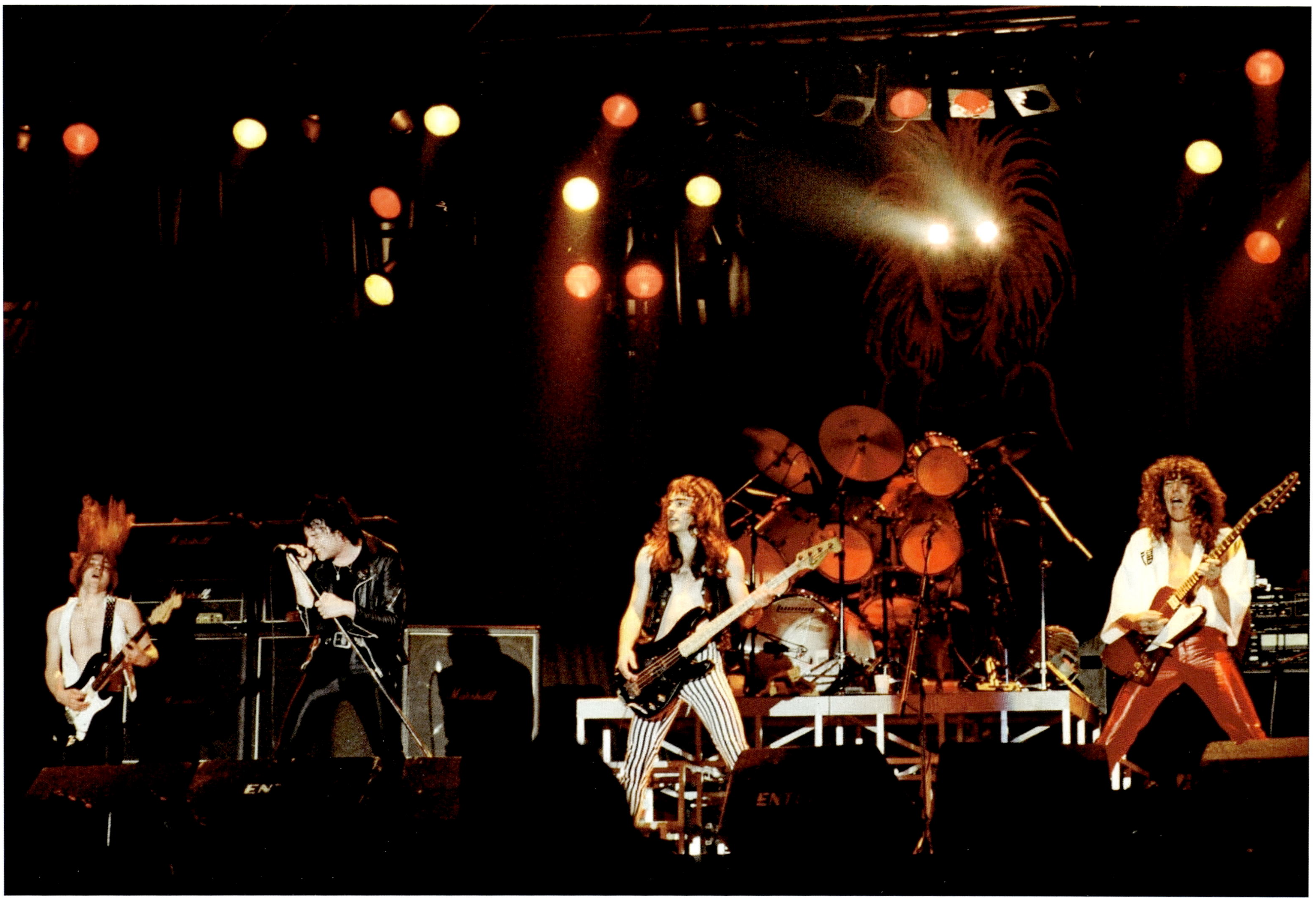

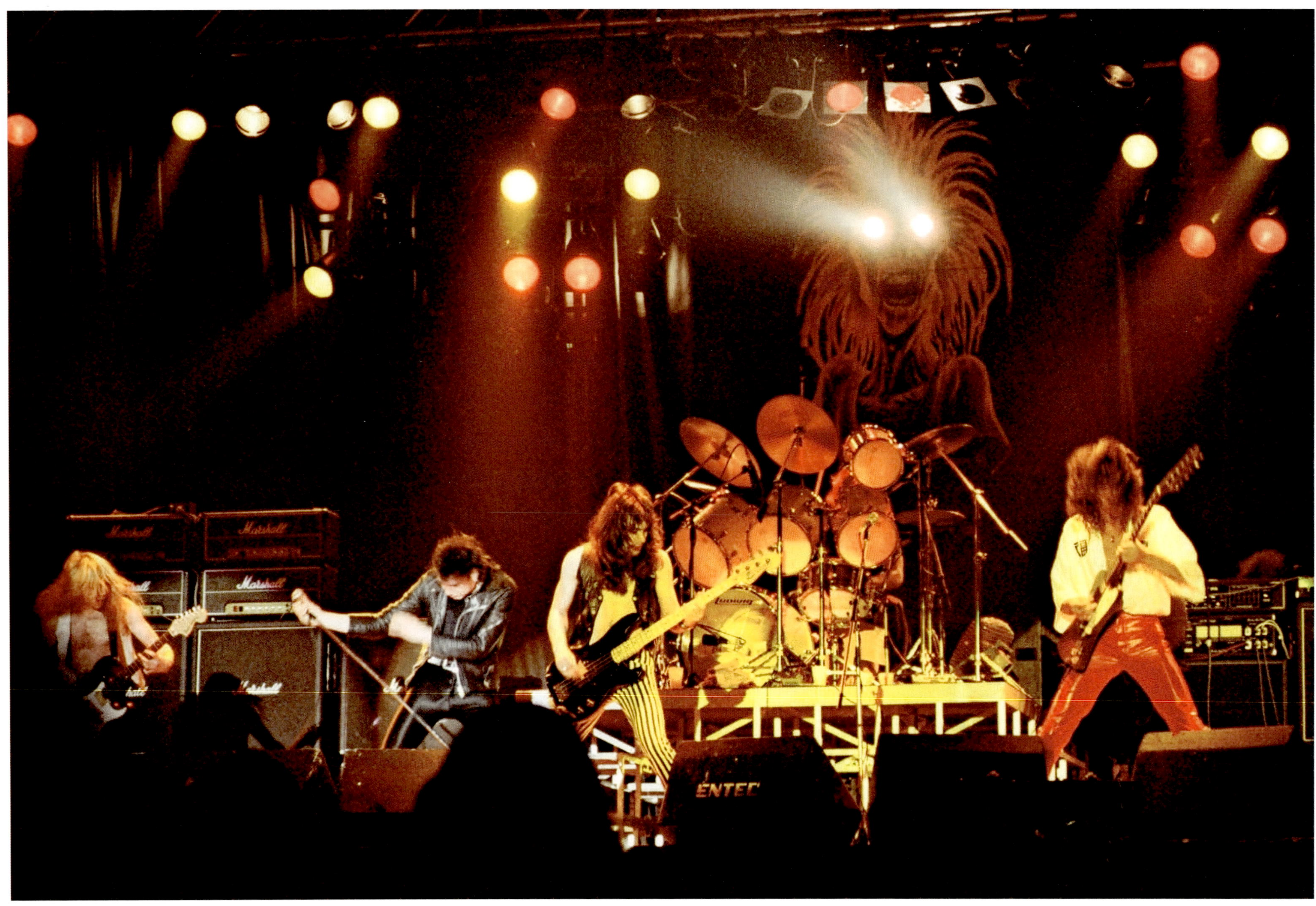

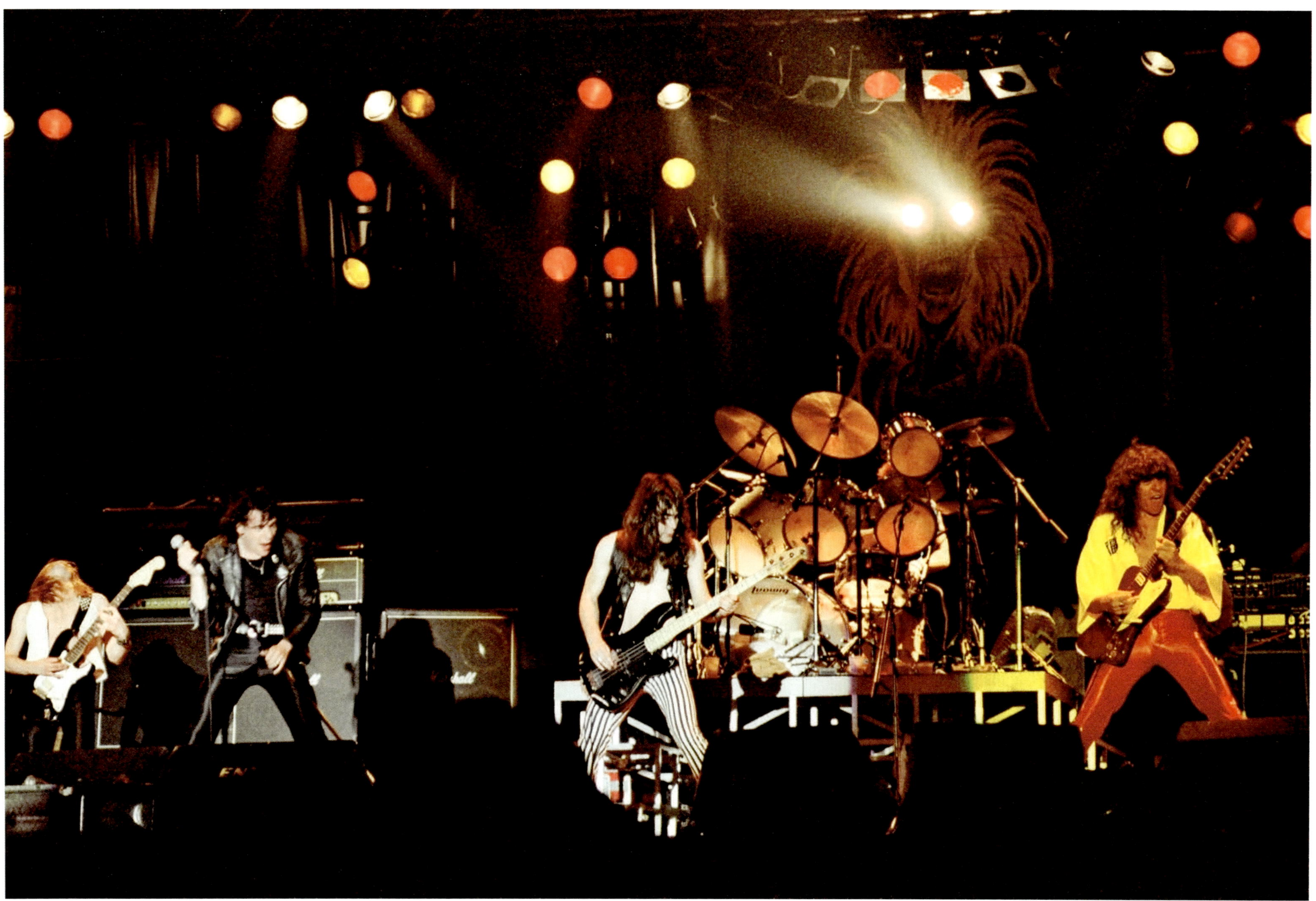

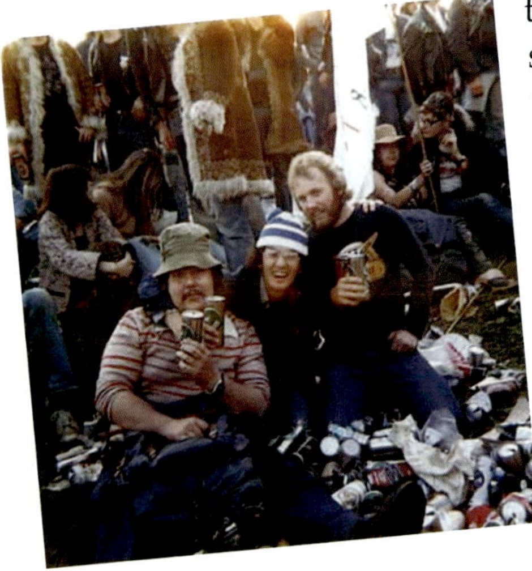

the show for about an hour or something, while they changed all their make-up and everything 'cause we made a lot of mess with them, as well. And good, good fun, it was a really fantastic tour."

"…when the band were touring with KISS in Paris," early fan club runner Keith Wilfort remembers, "Paul Di'Anno fancied a beautiful girl at the bar in a club, he spent most of the evening chatting her up. The local promoter tried to warn him off, but he wouldn't have it, it turned out later that he'd spent the evening trying to make out with a transvestite. Fortunately it was discovered before he went back to 'her' place… but he got endless stick from the rest of the band and crew for a while."

The road jaunt gave Maiden some major exposure outside of the British Isles. However, in October after the end of the tour Dennis Stratton left over perceived musical differences with the band and manager Rod Smallwood. Stratton's last show with the band was in Drammen, Norway on the final night of the KISS tour.

The band felt that it would be beneficial to play some shows with Stratton prior to working on their upcoming second album. Metal fans could not wait for a new album after witnessing the band at Reading.

The entire *Iron Maiden* Tour lasted for over seventy shows and saw the band's fanbase grow dramatically. Maiden's gig at the Rainbow on December 21 was filmed and released in May the following year as *Live At The Rainbow* featuring the songs 'The Ides Of March', 'Wrathchild', 'Killers', 'Remember Tomorrow', 'Transylvania', 'Phantom Of The Opera' and 'Iron Maiden'.

The experience was certainly life-changing for Adrian Smith, the newcomer to the band's camp. He'd never been given the opportunity to tour properly before having played mostly pub gigs in and around London.

Steve Harris had been the only member to have played in every incarnation of Iron

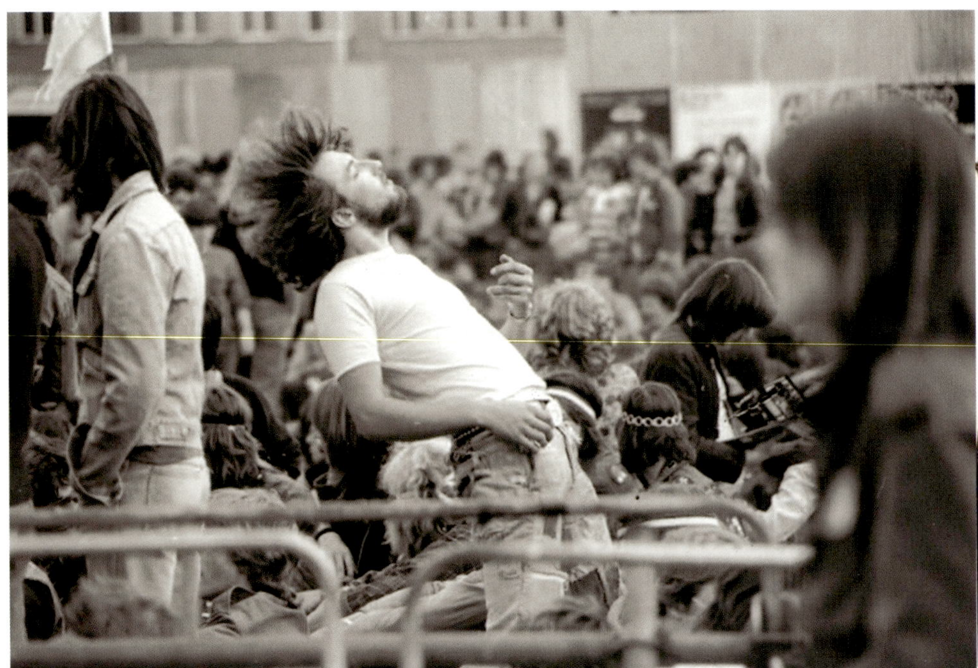

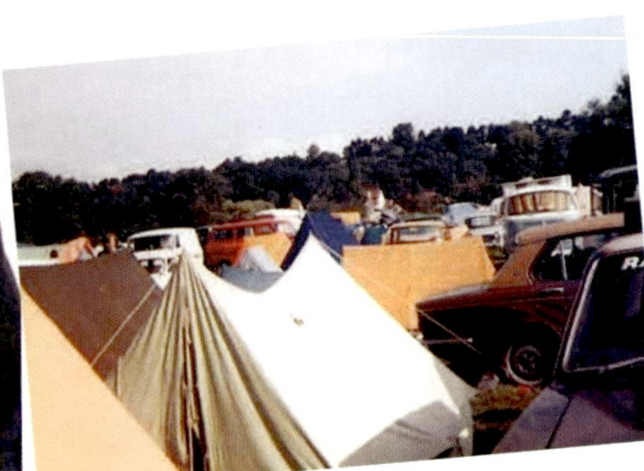

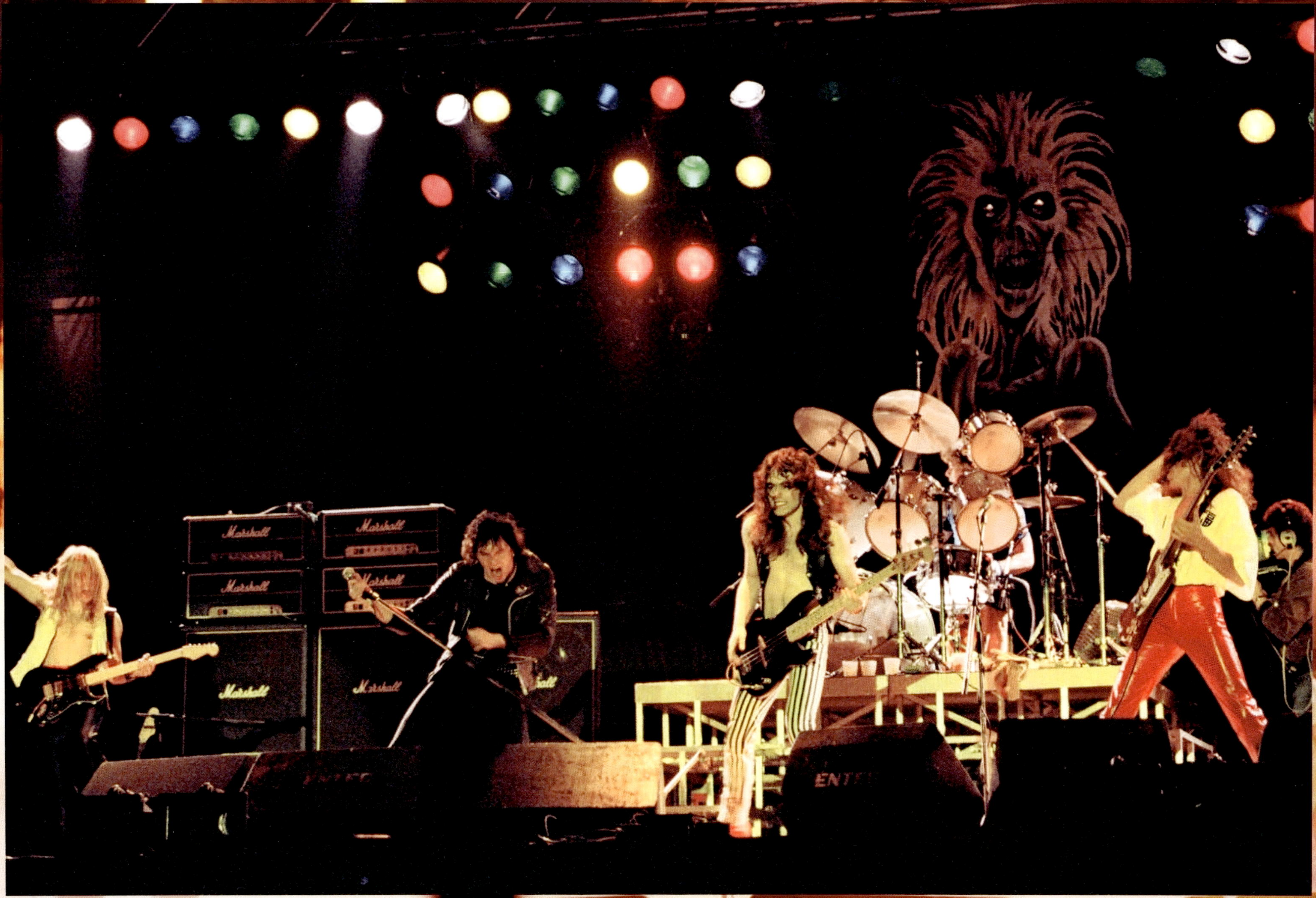
Marshall
Marshall
Marshall
Marshall

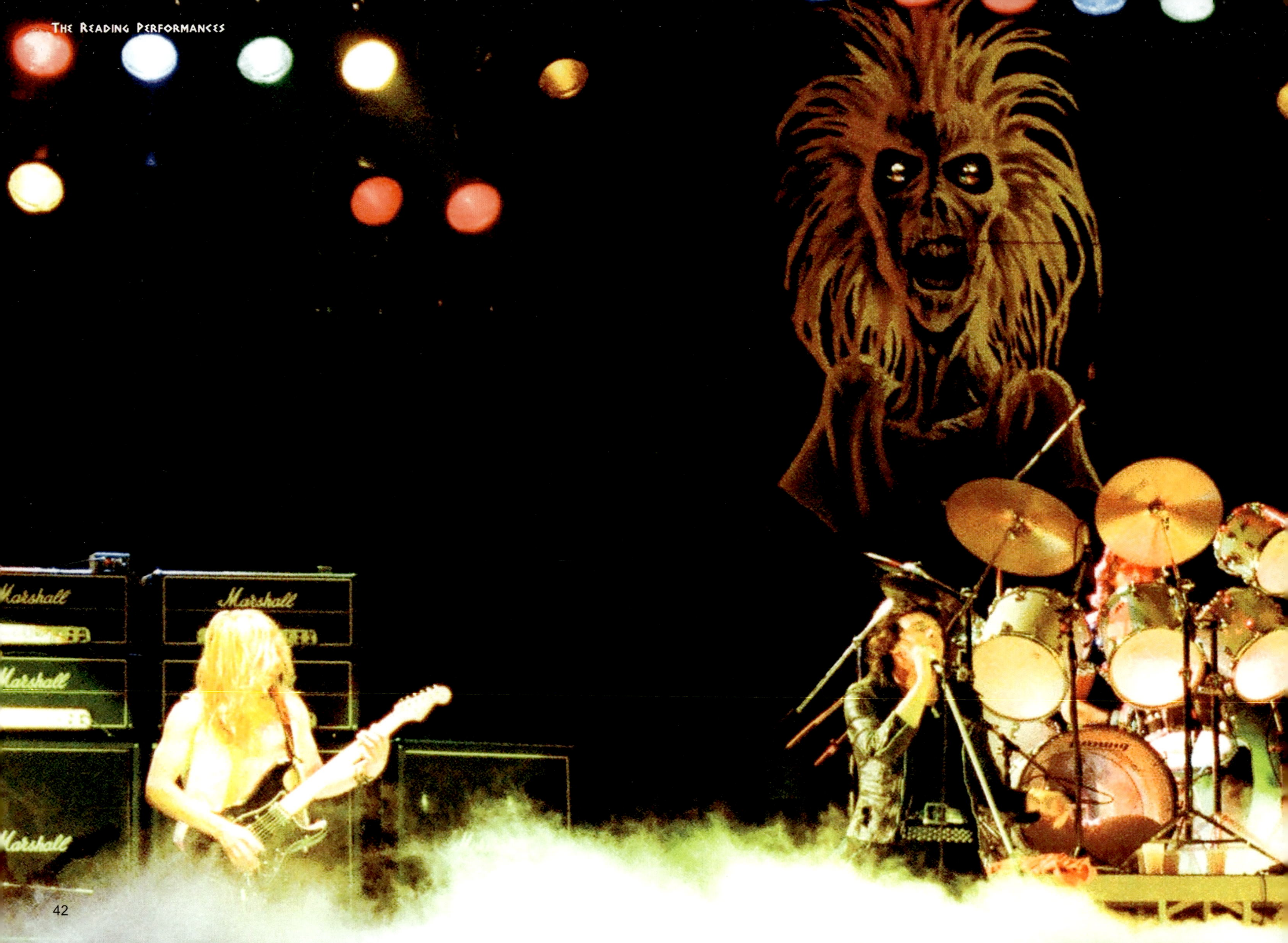

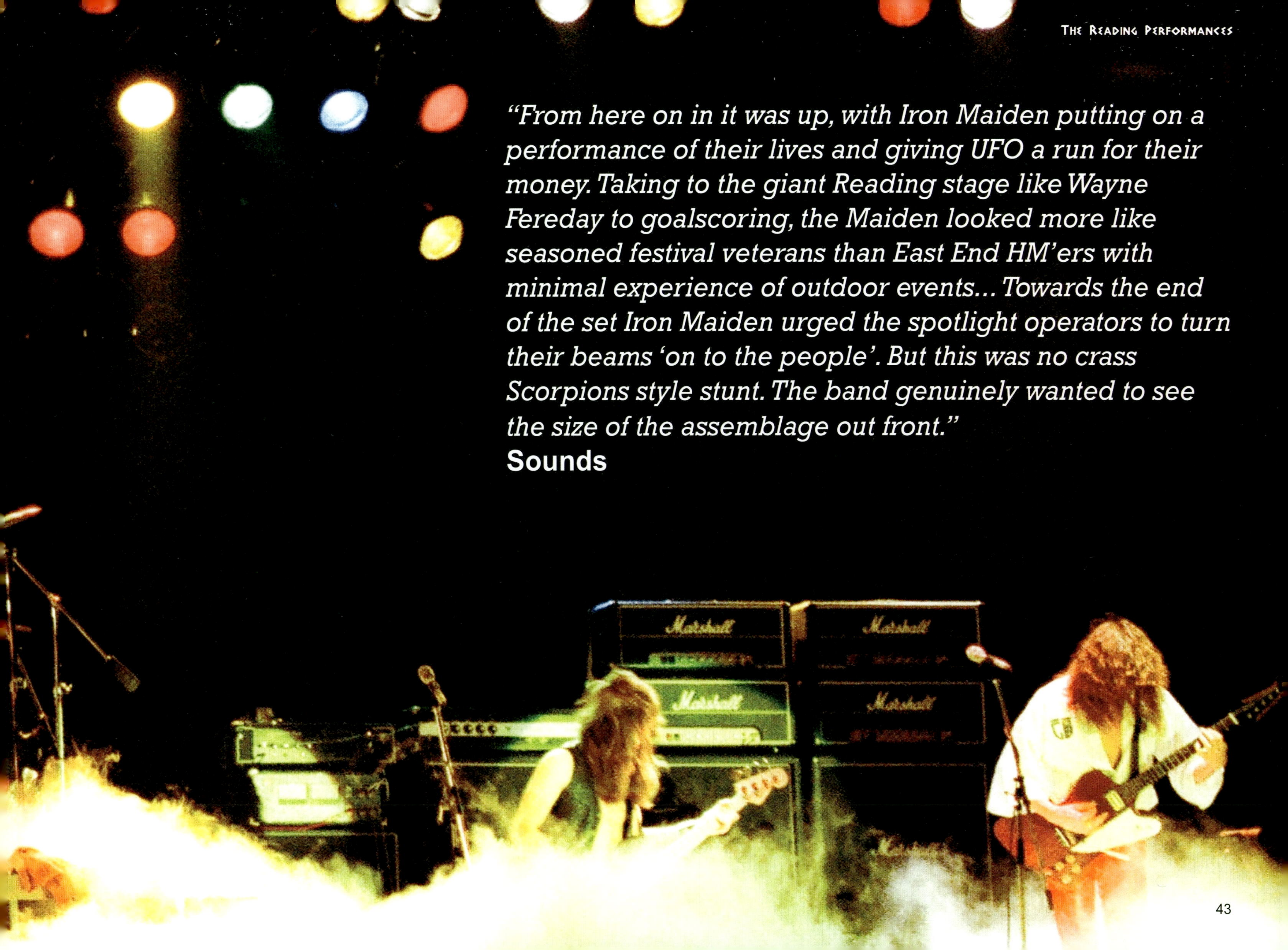

"From here on in it was up, with Iron Maiden putting on a performance of their lives and giving UFO a run for their money. Taking to the giant Reading stage like Wayne Fereday to goalscoring, the Maiden looked more like seasoned festival veterans than East End HM'ers with minimal experience of outdoor events... Towards the end of the set Iron Maiden urged the spotlight operators to turn their beams 'on to the people'. But this was no crass Scorpions style stunt. The band genuinely wanted to see the size of the assemblage out front."

Sounds

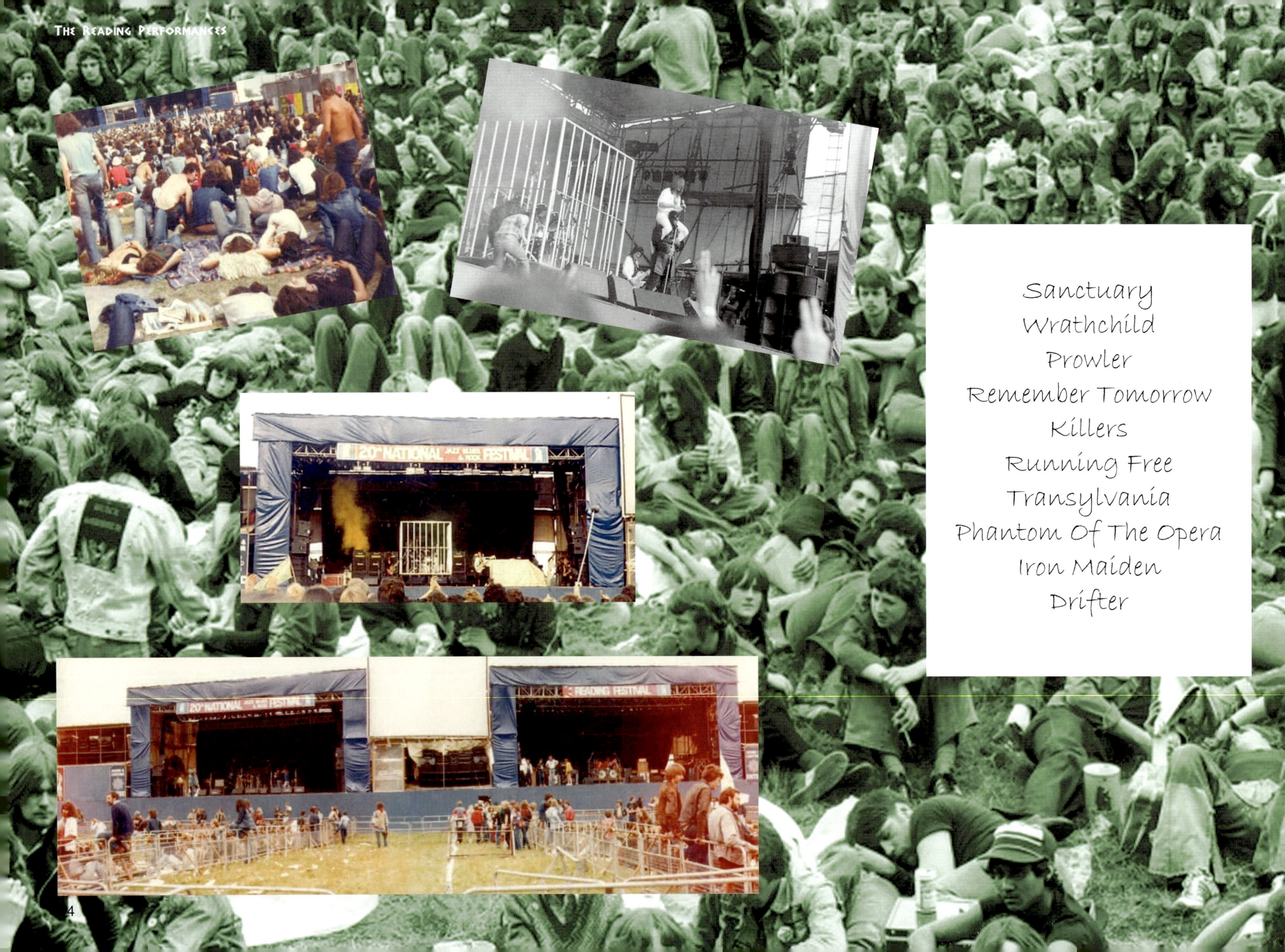

Sanctuary
Wrathchild
Prowler
Remember Tomorrow
Killers
Running Free
Transylvania
Phantom Of The Opera
Iron Maiden
Drifter

Maiden, of course it is his band. It always has been. There had been many changes in the early days of the band. Many of the situations that Harris found himself in were very frustrating especially as he was so dedicated to the band. Some of his former cohorts didn't have the time to spend on the band that Harris was able or willing to commit and some of them didn't have the money to help pay for equipment and such. But with each different set of circumstances Harris knew that he was going to make changes for the better; that his vision for Iron Maiden would one day become a reality. Some lesser minded and dedicated musicians would have fallen at the first hurdle and moved on to something else, but Harris was never going to fall down. In just a few short years Iron Maiden had already had their fair share of line-up changes. Regardless of which ever incarnation of the band there had been.

However, the seemingly steady line-up would be shaken up once more and once again, Reading would play a vital part in Iron Maiden's transformation.

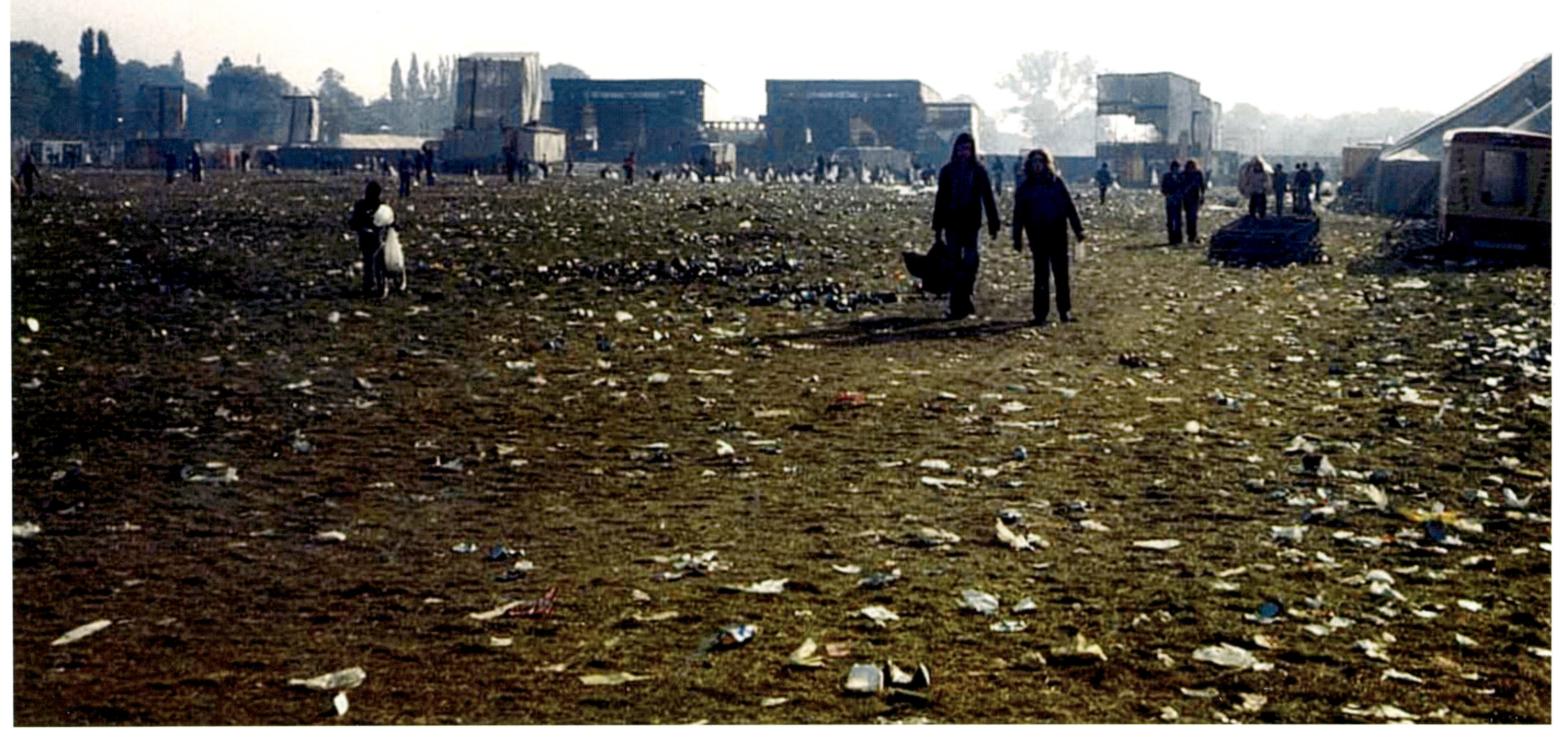

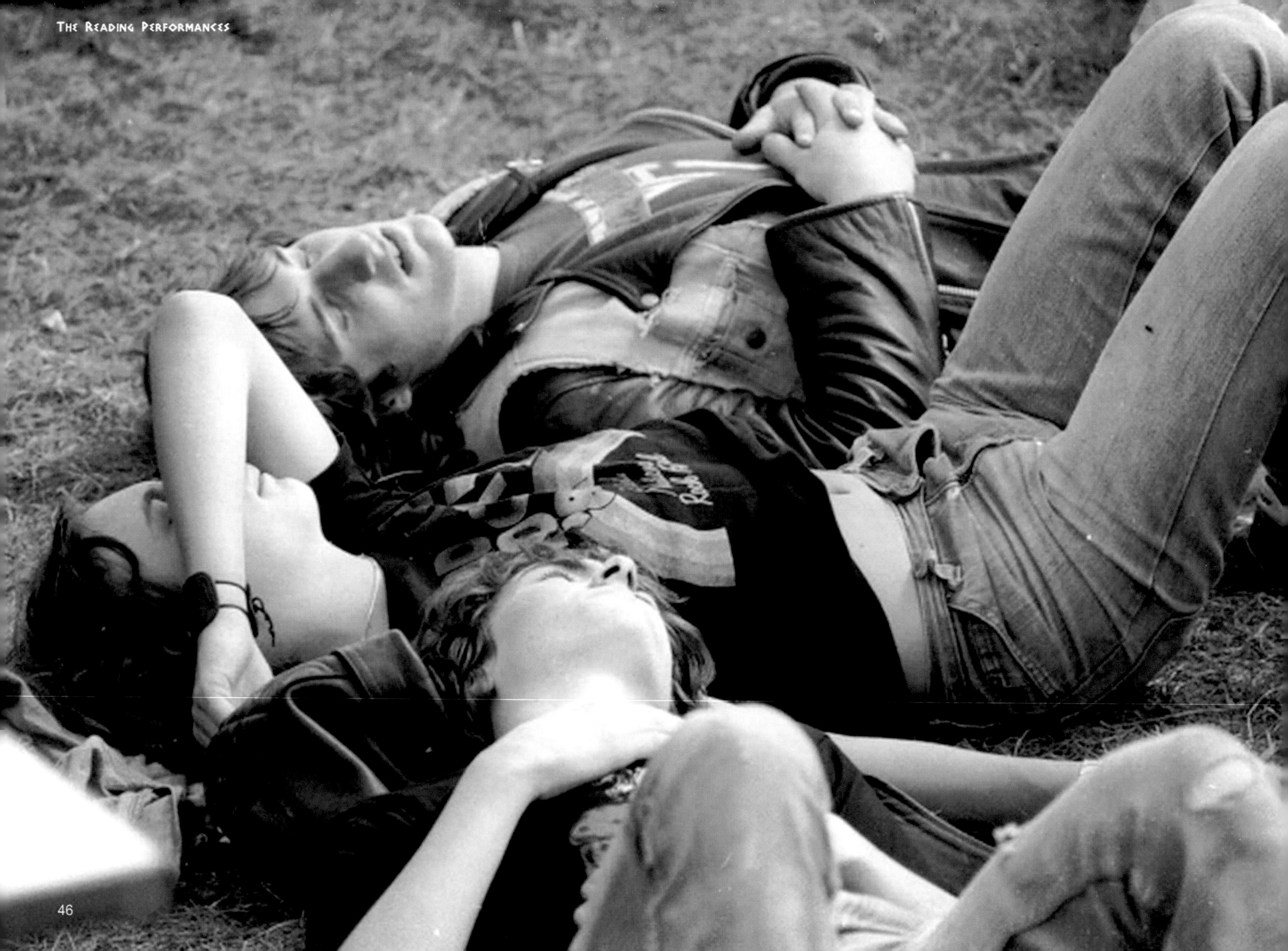

Reading Festival 1982

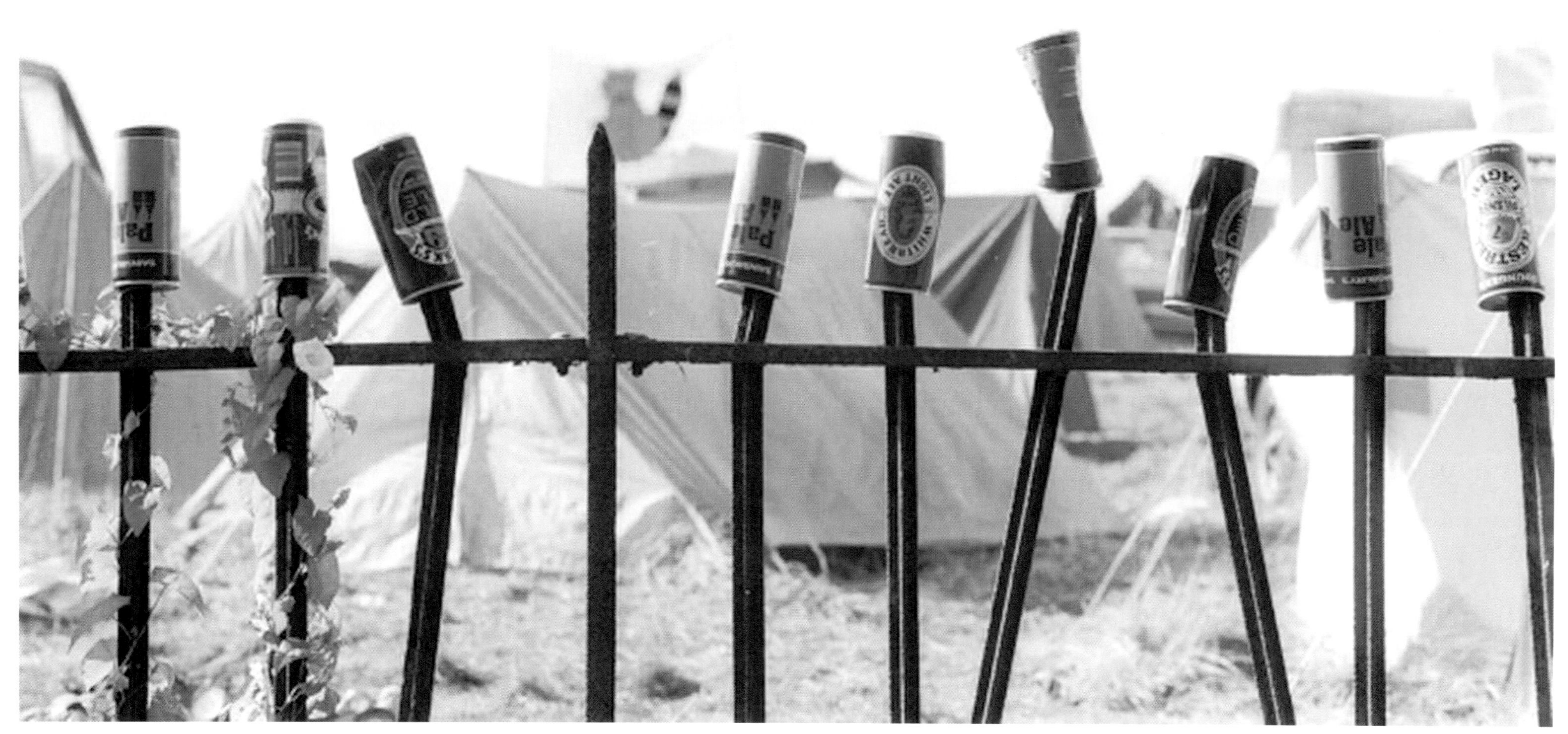

When cult metal band Samson first supported Iron Maiden at The Music Machine in 1980 Bruce Dickinson knew he wanted to move on to pastures new although he stayed in the outfit for their third album, *Shock Tactics* in 1981.

"At a relatively early age, when I was in Samson," Dickinson said to John McMurtrie of *Billboard*, "A&M Records wanted to sign me as a solo artist. And I was like, 'I'm 20 years old, I don't want to be a solo artist! Are you kidding me? I want to be a singer in a rock 'n' roll band!' And I've always pretty much been that way. I love working with bands, and I love the interaction and the banter and everything. It's great."

Samson, however, entered a messy legal situation after their label Gem went bust and thus could not finance a European tour in support of Maiden. Samson then switched to RCA Records but they had little interest in the band and so they last performed with Dickinson at Reading Festival in 1981, which was recorded by the BBC and later released as *Live*

> *"We went down really well and Steve Harris and Rod Smallwood were in the audience to check out the singer with this band called Samson. So it was a quite eventful day,"*
> **Bruce Dickinson**

At Reading 1981. That year also saw Gillan, The Kinks and Girlschool on the bill.

It was at Reading on August 29 1981 where Rod Smallwood first approached Dickinson about the idea of auditioning for Maiden. Yet another reason why Reading remains important in the history of Iron Maiden.

"We went down really well and Steve Harris and Rod Smallwood were in the audience to check out the singer with this band called Samson. So it was a quite eventful day," Dickinson enthused to esteemed music writer Chris Welch in 1989.

Dickinson jumped at the chance. It was for the best, really. They say things happen for a reason, don't they? Dickinson and Paul Samson did some work in the studio for vocal and guitar parts on September 9 1981. He announced he was leaving Samson on September 16 1981 and so in that month an enthusiastic and ambitious Bruce Dickinson turned up for an audition at a rehearsal room in Hackney and sang 'Killers', 'Twilight Zone' and 'Remember Tomorrow'.

Dickinson said to John McMurtrie of *Billboard*: "But I think that because we spent a lot of time rehearsing together, we also had this confidence that had grown even in just the rehearsal room. At the same time, I was aware that at the very beginning of the shows, I was going out to an audience that knew the previous singer, and we were doing material that they didn't know. We were doing new material that wasn't even released yet when we did our first five or six shows, when I first joined the band. And it was kind of nerve-wracking. I was like, 'I'm really not sure where we're going with this,' but I think the vocal approach was so different that people

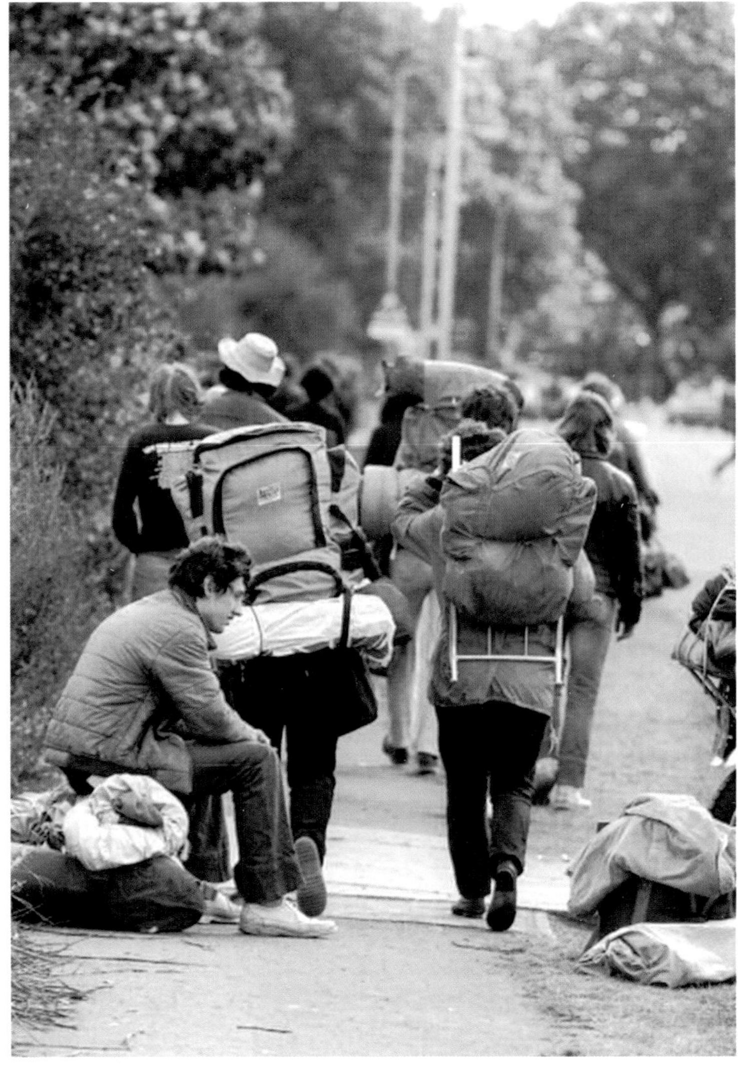

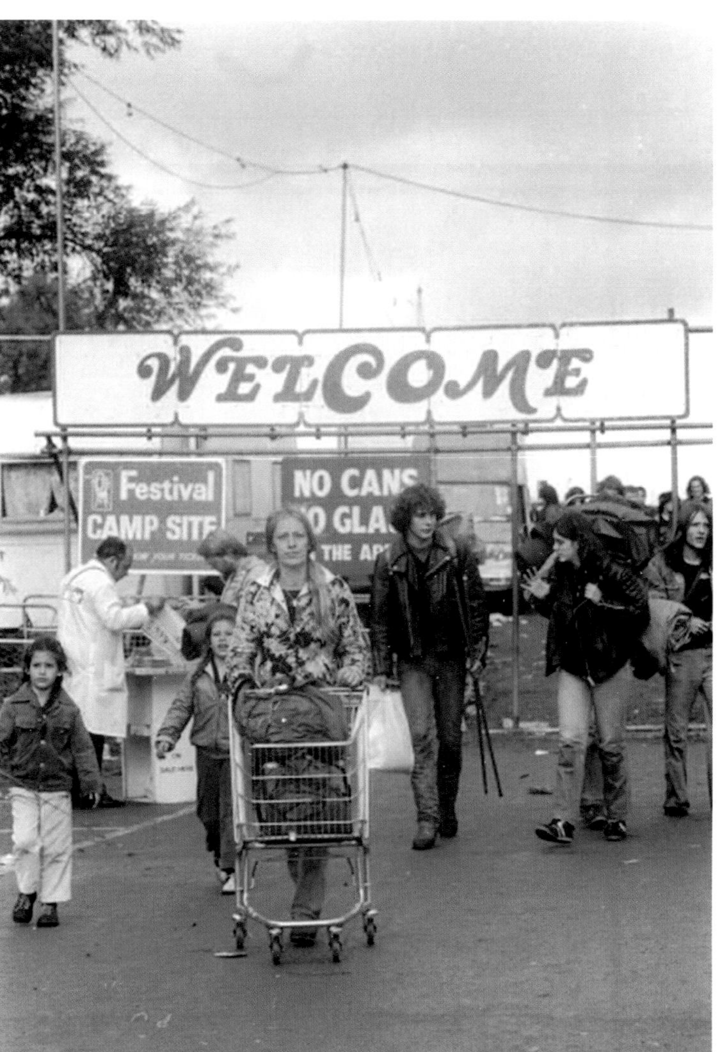

but the British metal scene was an incestuous world back then.

Steve Harris said to *Planet Rock*'s Paul Brannigan: "I'd never been much into Samson, but I'd always thought their singer was good. I thought, 'Yeah, the bloke's got a really good voice, and he knows how to work a crowd.' I thought he sounded a bit like Ian Gillan, actually. When the shit really hit the fan with Paul, he was one of the first people I thought of. Rod wasn't keen."

Smallwood also hated the name "Bruce Bruce" and didn't like Dickinson's white gown that he wore onstage.

Even Rod Smallwood admitted to Brannigan: "I hadn't even met Bruce, but I didn't really like him. I thought Bruce Bruce was a stupid name, I thought the white thing he used to wear on stage looked really naff, and also Samson had messed about with Maiden before I got involved; I do bear grudges."

kind of stood back and went, 'Wow. This is kind of cool. This is totally different.' But I think the audience was just as surprised as I was."

Dickinson had rehearsed a lot more songs than he was asked to do. He immediately impressed both Harris and Rod Smallwood though Smallwood reportedly had reservations because of the Samson connection; a band he no longer wanted anything to do with

Iron Maiden impressed Dickinson, though. "When I first heard Maiden I got the same buzz of them I did when I heard *Deep Purple In Rock*," Dickinson said to Chris Welch. "It was like a steam train coming at you and none of the other bands did that any more. I really wanted to be the in their band. When I did *The Number Of The Beast* we went in with all guns blazing. The rest is... newspaper clippings. Paul wasn't surprised when I left and it was a relief to him because he wanted to be more in control."

It has to be said though that without Samson Maiden would possibly have never come across, Thunderstick, Clive Burr or Bruce Dickinson, so Samson does have a rightful place in heavy metal history. And it sort of all came together at Reading Festival. Dickinson got the gig before they asked Dickinson to sing the songs again. Dickinson was impressed by the strict professionalism of Maiden and knew it would be his rightful home for the long-term.

"When he joined the band, it was a huge relief for us," Harris admitted to Philippe Touchard of *Enfer Magazine* in 1985. "We'd known him a long time and he'd always been a great fan of Iron Maiden. Right from the first rehearsal, he gave us a brand new conviction and we were back in business again. Because, even if we weren't worried about the music — at that time, I was writing almost all the songs — there was a general feeling of discouragement that worried me, and that if the *Killers* album was doing really well and bringing us more and more success."

The former Samson frontman made his debut appearance with Maiden in Bologna, Italy on October 26, 1981.

It was to be with Dickinson that the East End lads would achieve their greatest success. Dickinson hits the falsettos with ease and runs around the stage like an escaped madman proving himself to be a vastly different presence than Di'Anno; who had much more of a punky, tougher attitude that was in many ways similar to the late AC/DC singer Bon Scott.

With Bruce Dickinson Iron Maiden would become the consummate professional metal band that they remain to this very day. They would become a totally different beast from the Paul Di'Anno incarnation.

Bruce Dickinson truly showed his majesty as a heavy metal front man when Maiden made an all-important performance at the 1982 Reading Festival during August 28 Bank

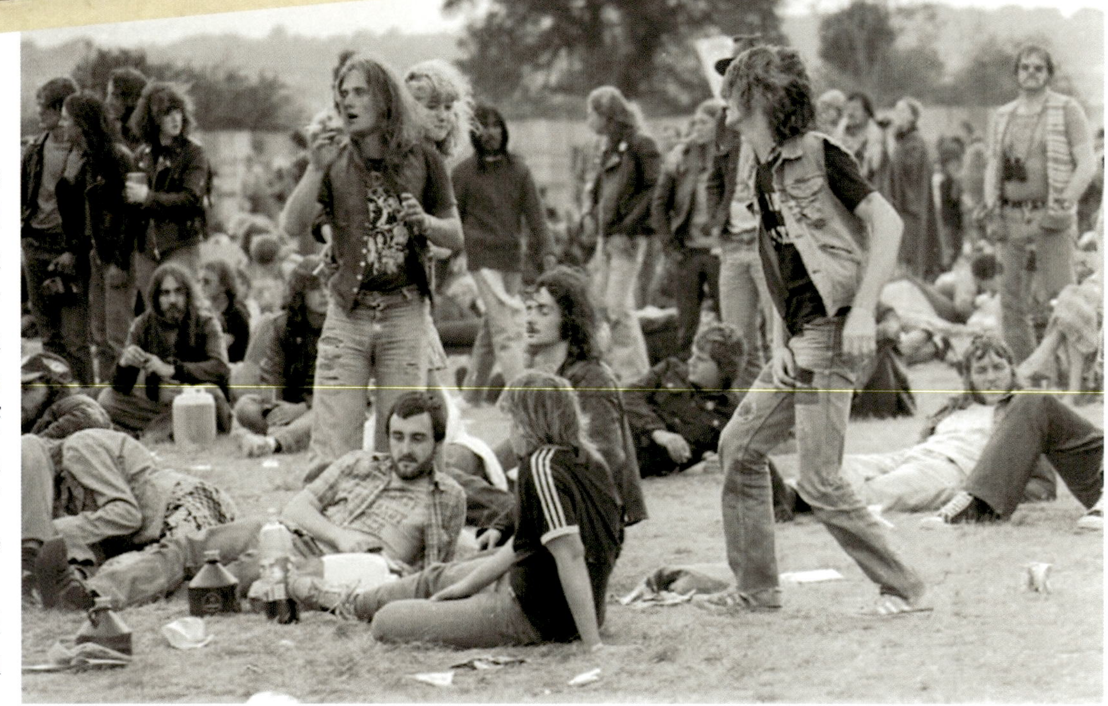

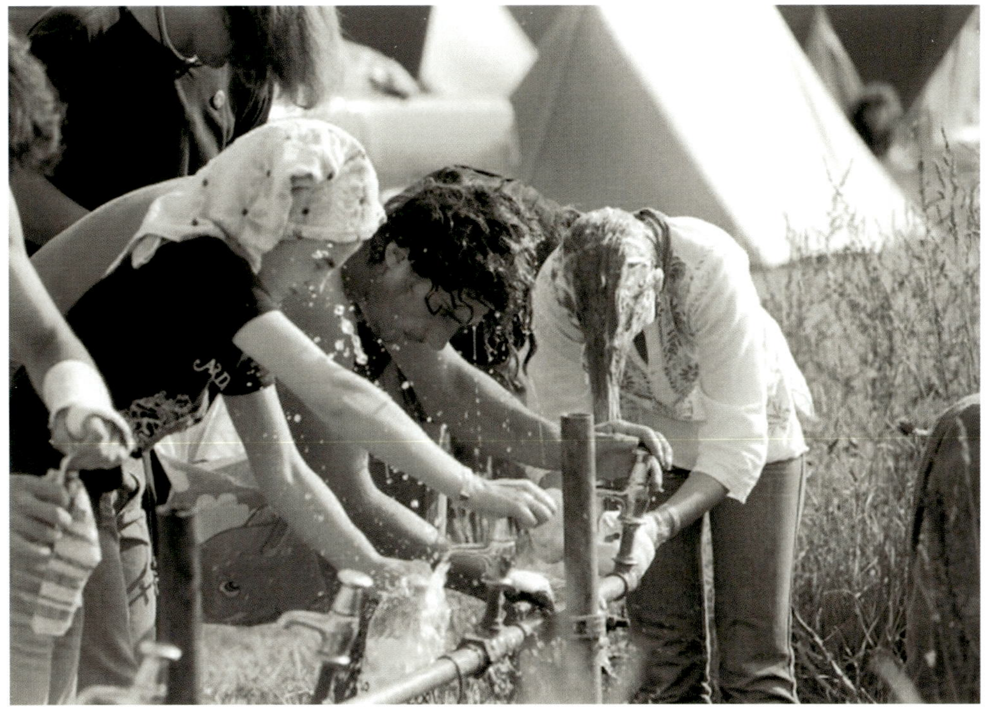

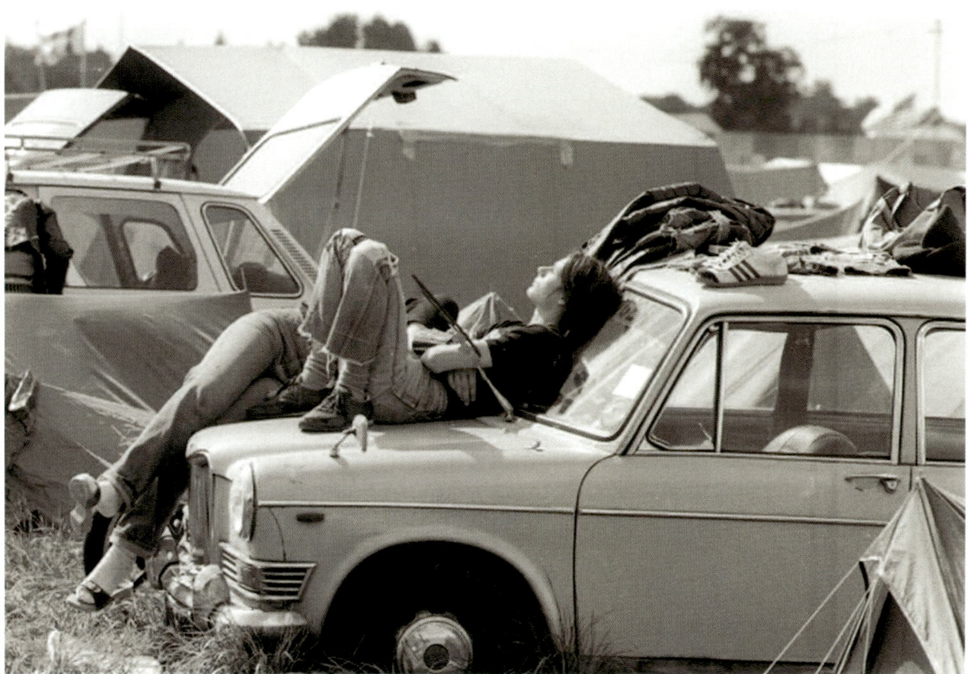

Holiday.

Budgie and The Michael Schenker Group were also on the bill that long weekend along with such artists as Twisted Sister, Tank, Marillion, Overkill, The Angels, Dave Edmunds, Blackfoot, Y & T, Wilko Johnson, Baron Rojo, Tygers Of Pan Tang, Spider, Cheetah, Praying Mantis, Chinatown, Against the Grain, Bernie Tormé, Stampede, Randy California, Rock Goddess, Terraplane, Grand Prix, Ore, The Gary Moore Band and Bernie Marsden's SOS. What a bill!

Obviously the band's 1982 appearance was significantly different from their first show at Reading back in 1980. Di'Anno and Stratton were both gone and replaced with Dickinson and Smith, respectively.

The band flew 12,000 miles in a round trip for the festival spot from El Paso, Texas to London, England and then to Los Angeles, California. Legend has it that before the flight Dickinson and roadie Dave Lights took three horse tranquillizers and didn't wake up properly for days. Maiden did find time to play a few small warm-up gigs as Dickinson was nervous about the performance.

Only 36 hours before Reading he'd lost his voice. Ricky Medlocke of Blackfoot joined them onstage for a quick jam. The event was headlined by Budgie with Maiden second on the bill and also featured Michael Schenker, Twisted Sister, Blackfoot and Marillion.

The Dickinson/Harris/Murray/Smith/Burr line-up was on fire and can be heard as part of the 2002 *BBC Archives* release. The band blitzed through 'Wrathchild', 'Run To The Hills', 'Children Of The Damned', 'The Number Of The Beast', '22 Acacia Avenue', 'Transylvania', 'The Prisoner', 'Hallowed Be Thy Name', 'Phantom Of The Opera' and 'Iron Maiden'.

An important gig for the band was at Reading Festival on August Bank Holiday where Bruce Dickinson made his presence felt in front of thousands of music fans. They toured extensively around the USA where they supported Rainbow on their *Straight Between The Eyes*

tour and Scorpions on their *Blackout* tour, and also Judas Priest on their *Screaming For Vengeance* trek. Maiden also played some of their own headlining shows in the USA. It opened up a huge market for the band but it wasn't an easy task. Maiden were more than prepared to put the hard work in.

Maiden proved to the Reading audience that Bruce Dickinson was now their one and only frontman; the Paul Di'Anno years were a thing of the past. Fans needed to get over it, and move on. Dickinson hit those notes with ease and commanded the audience's attention like a heavy metal Freddie Mercury. The rest of the band offered a blistering attack on the senses. Man, this was HEAVY METAL. There was nothing else like it in Britain. Somehow, Maiden managed to stay true to the heavy

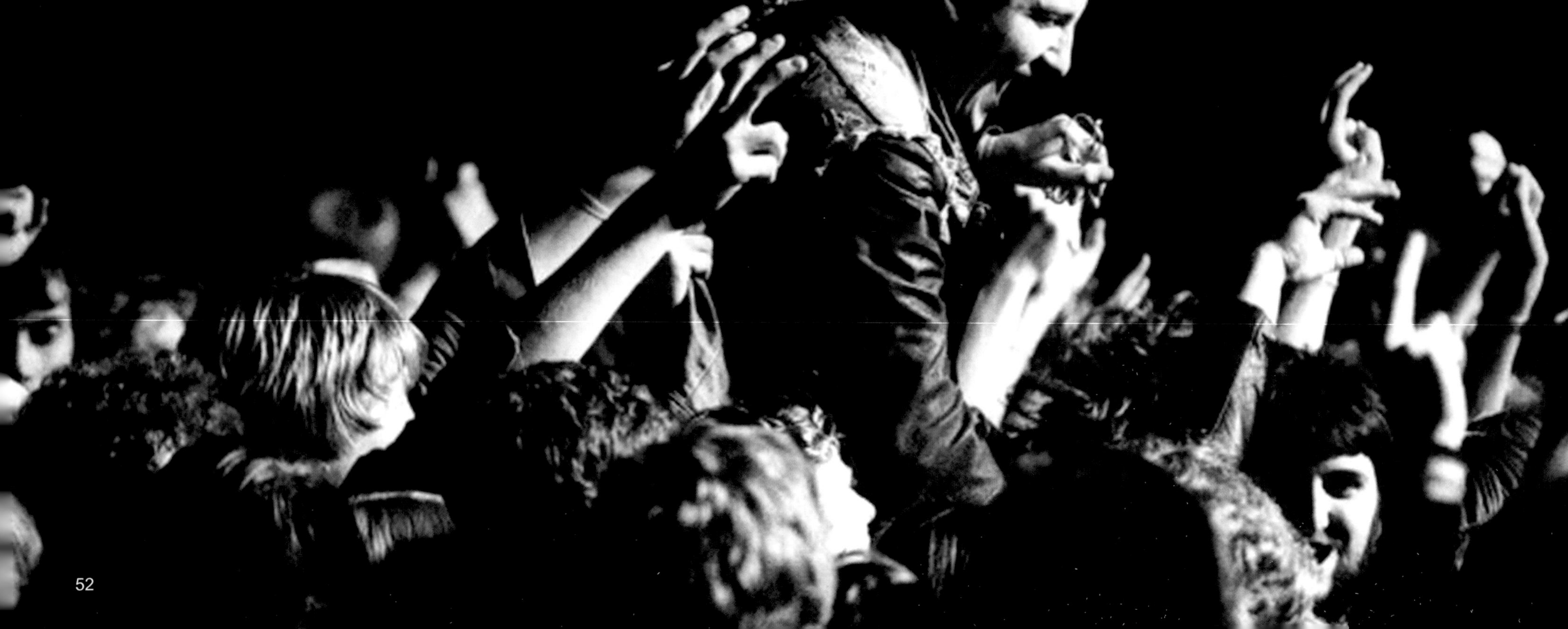

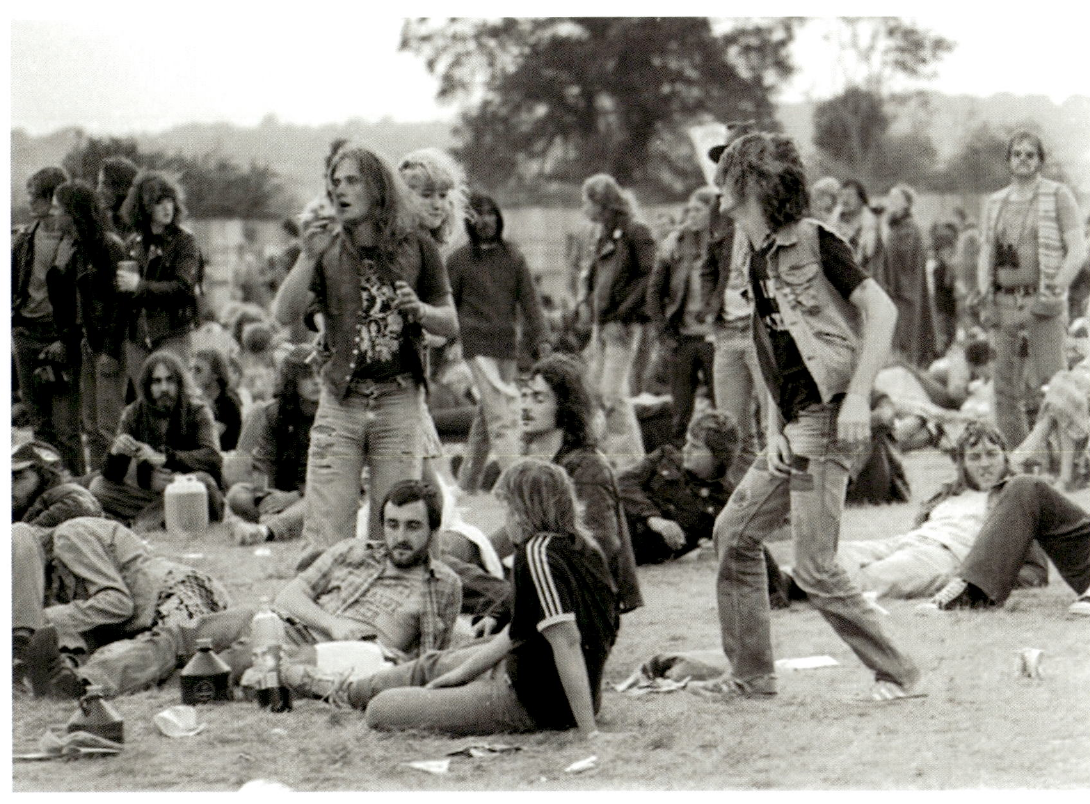

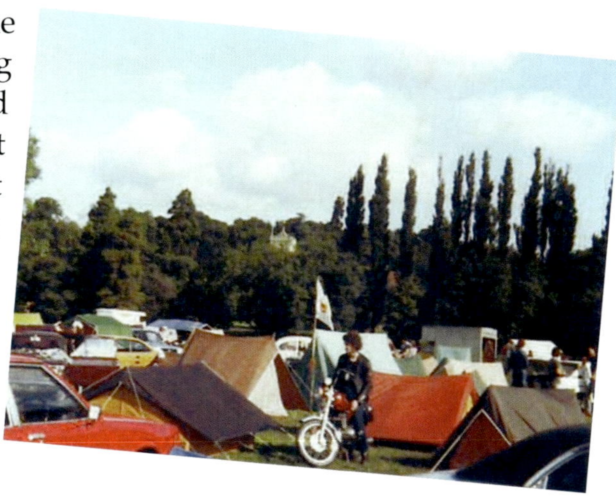

and 'Prisoner' - outline their expanding musical scope, and mindful of this slot being taken straight out of the middle of a gruelling world tour, Iron Maiden still managed to inject sheer sparkle into a set that they've been performing since Easter!"

Guitarists Dave Murray and Adrian Smith made a huge impression on the metal scene and could be mentioned in the same breath and tones of reverence as Judas Priest's master shredders K.K. Downing and Glenn Tipton.

Smith told respected rock historian Steve Rosen of *Ultimate-guitar.com* in 1982: "Dave grew up with a lot of Hendrix. You go down to his house anytime and he'll be playing that. So his approach is wah wah and lots of whammy bar, very, very fast. I tend to, when I do a solo in the studio, I'll just like work it out. Then I'll put it down and maybe I'll keep it. Dave will just rip it out three

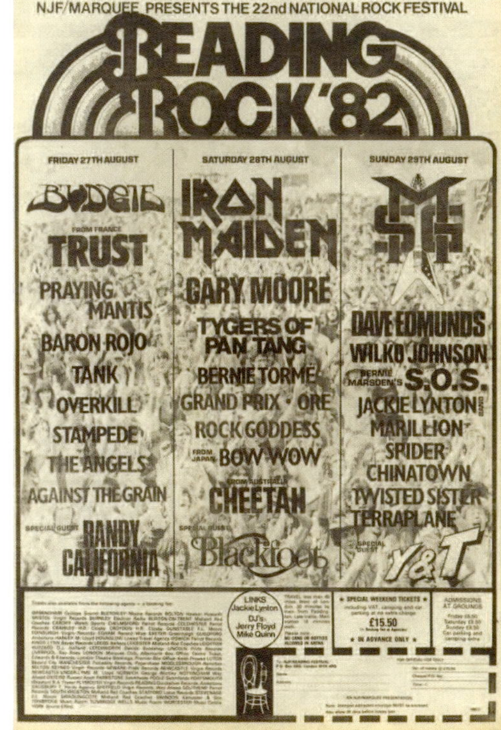

metal sound of authenticity but also have enough guts and glory about them to appeal general rock fans. They dominated the Reading audience and did not look back. Why would they? They had become the biggest metal band in Britain.

Reviewing the band's Reading performance Robbi Millar of *Sounds* wrote: "The US experience in front of the mega audience is clear: while the band have built up a show that is visually stimulating and sharp, their music shows no sign of being left behind. Selections from 'Beast' – namely 'Run To The Hills'

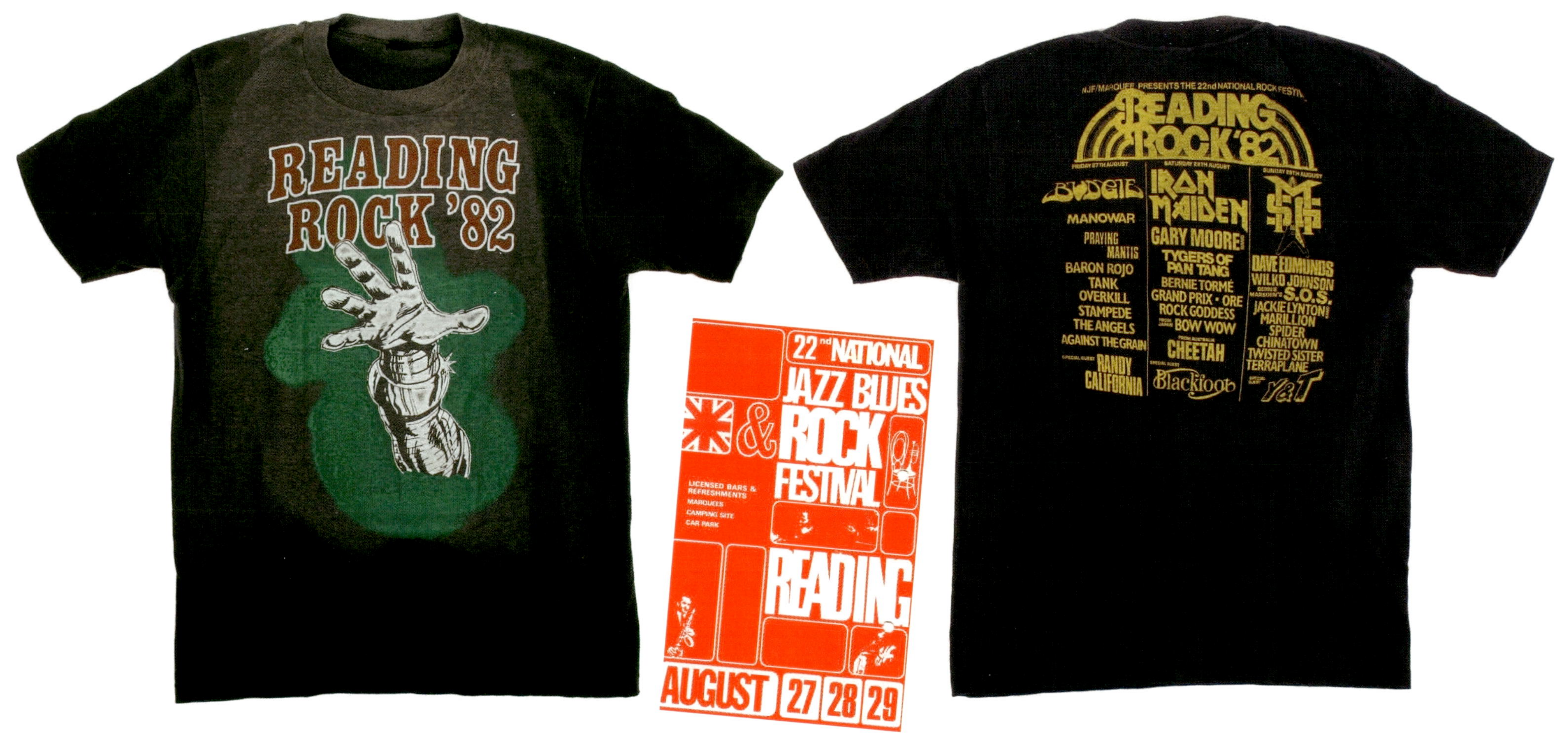

or four at once." After Reading there would be yet more changes.

As 1982 was drawing to a close the band took a break in Honolulu in October. However, drummer Clive Burr announced his departure from the band due to personal reasons and the hectic nature of the band's touring rota. After a tour of Australia and East Asia in November through to December the band brought The Beast On The Road Tour to a close in Japan at Niigata Prefectural Civic Centre on December 10, which was Burr's last gig with Maiden. The band subsequently, and predictably, hired Michael Henry "Nicko" McBrain, who has been Maiden's drummer ever since. A few years older than Harris, McBrain's heavier, faster style of drumming would take Maiden onto a whole new level of performance.

Photographer and *Fireworks* magazine contributor Ian Parry says: "The arrival of Bruce Dickinson immediately changed that. Even though the tour kicked off before the release of the full 'Number Of The Beast' album, 'Run To The Hills' was already in the charts and the Liverpool Empire, a step up in capacity from previous local gigs was packed to capacity. My overriding memory of the show is of Bruce, full of energy and enthusiasm, bouncing around the stage like the proverbial kid in a sweet shop. Vocally on another level from

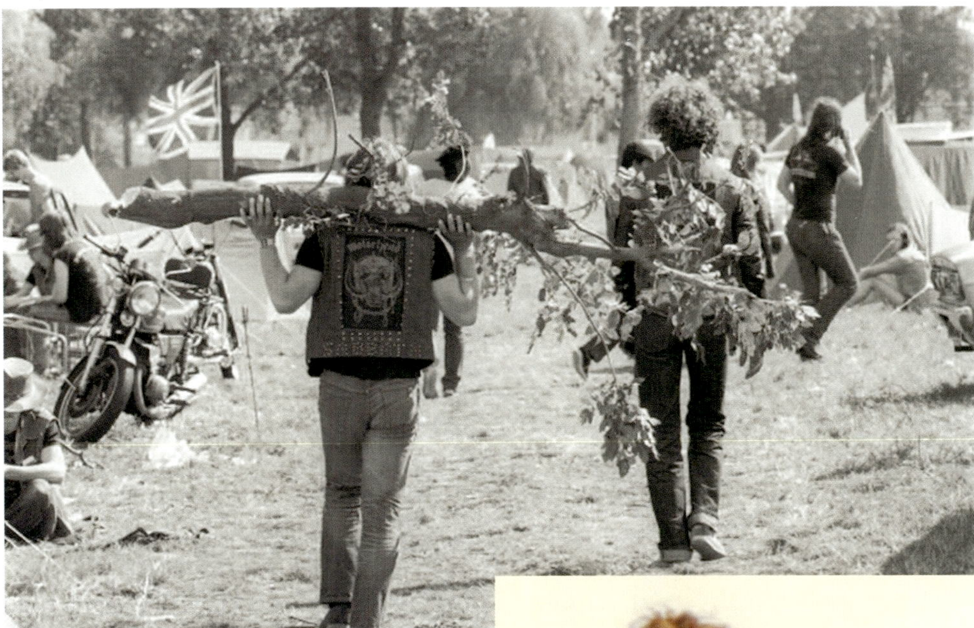

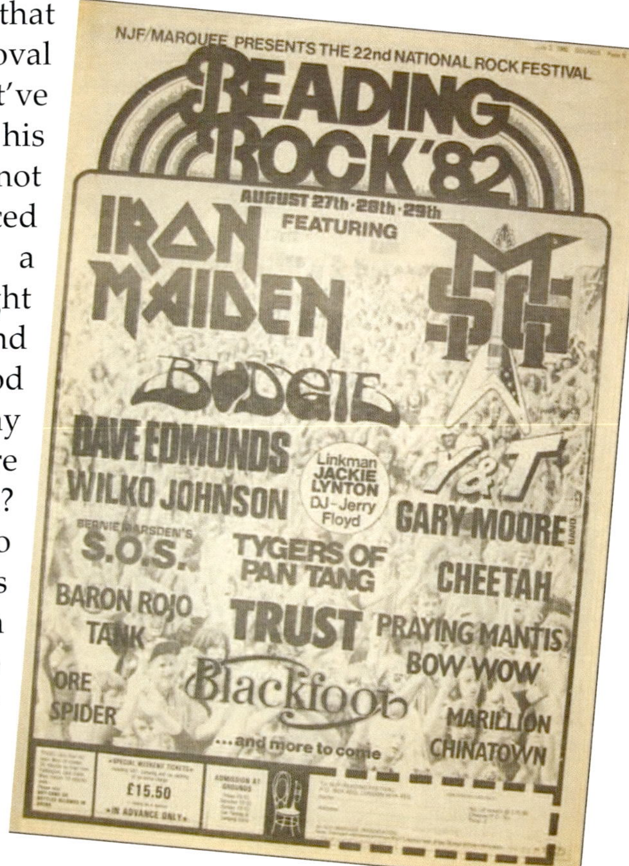

Di'Anno, songs old and new were handled as if his own whilst also connecting with the audience with ease. 'Run To The Hills' was introduced as 'Our latest cowboy film' proudly announcing its rise to Number 11 in the charts 'to show Adam and the Ants a fucking thing or two'. After that there was never any doubt which way Iron Maiden's career was heading, even thirty years on, memories of that first encounter are clear."

Renowned American metal writer Ray Van Horn, Jr comments: "Being a near-lifelong Maiden fanatic, I feel that Paul Di'Anno's removal from the band might've been necessary to his personal survival. If not for a reported forced resignation from a difference of thought with Steve Harris and band manager Rod Smallwood, who's to say what either side's future would've been? Unfortunately, Di'Anno hardly profited from his ejection, while Iron Maiden went the opposite route. Their division, however, seemed not only inevitable but appointed.

More of a roughneck street punk in visual and vocal projection, Di'Anno's chiselled pipes were befitting of Iron Maiden's initial merge of punk, hard rock and heavy metal. 'Prowler' might be the best song Motörhead never wrote, while 'Sanctuary' remains Iron Maiden's snaggletooth response to Judas Priest's 'Breaking The Law' released the same year. No matter how sharp Dickinson wields 'Sanctuary' onstage, the song was made for Di'Anno's huffing rasps. In his hands, 'Sanctuary' sounds as dangerous as it was intended. With Dickinson, the same song comes off as a polished-up nostalgia trip, vivid a singer as Dickinson is."

He continues: "The move from Di'Anno to Dickinson may look

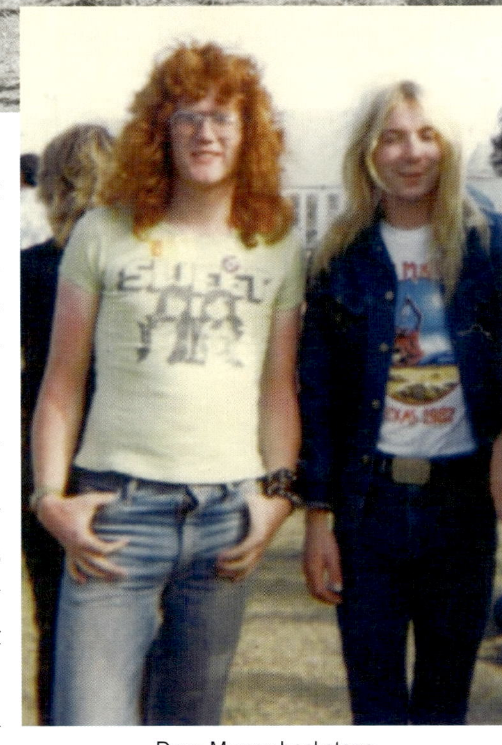

Dave Murray backstage
with music journalist Dave Ling.

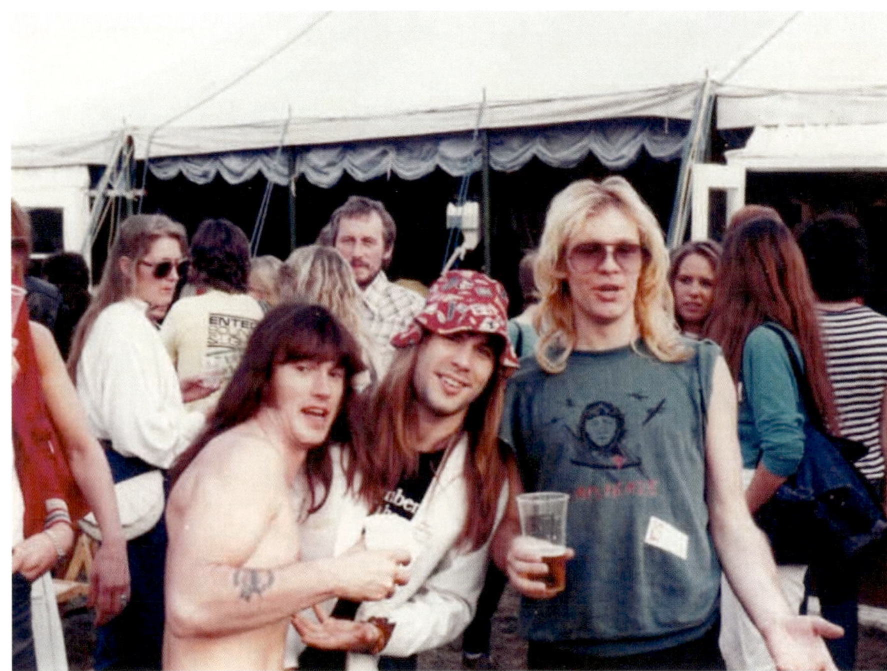

Bruce Dickinson backstage with Colin Bond from Stampede.

unfair on paper given the dubious circumstances, but with Di'Anno's recounted substance abuse at the time of *Killers*, there was no remembering tomorrow for him. As one of his finest hours on the mike, 'Remember Tomorrow' continues to remain isolated unto Di'Anno's era, just as 'Charlotte The Harlot,' 'Women In Uniform', 'Innocent Exile' and 'Wrathchild' are bona fide *Di'Anno*. Malleable as Bruce Dickinson is with 'Running Free', 'Murders In The Rue Morgue' and 'Iron Maiden'' those preceding cuts are nearly sacred and untouchable, regardless of where you stand on the topic of Di'Anno's tenure.

The two Reading Festivals brought together two very different incarnations of Iron Maiden yet both versions were forces to be reckoned with. It would be quite some time before Maiden would visit Reading again.

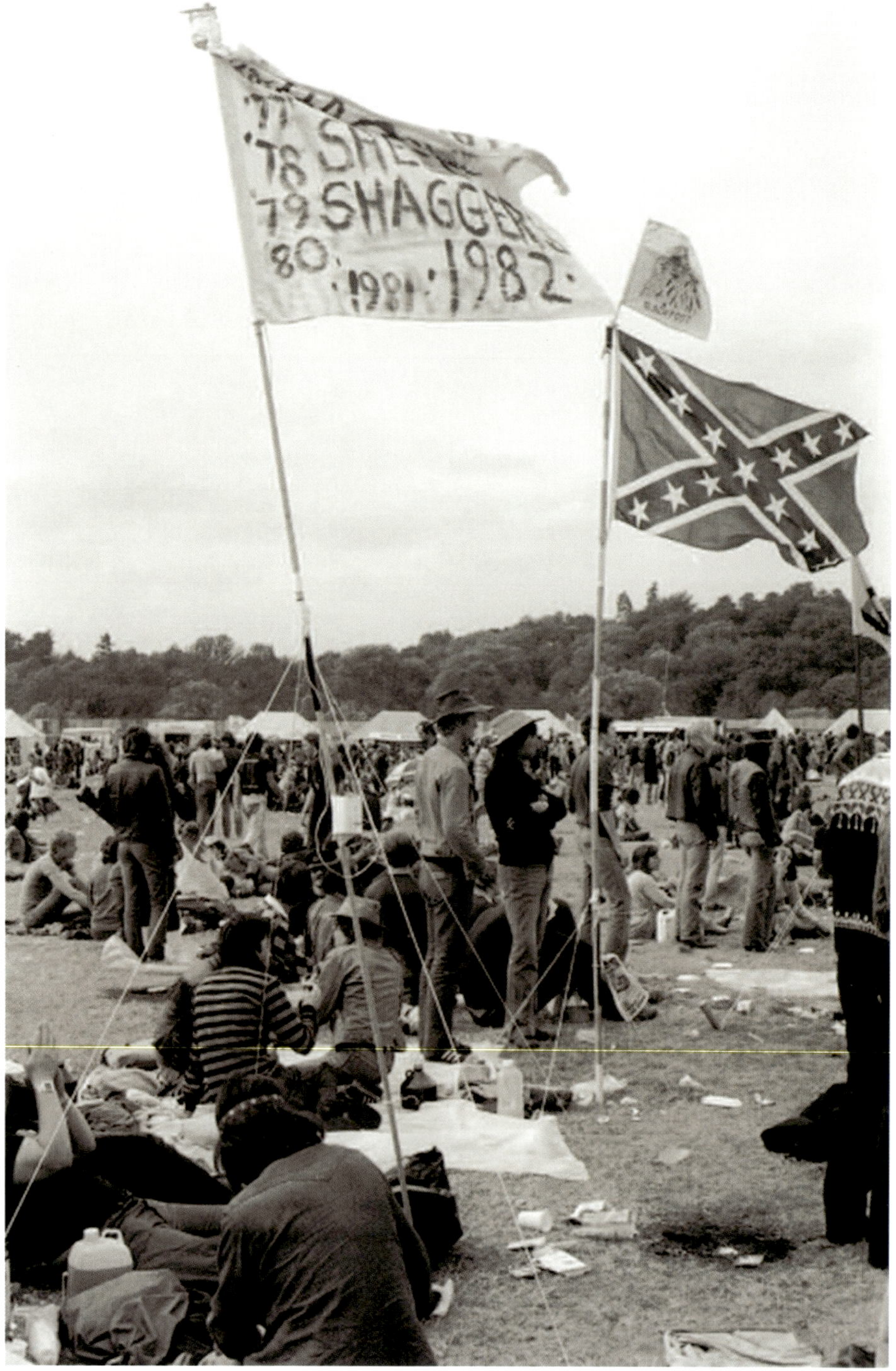

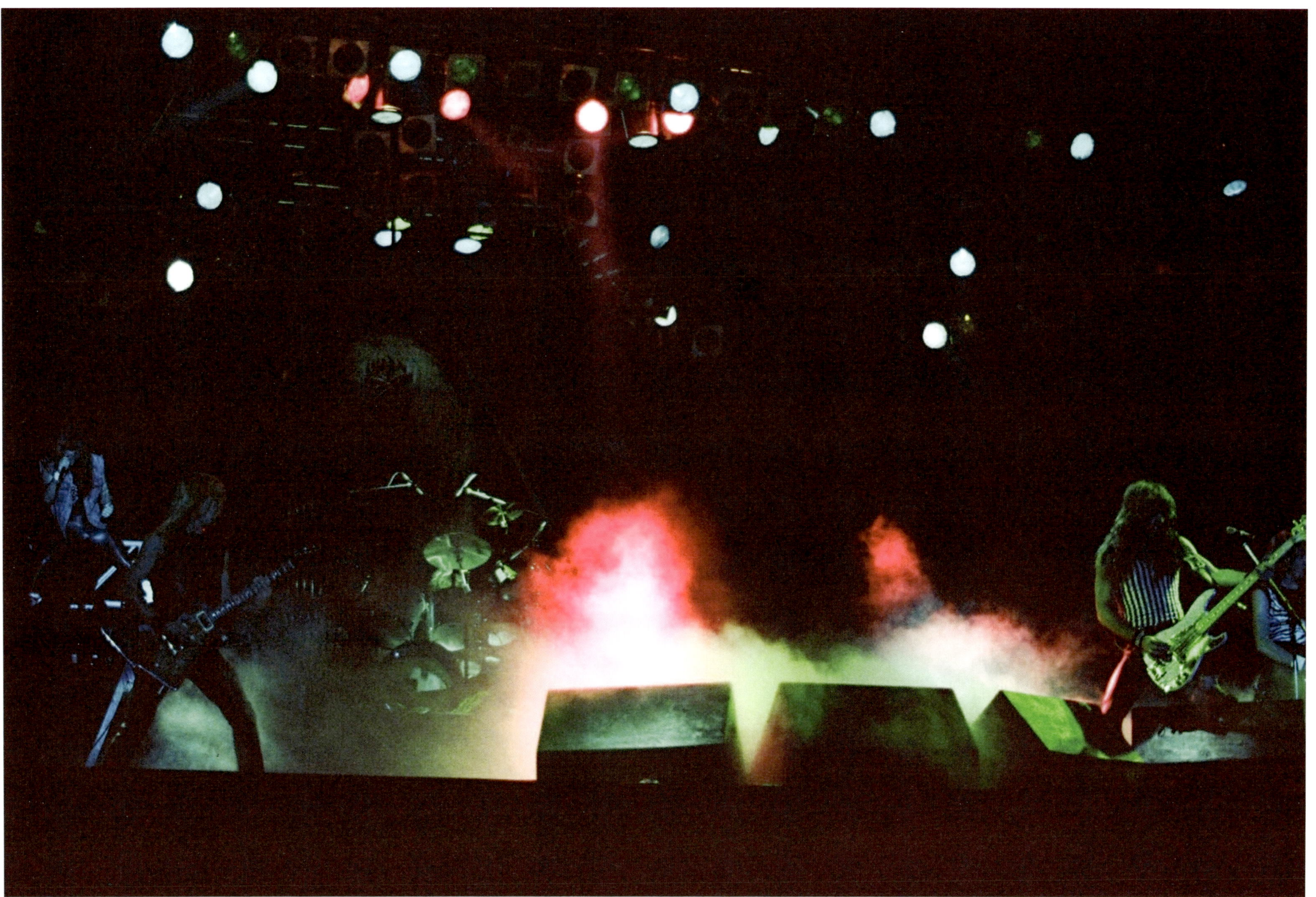

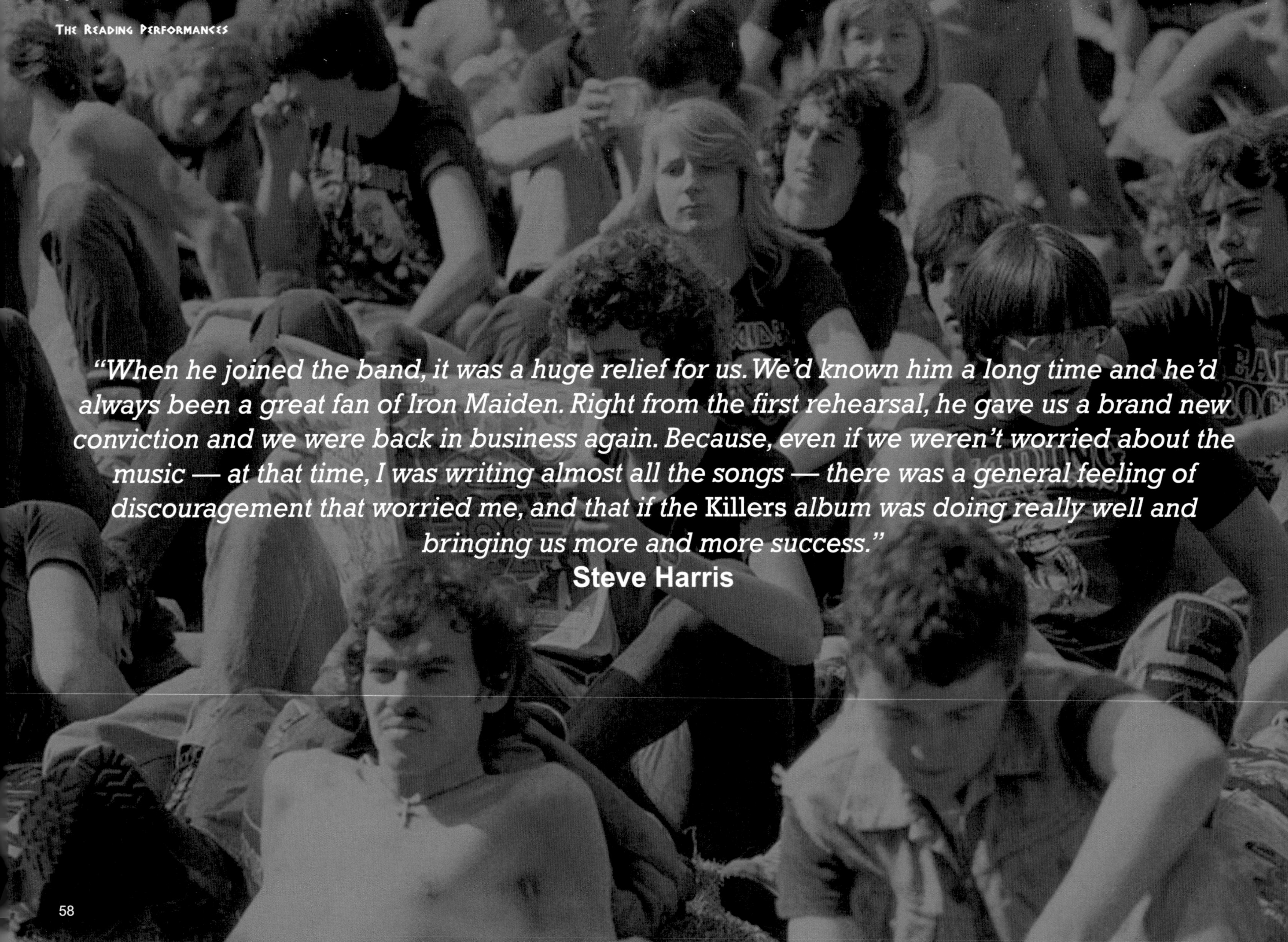

"When he joined the band, it was a huge relief for us. We'd known him a long time and he'd
always been a great fan of Iron Maiden. Right from the first rehearsal, he gave us a brand new
conviction and we were back in business again. Because, even if we weren't worried about the
music — at that time, I was writing almost all the songs — there was a general feeling of
discouragement that worried me, and that if the Killers album was doing really well and
bringing us more and more success."
Steve Harris

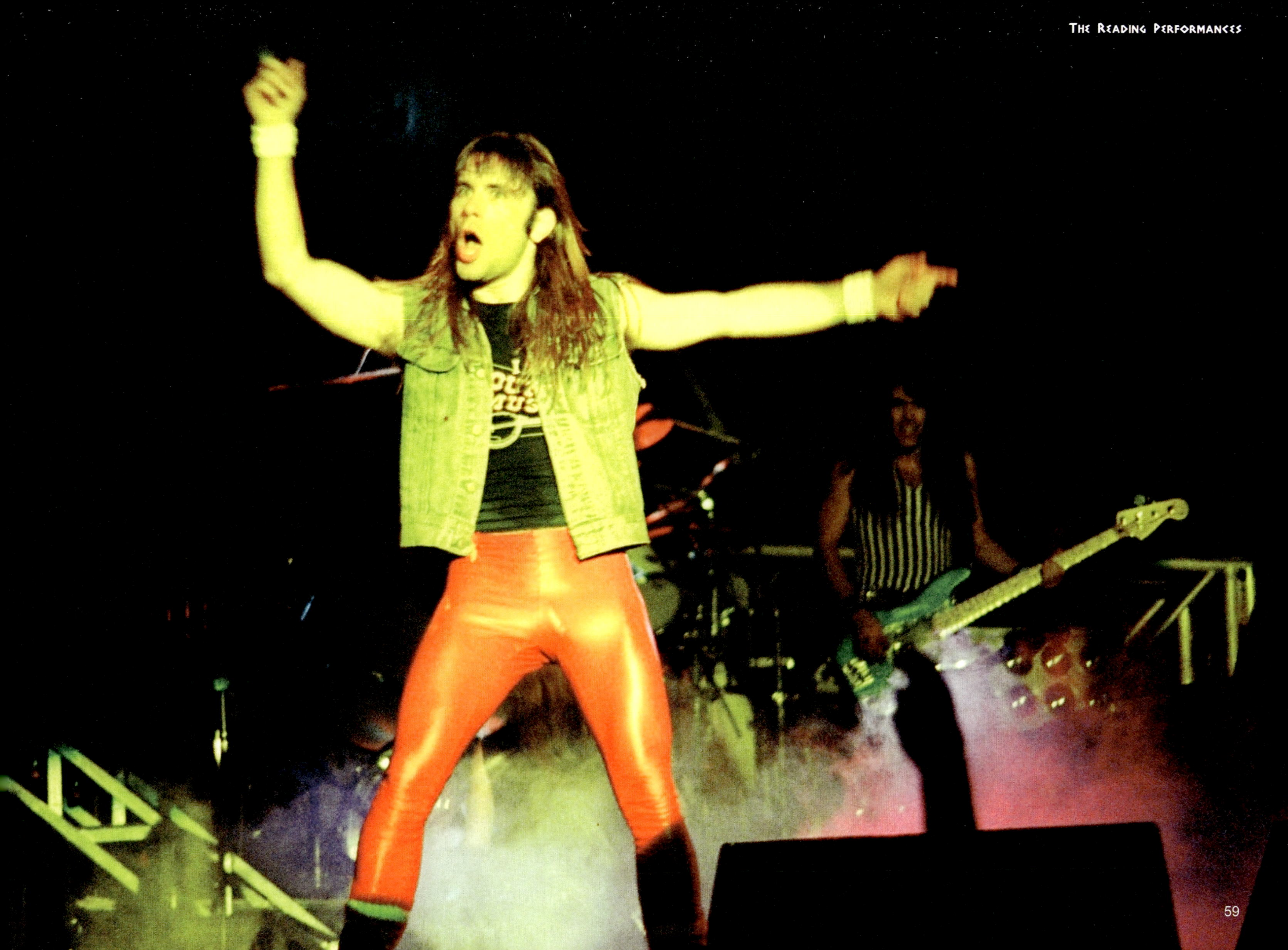

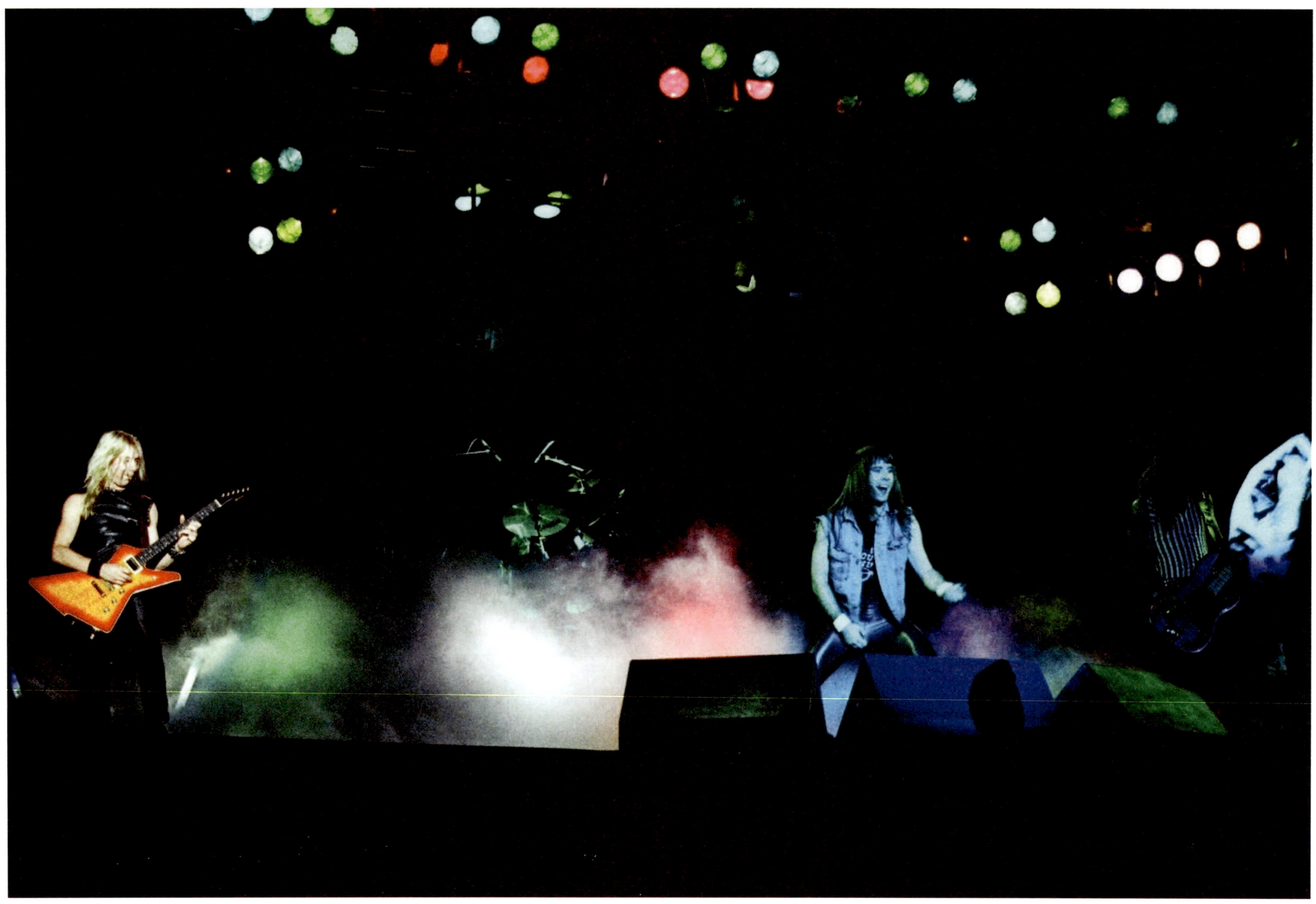

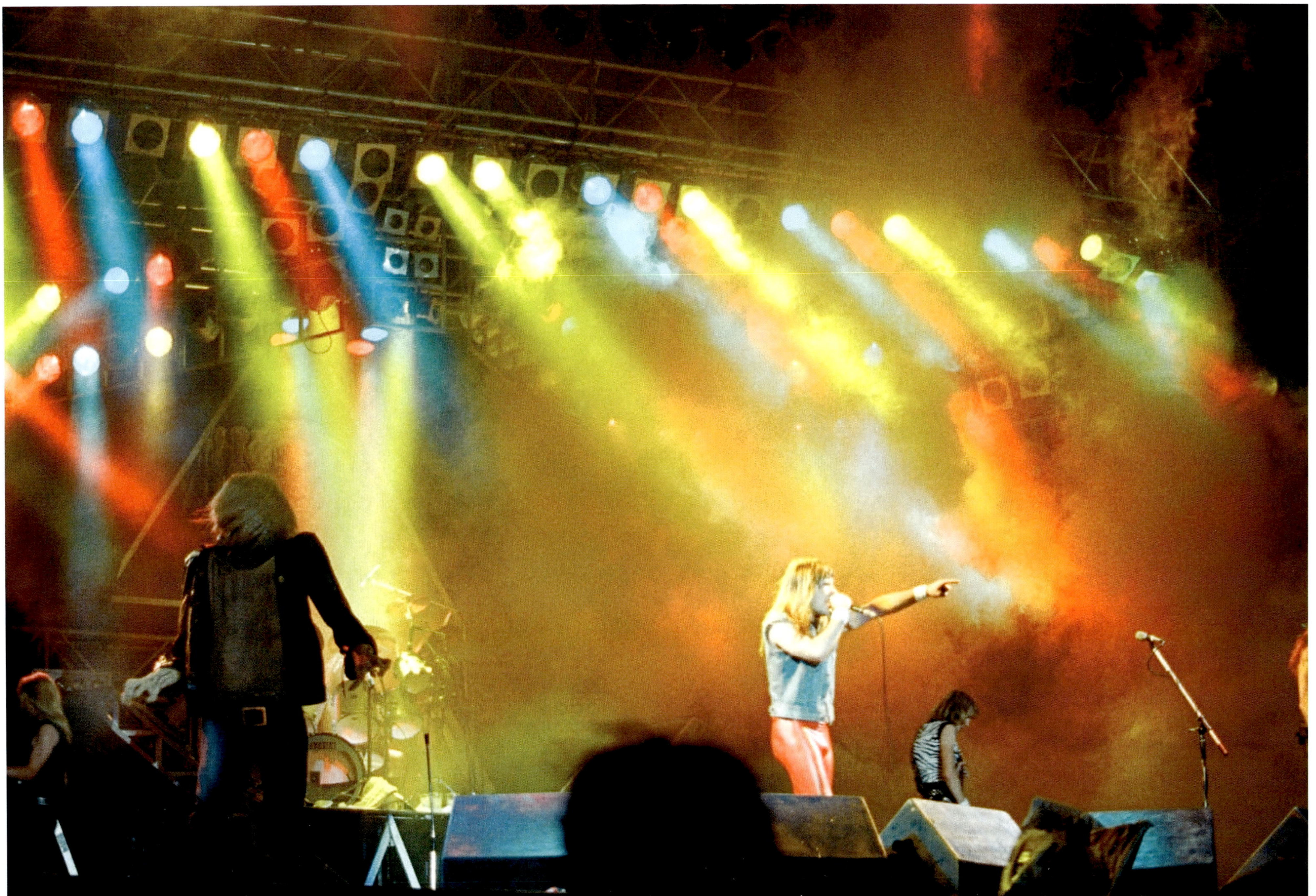

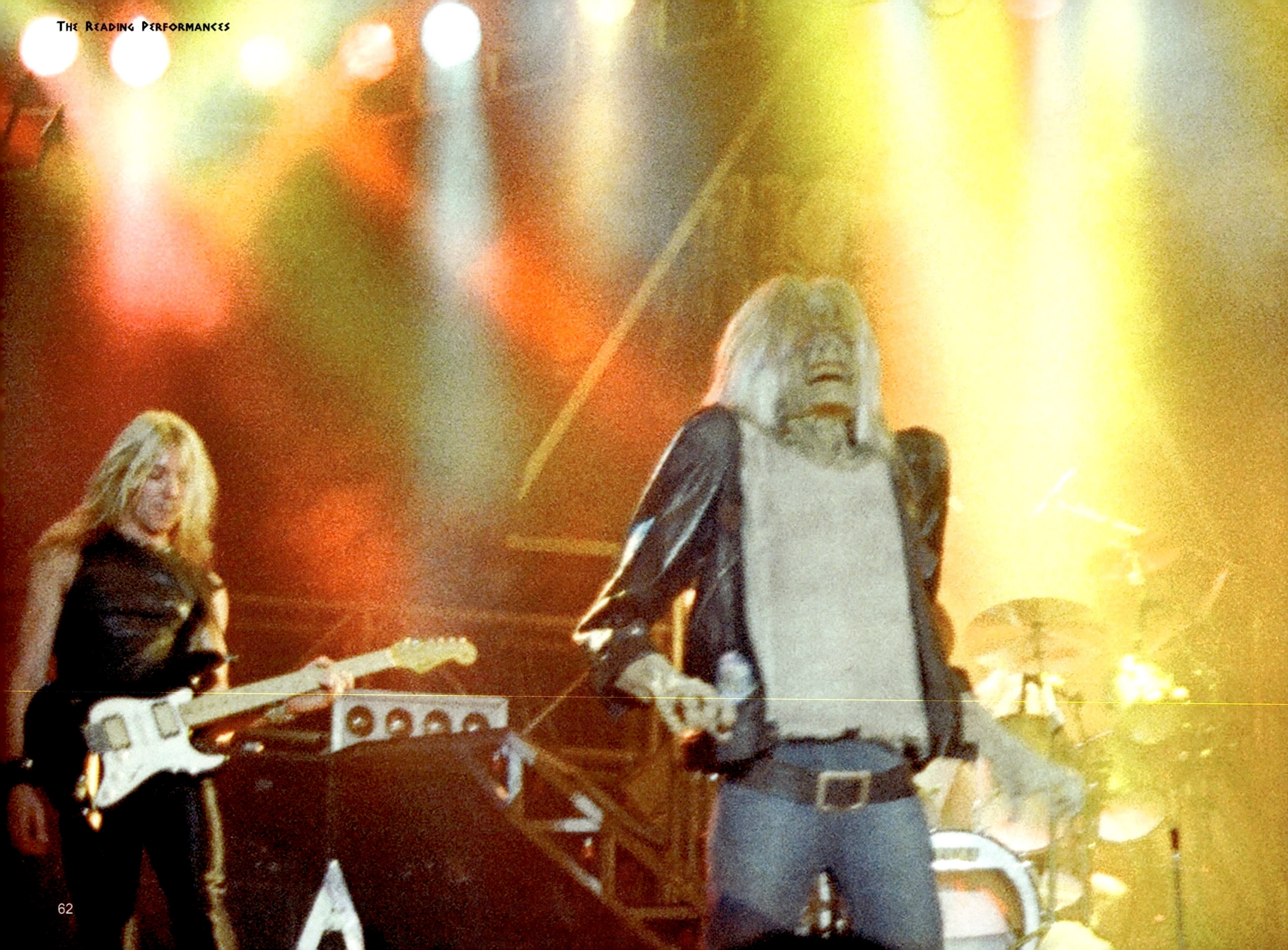

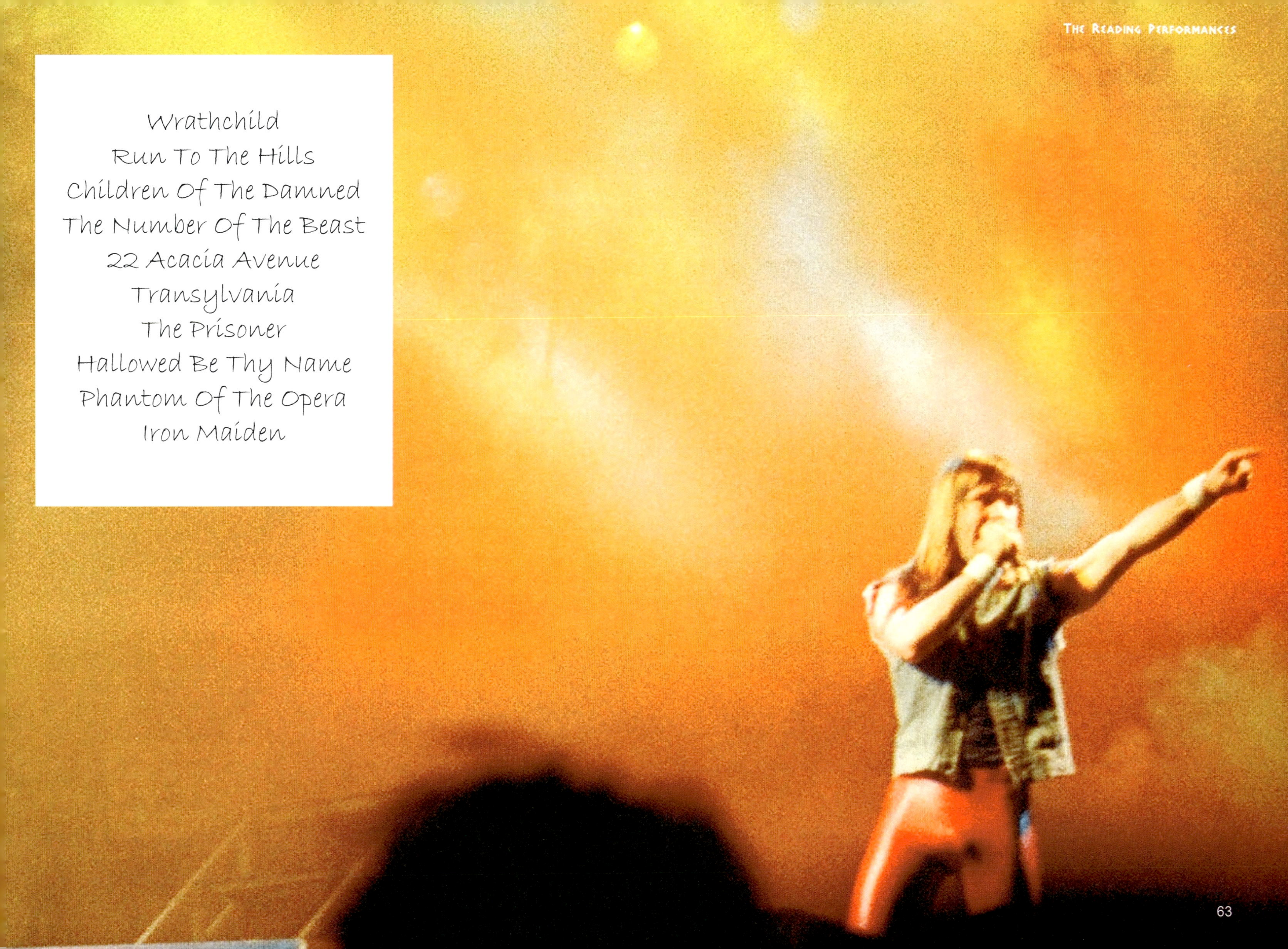

Wrathchild
Run To The Hills
Children Of The Damned
The Number Of The Beast
22 Acacia Avenue
Transylvania
The Prisoner
Hallowed Be Thy Name
Phantom Of The Opera
Iron Maiden

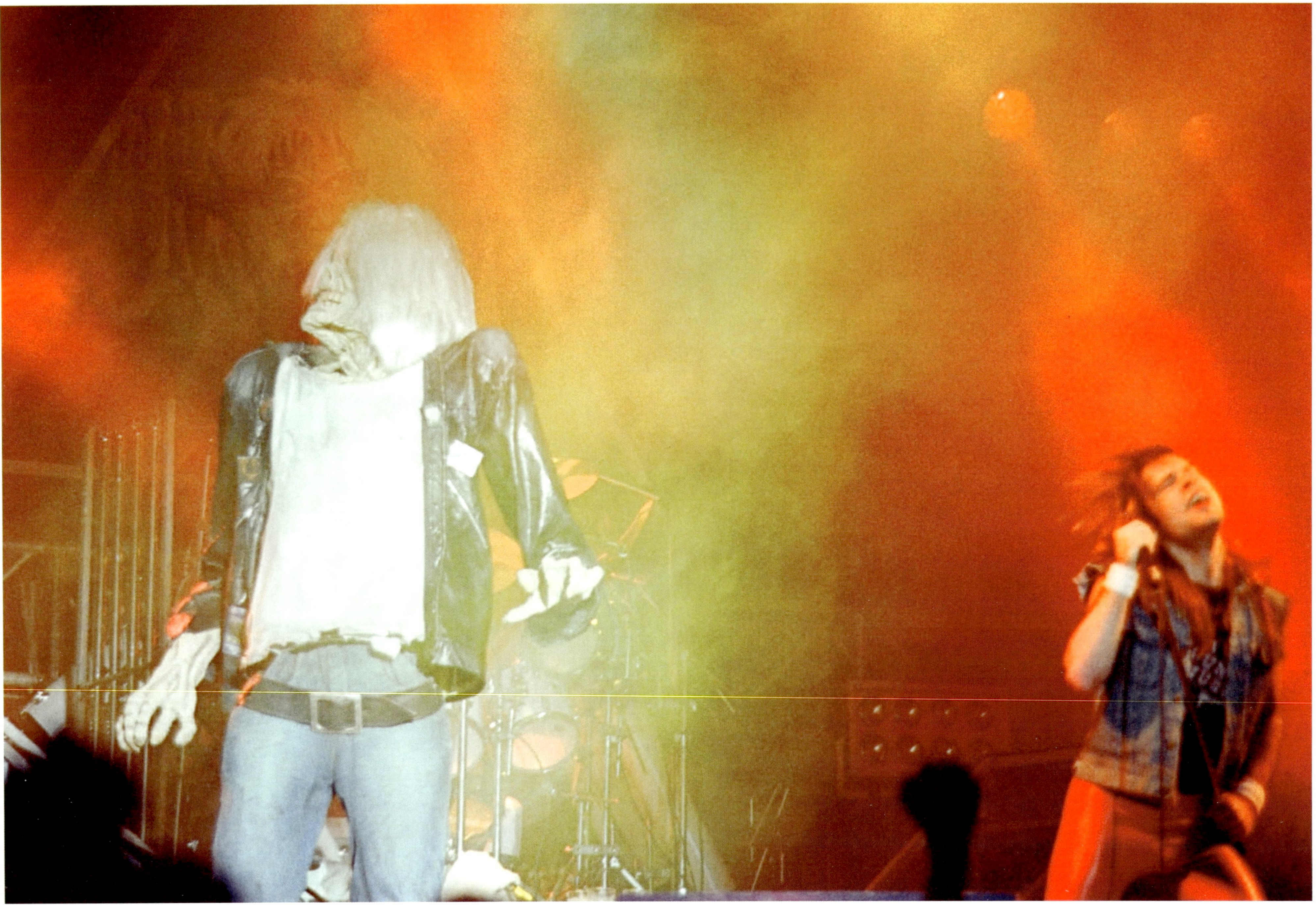

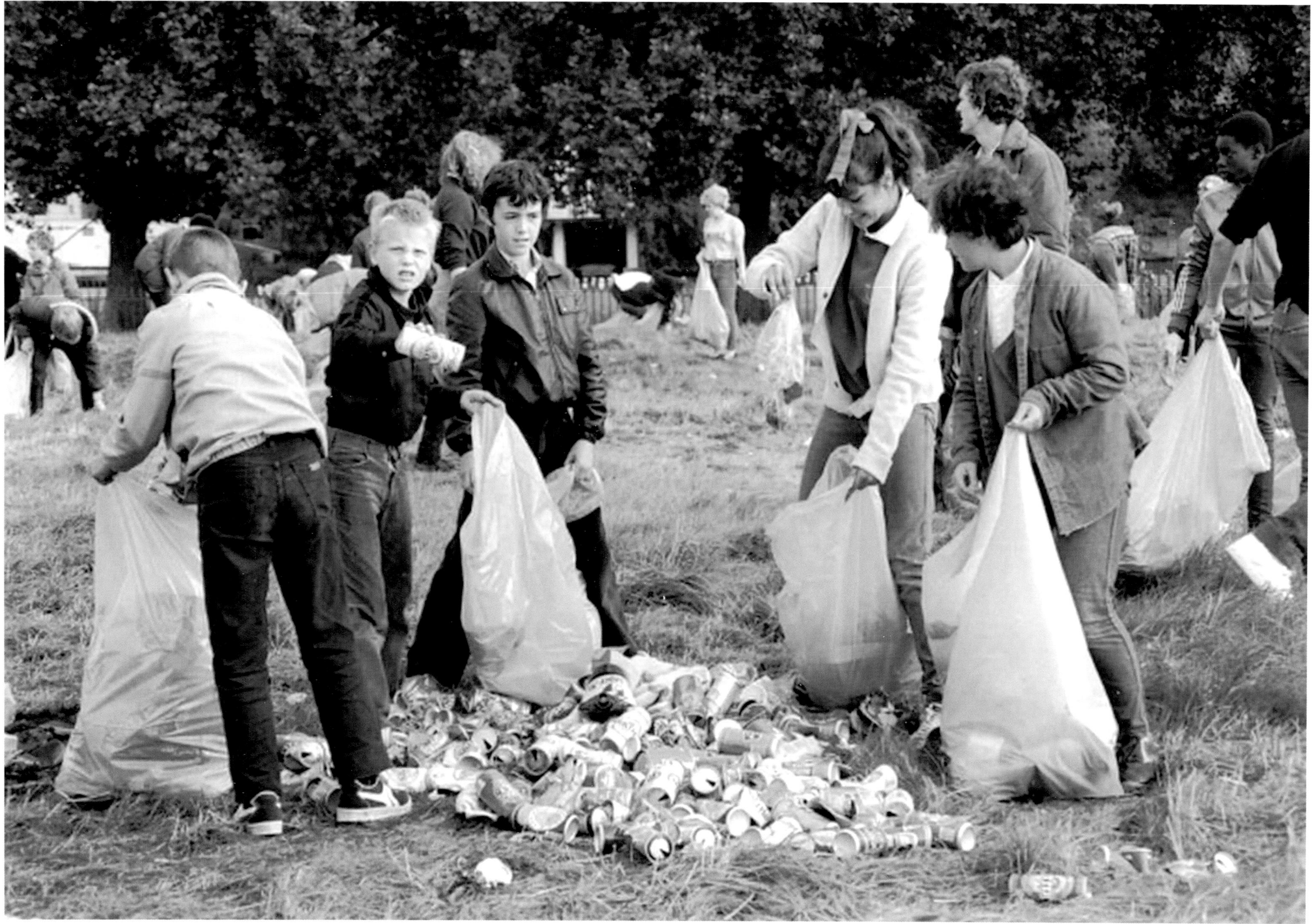

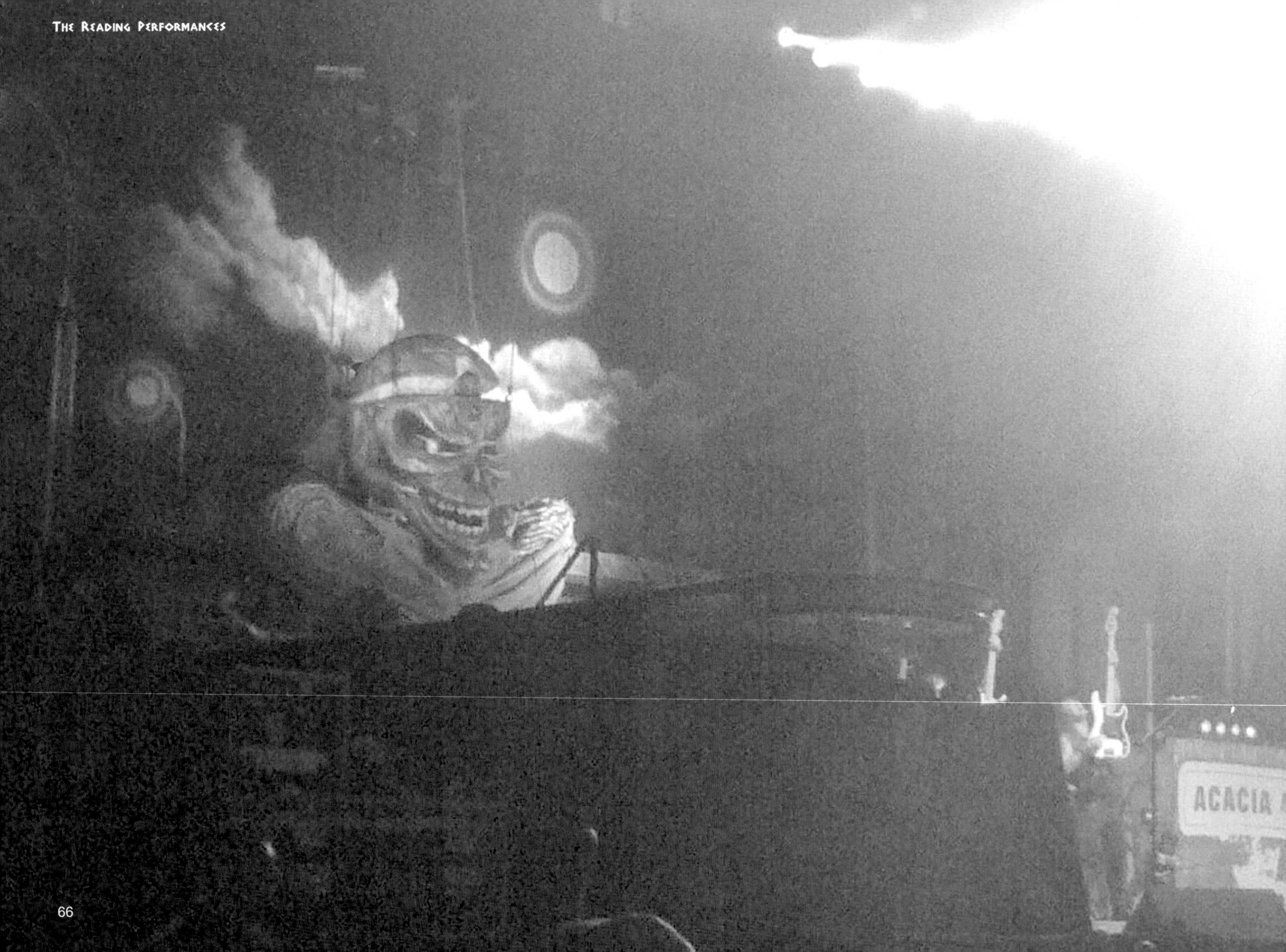
ACACIA

Reading Festival 2005

Reading had changed significantly since Maiden's last appearance. Donington had become the hallowed grounds of rock and metal as far as live appearances were concerned hosting the once annual Monsters Of Rock Festival. Reading had shifted it's musical direction focussing on pop artists of the day such as Squeeze. However Meat Loaf and Bonnie Tyler performed there though both of them in their separate sets did not go down well with the crowd. By the 1990s the music scene had changed and festivals had to change too. Reading was the last stage Nirvana performed on in the UK and it would become one of the band's most famous performances. Reading embraced Britpop and indie music throughout the 1990s and by the noughties Reading hosted a sister festival in Leeds and thus Reading-Leeds festival was born. Reading now sees such varied artists a Metallica, the Foo Fighters, Eminem and Muse perform. Reading embraces all kinds of pop music sub genres. It is a different festival from what Maiden are used to.

"I've been to the Reading festival twice before - as a punter, though I stayed backstage in the hospitality tent!" Dickinson said to the BBC's Linda Serck and Catherine Turner.

One would think that Maiden are more synonymous with Castle Donington, the hallowed grounds of the famed Monsters Of Rock Festival, than with Reading but Maiden's three Reading shows are vital to their history.

It was probably hard to believe that by the time the New Year had arrived Iron Maiden would soon be celebrating 25 years since the release of their debut album and what a journey it had been. They launched Eddie Rips Up The World Tour to celebrate 25 years and to also highlight the 2004 DVD release *The Early Days,* which covered the band's career from their inception in 1975 to the release of 1983s *Piece Of Mind.*

They began in Prague on May 28 2005 and finished in London on September 2; it included many stadium dates and festival appearances. Throughout the tour Maiden were supported by Mastodon, DragonForce, Dream Theater, Marilyn Manson and

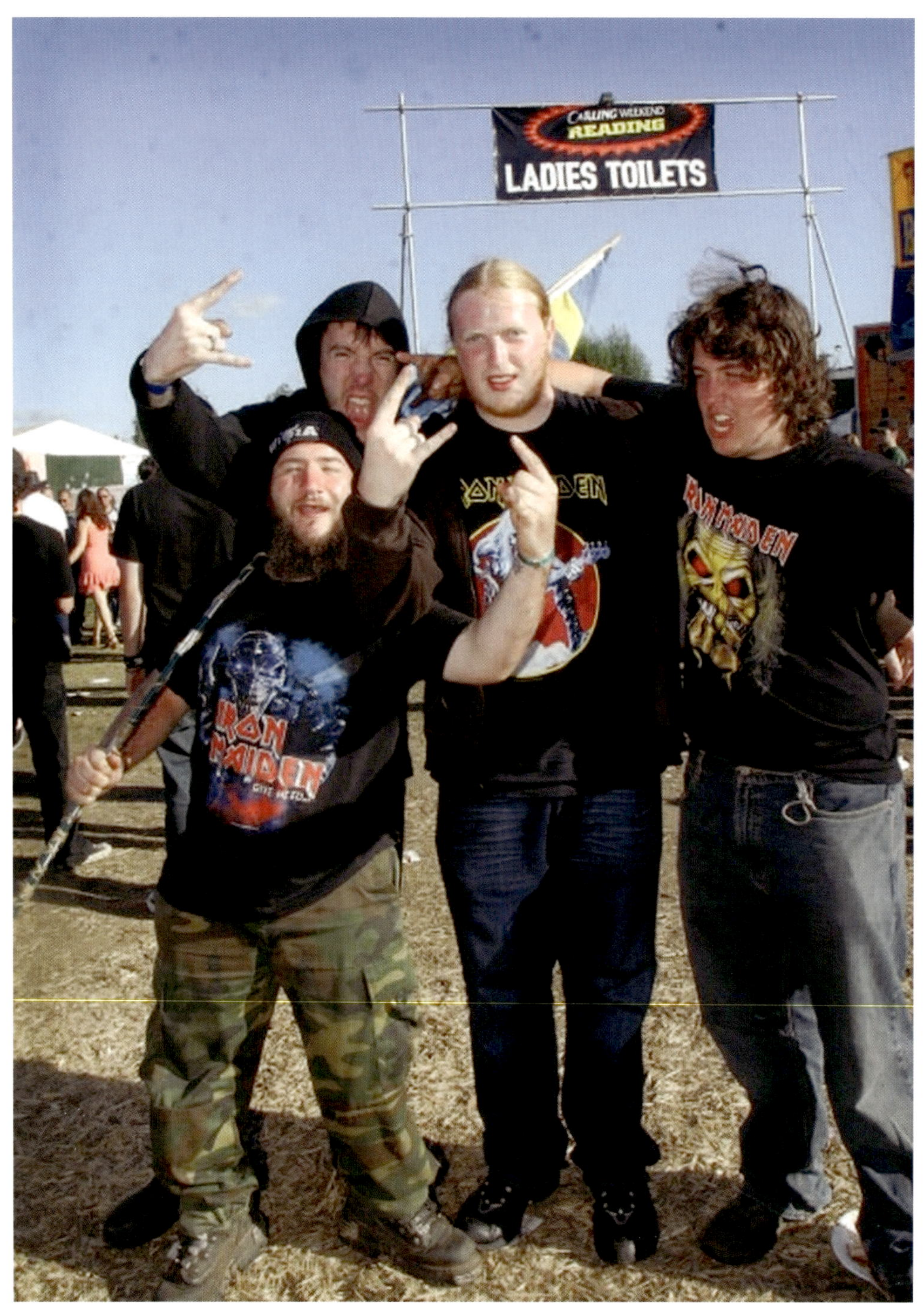

Turbonegro. The road jaunt included many stadium dates and festival appearances, including Rock Am Ring and Rock Im Ring festivals in Germany, Gods Of Metal in Italy and the coveted Reading and Leeds festivals in England which were major coups for the band in exposing their music to a mainstream audience in their native island; they played to a combined audience of 130,000 fans!

Yes! Maiden were back at Reading, this time with fellow headliners Foo Fighters and Pixies; both American. Maiden, however, were on their home turf. Maiden proved that they were still a relevant band by appearing at one of the UK's most coveted (and mainstream) festivals. The Killers, Razorlight and Queens of the Stone Age were playing at Leeds and Reading festivals too, which were staged on August 26-28. How many bands from Maiden's era could headline Reading Festival? Answers on a postcard.

Dickinson said to the Reading crowd: "Ten years ago they wouldn't have believed we'd be still going, and playing to more fucking people than ever!"

On the other side, Maiden were full of speed and enthusiasm and stamina. Maiden's work ethic had definitely not become sluggish; in fact it was on warp speed ahead. Reading loved them just as they had back in 1982.

Dickinson had, in fact, never sounded or looked any better. He was on fire during that tour. He kept himself in rigorous shape by fencing and eating healthily and generally looking after himself and it worked out great for the singer. Touring is hard work for everyone involved but especially the frontman who not only has to sing but has to keep the audience interested which in itself is often a difficult

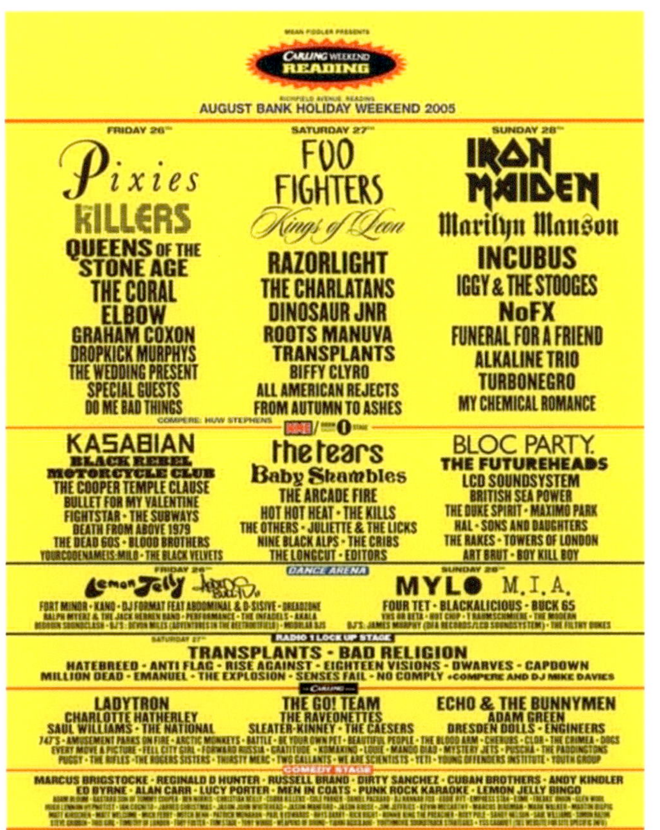

task. The fans loved having Dickinson back and appreciated every moment he was on stage by cheering to the top of their lungs. But they still craved for the older material rather than the new stuff. Dickinson was ready for Reading but the non-Maiden fans in the crowd were not prepared for just how good a singer and frontman Dickinson is.

Bruce Dickinson biographer and rock writer Joe Shooman who attended Reading's sister festival up in Leeds says: "Maiden's day in particular featured some ace rock/metal/punk acts including Iggy & The Stooges, Marilyn Manson, NoFX etc so the line-up was definitely designed to accommodate their audience. Maiden headlined the whole thing at Reading and Fri night at Leeds, which was awesome. Foos headlined the Sunday up in Yorkshire. If you look at the line-up in general it's a much more rock-oriented year than others had been. Iron Maiden in 2005 were touring the classics to promote that ace *Early Days Part 1* DVD so it was definitely going to always provide a set of crowd-pleasers wasn't it, rather than a bunch of new tracks."

He continues: "The whole thing really did ramp up the excitement throughout the day for their performance. Obviously there are several stages at these fests so it's a case of take your pick of what to see. But by that point the band were absolutely at the height of their powers since Bruce/Adrian came back. All the niggles/weird bits had been ironed out in those preceding five years or so."

How did they go down with the crowd?

"Amazing. Incredible. Fabulous. Incendiary. I lost all my friends and didn't care. Found them afterwards similarly up in the skies after a set of classics from one of the best bands in the world. It was almost

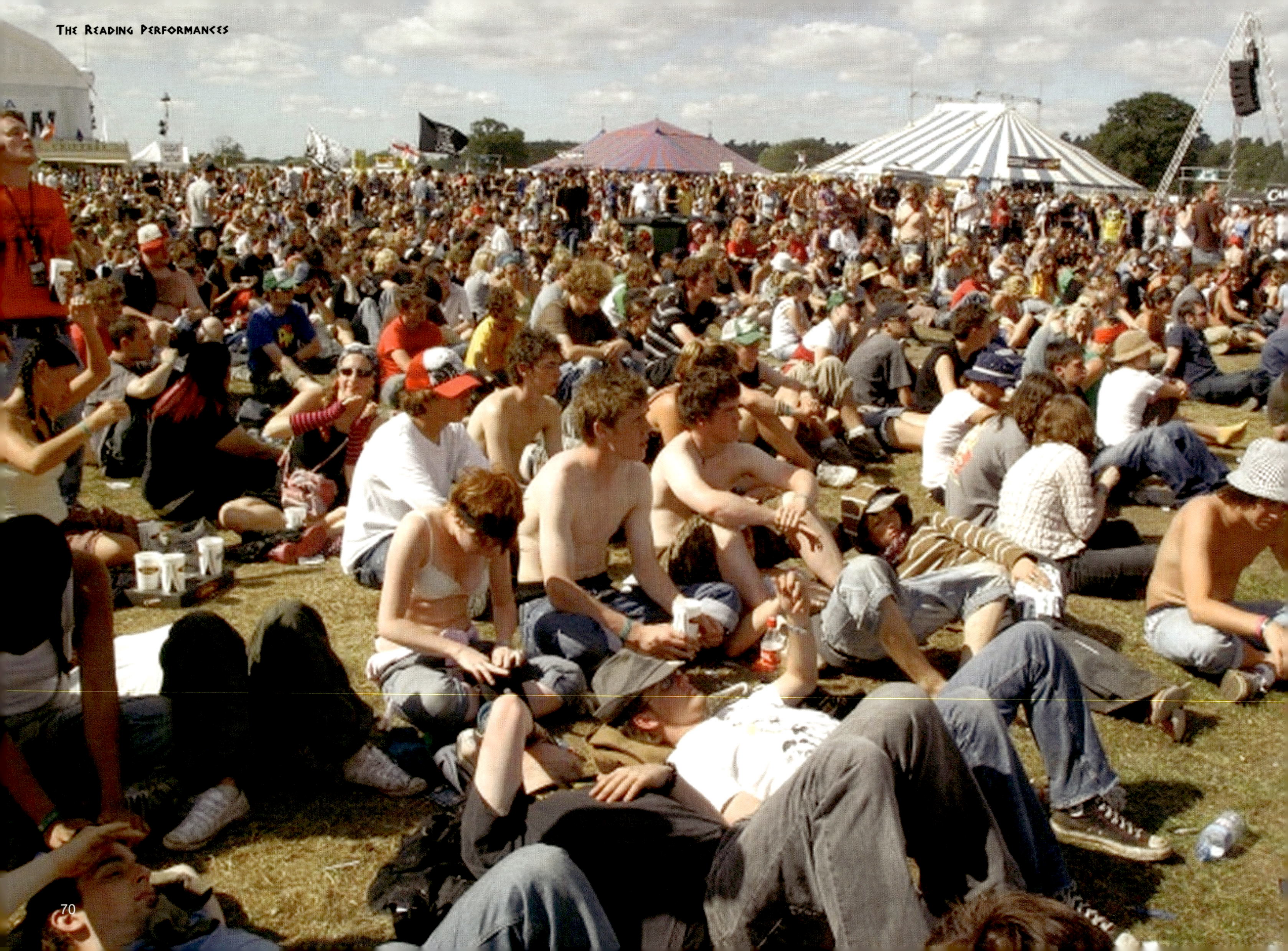

indescribable, the atmosphere on the night. Festivals can be special just by dint of the experience but when you have the music, the spectacle and the legends in front of you too it's transcendent. I know that's all a bit OTT but sometimes words fail to capture just how significant a moment is — when you're with tens of thousands of other fans having that totally immersive visceral experience it is quite extraordinary. They were the world's best metal band. I can't help but thinking that the run-in they had with Ozzy a few days previously had put a real rocket up their arses. They had a real edge of self-belief and a little bit of danger about them again in the aftermath of all that nonsense. Britain's best band bar none, regardless of genre."

It was as if Dickinson's career had come full circle. He told *The Sun* newspaper, "(Reading) is where I was asked to join the band and it's also the first festival I went to and also played at. And this year it will be a big one… we'll be nervous."

With more new material the band's setlist was obviously much different from either of their 1980 and 1982 performances. After the taped intro of 'The Ides Of March' the band blitzed through 'Murders In The Rue Morgue', 'Another Life', 'Prowler', 'The Trooper', 'Remember Tomorrow', 'Where Eagles Dare', 'Revelations', 'Run To The Hills', 'Wrathchild', 'Die With Your Boots On', 'Phantom Of The Opera', 'The Number Of The Beast', 'Hallowed Be Thy Name' and 'Iron Maiden' with an encore of 'Running Free', 'Drifter' and 'Sanctuary'. So, there was a bit of old and a bit of new.

Reading Festival was a different experience from the days of olde. There where no concerns from fans

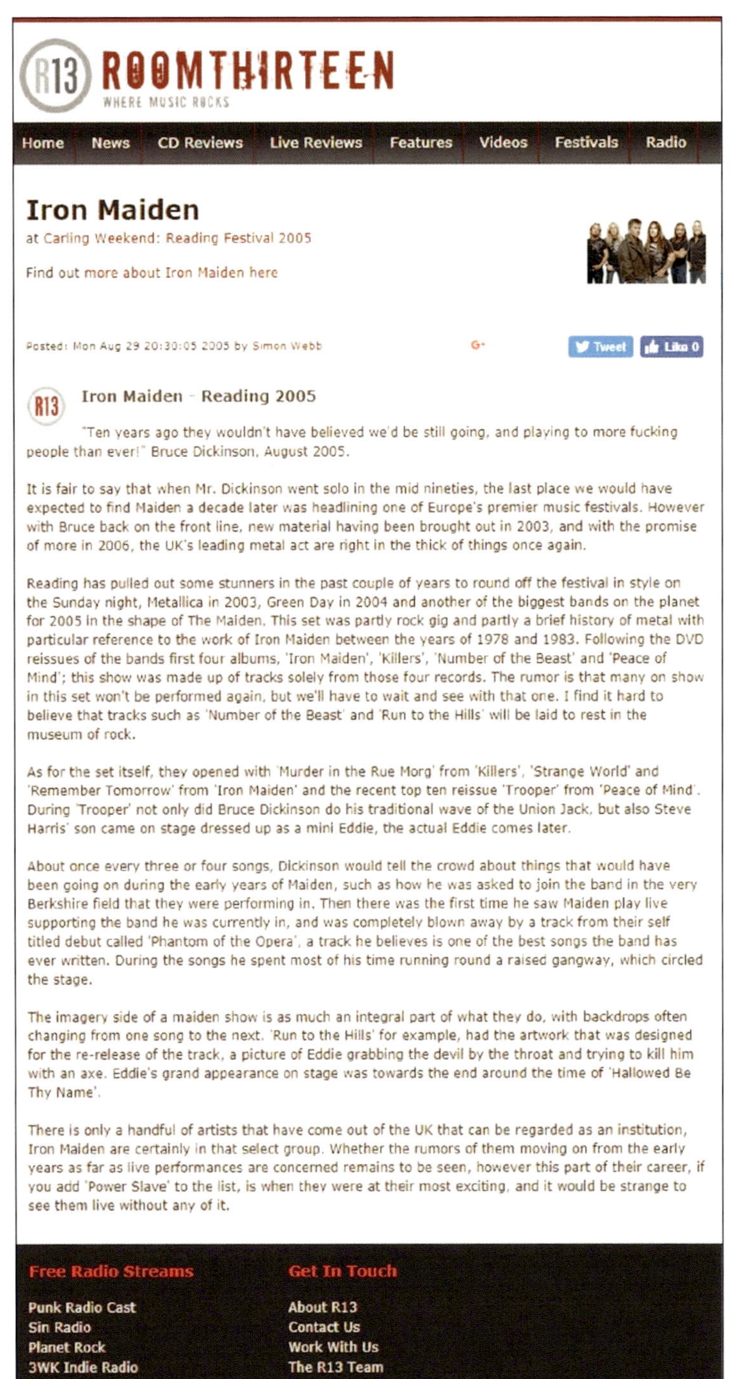

ROOMTHIRTEEN
WHERE MUSIC ROCKS

Home   News   CD Reviews   Live Reviews   Features   Videos   Festivals   Radio

Iron Maiden

at Carling Weekend: Reading Festival 2005

Find out more about Iron Maiden here

Posted: Mon Aug 29 20:30:05 2005 by Simon Webb

Tweet   Like 0

Iron Maiden - Reading 2005

"Ten years ago they wouldn't have believed we'd be still going, and playing to more fucking people than ever!" Bruce Dickinson, August 2005.

It is fair to say that when Mr. Dickinson went solo in the mid nineties, the last place we would have expected to find Maiden a decade later was headlining one of Europe's premier music festivals. However with Bruce back on the front line, new material having been brought out in 2003, and with the promise of more in 2006, the UK's leading metal act are right in the thick of things once again.

Reading has pulled out some stunners in the past couple of years to round off the festival in style on the Sunday night, Metallica in 2003, Green Day in 2004 and another of the biggest bands on the planet for 2005 in the shape of The Maiden. This set was partly rock gig and partly a brief history of metal with particular reference to the work of Iron Maiden between the years of 1978 and 1983. Following the DVD reissues of the bands first four albums, 'Iron Maiden', 'Killers', 'Number of the Beast' and 'Peace of Mind'; this show was made up of tracks solely from those four records. The rumor is that many on show in this set won't be performed again, but we'll have to wait and see with that one. I find it hard to believe that tracks such as 'Number of the Beast' and 'Run to the Hills' will be laid to rest in the museum of rock.

As for the set itself, they opened with 'Murder in the Rue Morg' from 'Killers', 'Strange World' and 'Remember Tomorrow' from 'Iron Maiden' and the recent top ten reissue 'Trooper' from 'Peace of Mind'. During 'Trooper' not only did Bruce Dickinson do his traditional wave of the Union Jack, but also Steve Harris' son came on stage dressed up as a mini Eddie, the actual Eddie comes later.

About once every three or four songs, Dickinson would tell the crowd about things that would have been going on during the early years of Maiden, such as how he was asked to join the band in the very Berkshire field that they were performing in. Then there was the first time he saw Maiden play live supporting the band he was currently in, and was completely blown away by a track from their self titled debut called 'Phantom of the Opera', a track he believes is one of the best songs the band has ever written. During the songs he spent most of his time running round a raised gangway, which circled the stage.

The imagery side of a maiden show is as much an integral part of what they do, with backdrops often changing from one song to the next. 'Run to the Hills' for example, had the artwork that was designed for the re-release of the track, a picture of Eddie grabbing the devil by the throat and trying to kill him with an axe. Eddie's grand appearance on stage was towards the end around the time of 'Hallowed Be Thy Name'.

There is only a handful of artists that have come out of the UK that can be regarded as an institution, Iron Maiden are certainly in that select group. Whether the rumors of them moving on from the early years as far as live performances are concerned remains to be seen, however this part of their career, if you add 'Power Slave' to the list, is when they were at their most exciting, and it would be strange to see them live without any of it.

Free Radio Streams

Punk Radio Cast
Sin Radio
Planet Rock
3WK Indie Radio

Get In Touch

About R13
Contact Us
Work With Us
The R13 Team

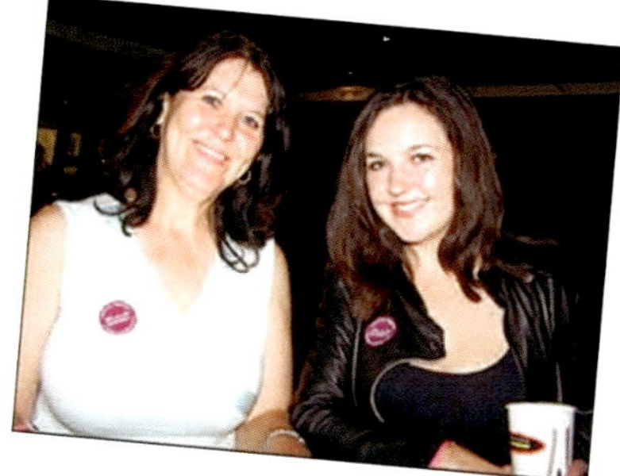

Former Reading Mayor, Councillor Jeanette Skeats was behind the main stage with her daughter during Iron Maiden's set. Had she brought her daughter to the slaughter?

about how Iron Maiden would "fit in" with the younger bands because Maiden is a professional unit. The most pro heavy metal band out there. They could tackle any audience. They've been around the block more than once and could again, hold Reading in the palm of their hands. Reading was no challenge for the mighty Maiden.

The Guardian's Betty Clarke wrote: "Bruce Dickinson is keener to talk about the past than comment on the current furore, recalling how he was first asked to join the band '100 yards' behind the huge stage set adorned by ramps and massive images of the band's mascot Eddie. 'This is the song that got me into Iron Maiden', he says of 'Remember Tomorrow'. 'If you haven't heard the band, it might get you into it

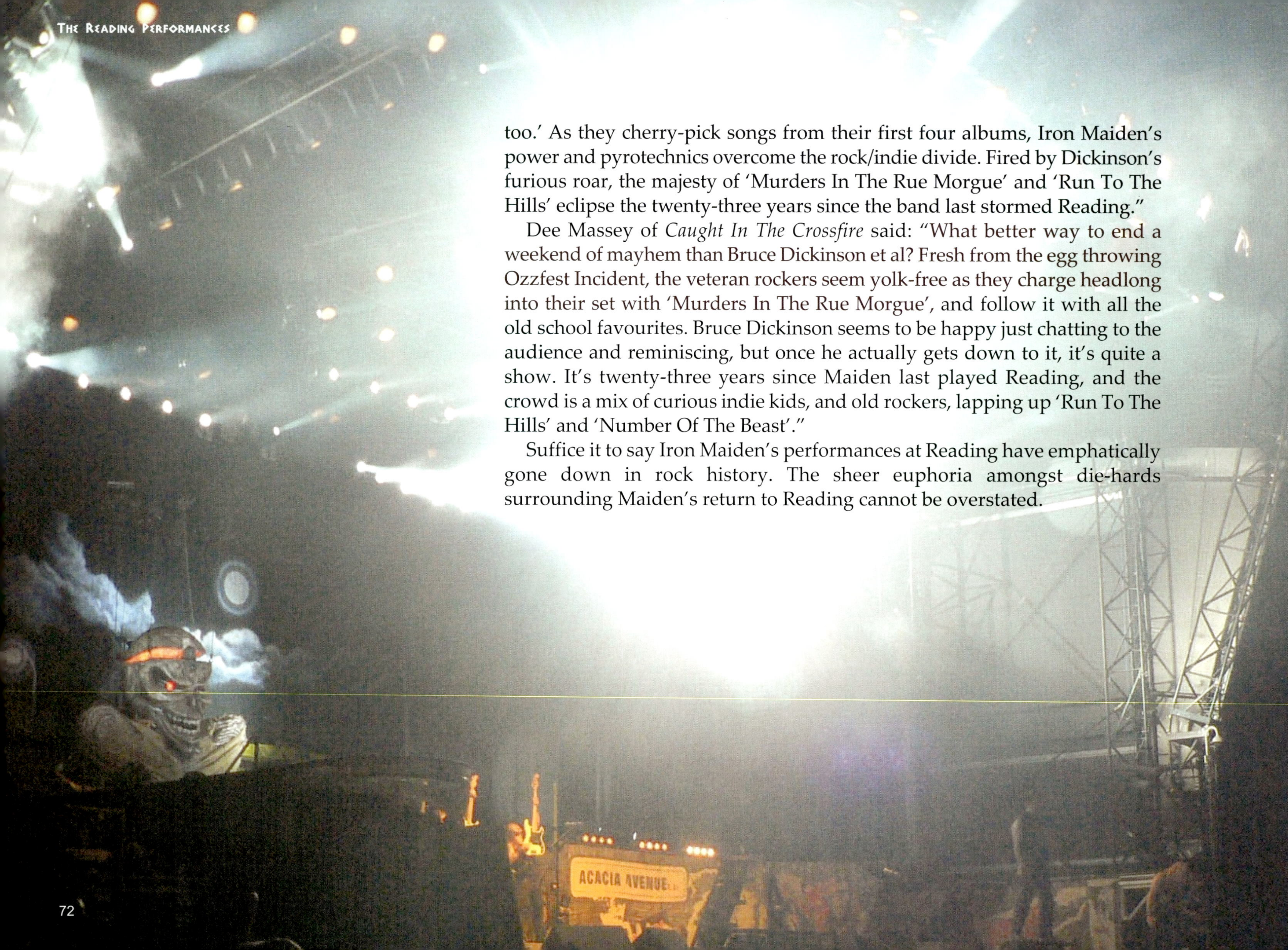

too.' As they cherry-pick songs from their first four albums, Iron Maiden's power and pyrotechnics overcome the rock/indie divide. Fired by Dickinson's furious roar, the majesty of 'Murders In The Rue Morgue' and 'Run To The Hills' eclipse the twenty-three years since the band last stormed Reading."

Dee Massey of *Caught In The Crossfire* said: "What better way to end a weekend of mayhem than Bruce Dickinson et al? Fresh from the egg throwing Ozzfest Incident, the veteran rockers seem yolk-free as they charge headlong into their set with 'Murders In The Rue Morgue', and follow it with all the old school favourites. Bruce Dickinson seems to be happy just chatting to the audience and reminiscing, but once he actually gets down to it, it's quite a show. It's twenty-three years since Maiden last played Reading, and the crowd is a mix of curious indie kids, and old rockers, lapping up 'Run To The Hills' and 'Number Of The Beast'."

Suffice it to say Iron Maiden's performances at Reading have emphatically gone down in rock history. The sheer euphoria amongst die-hards surrounding Maiden's return to Reading cannot be overstated.

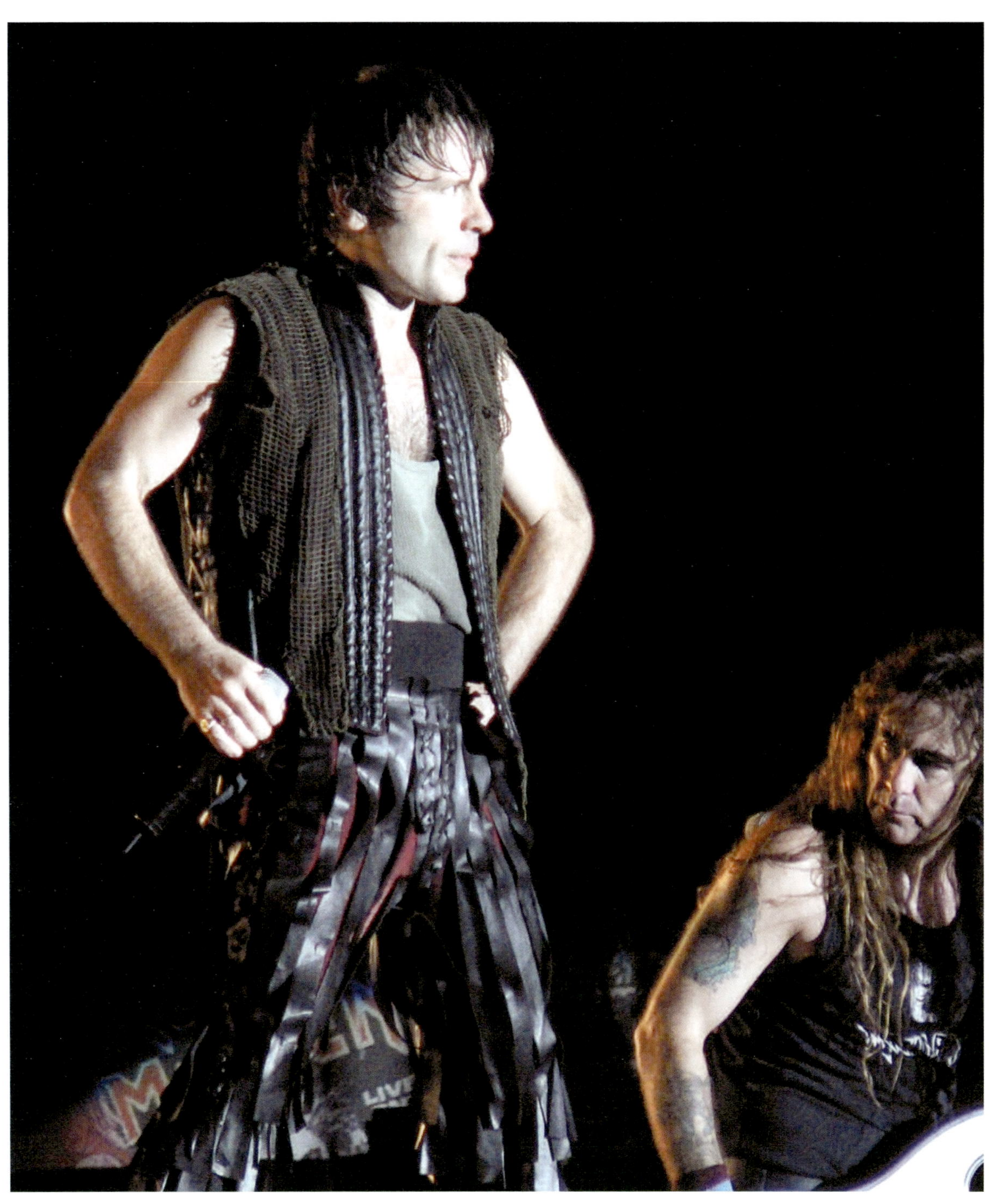

"Ten years ago they wouldn't have believed we'd be still going, and playing to more fucking people than ever!"
Bruce Dickinson

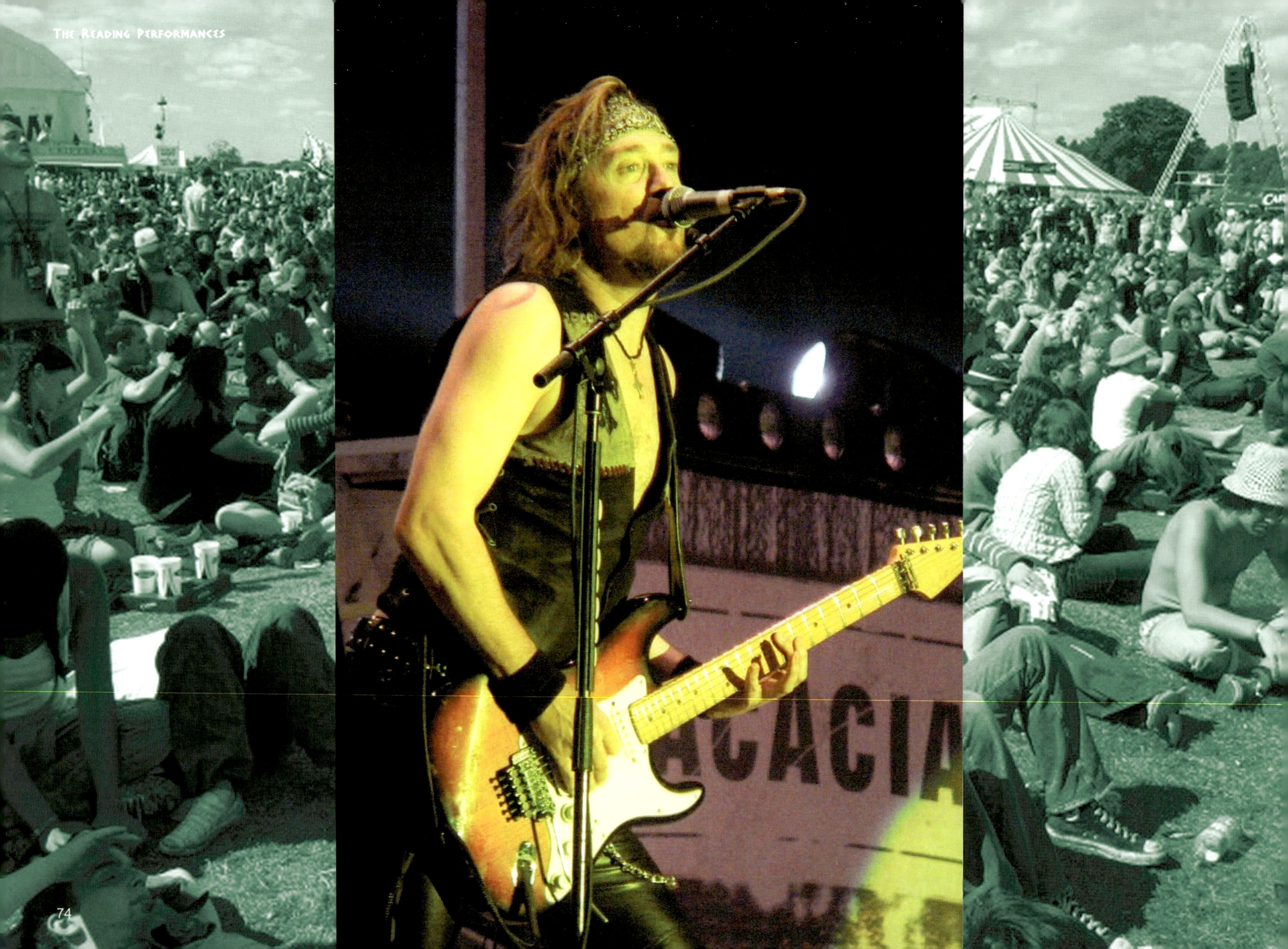
ACACIA

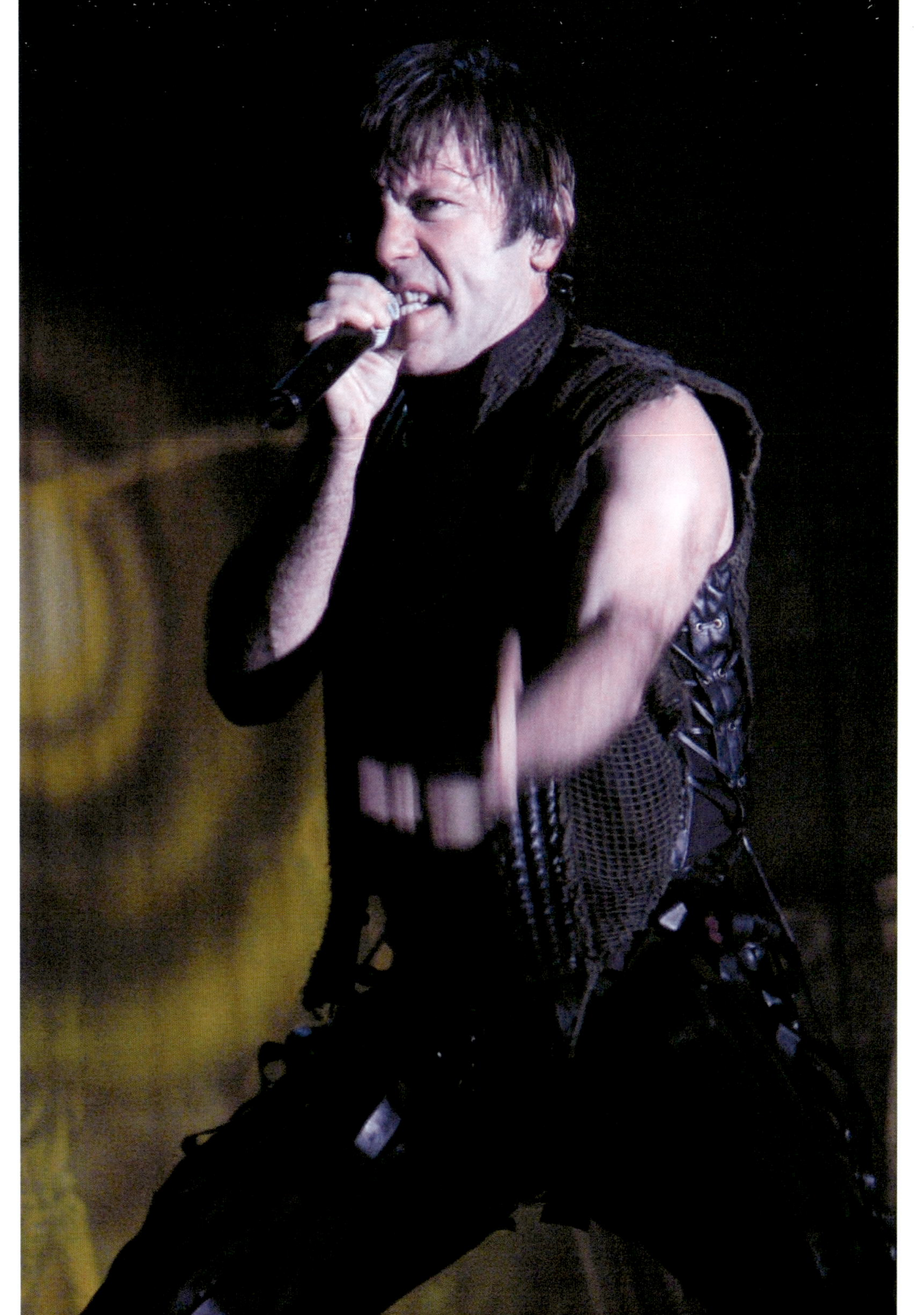

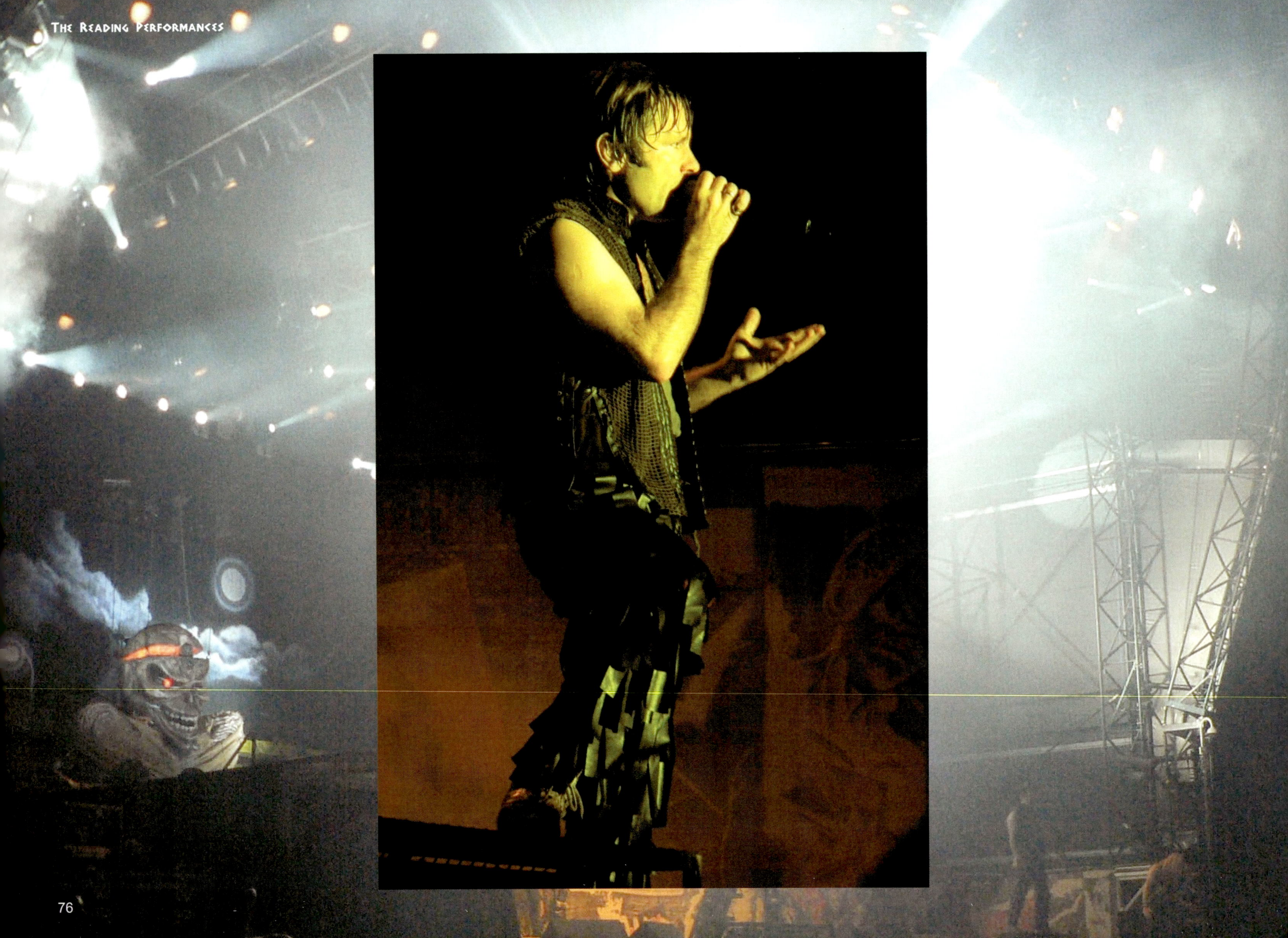

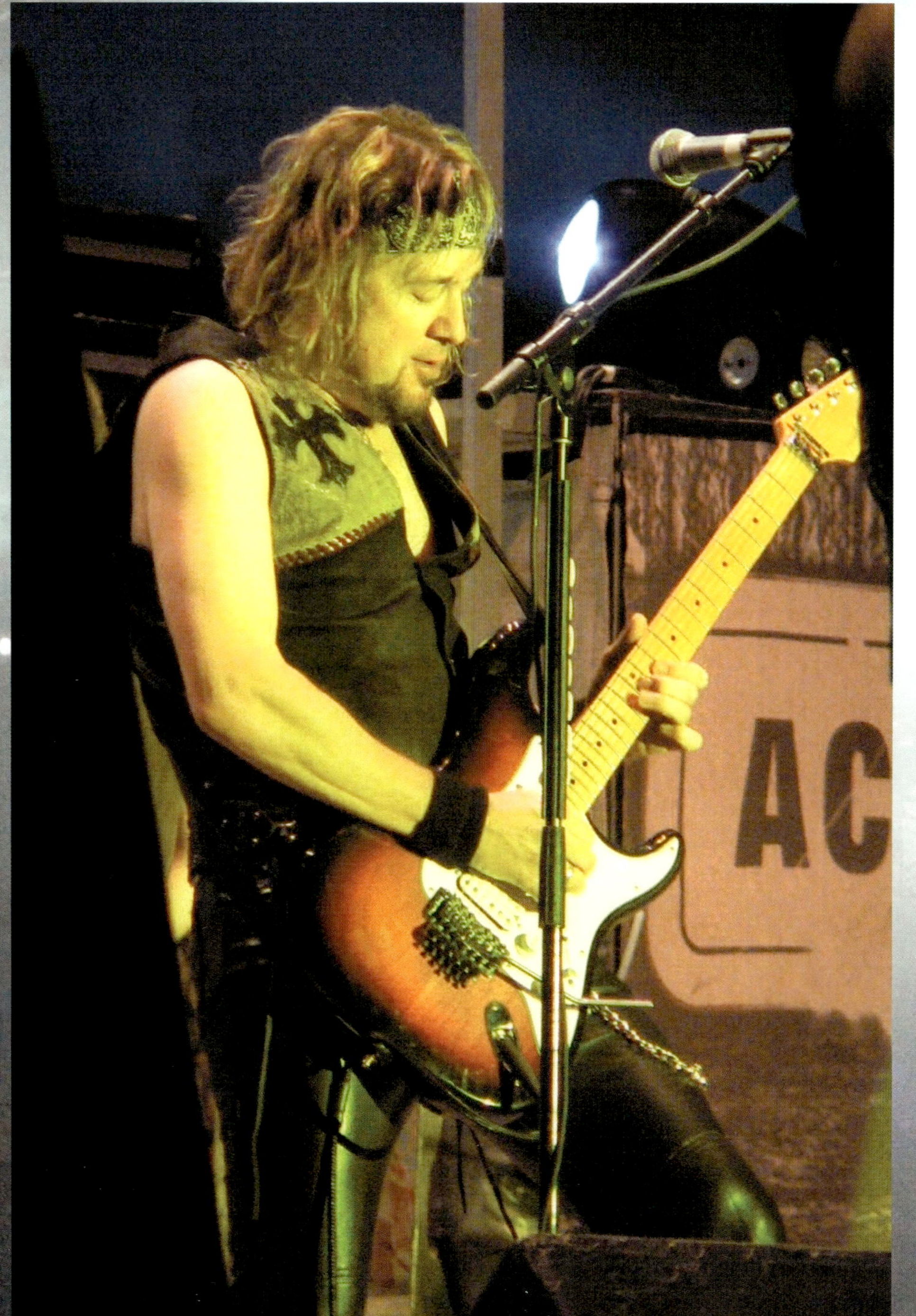

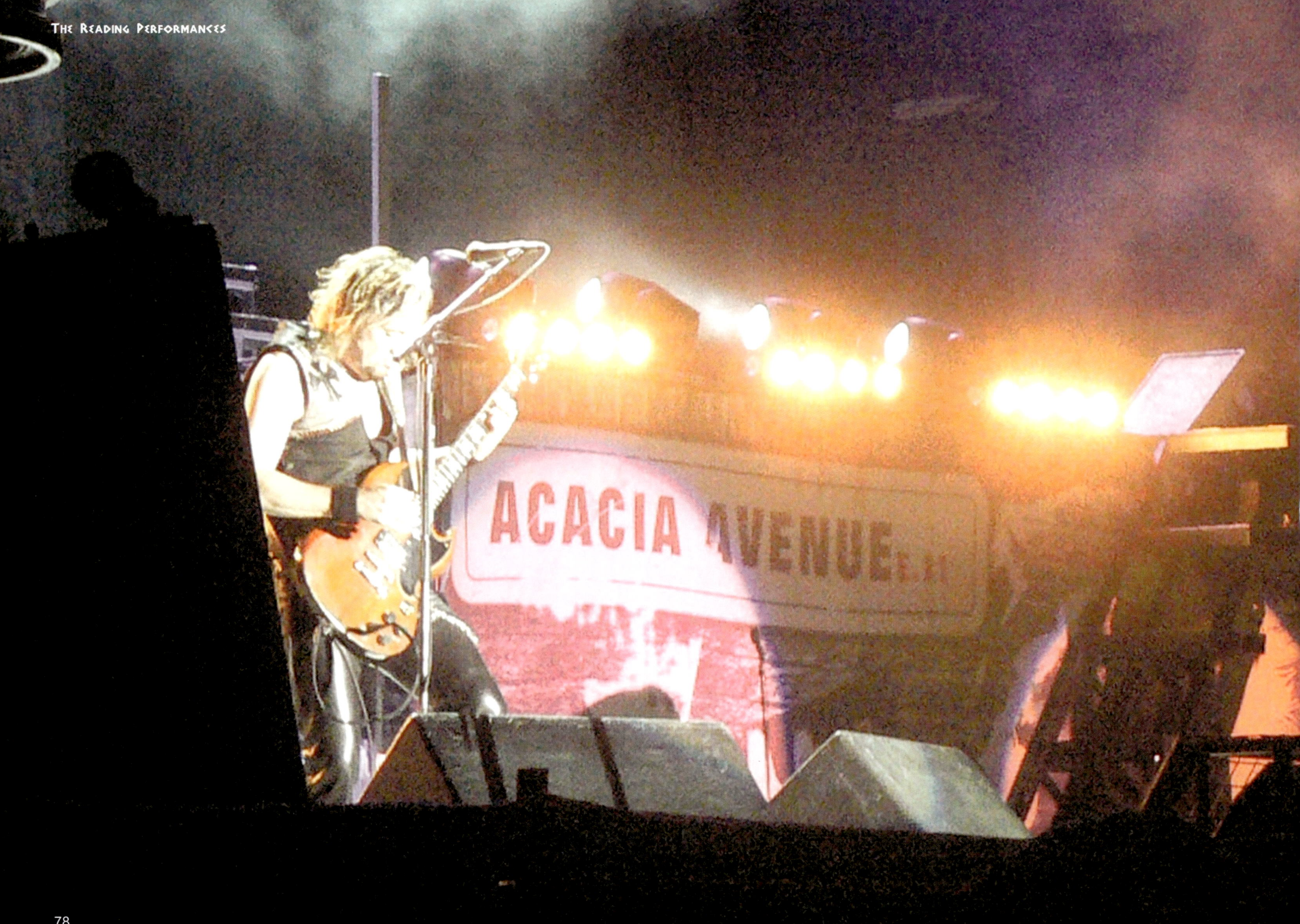
ACACIA AVENUE

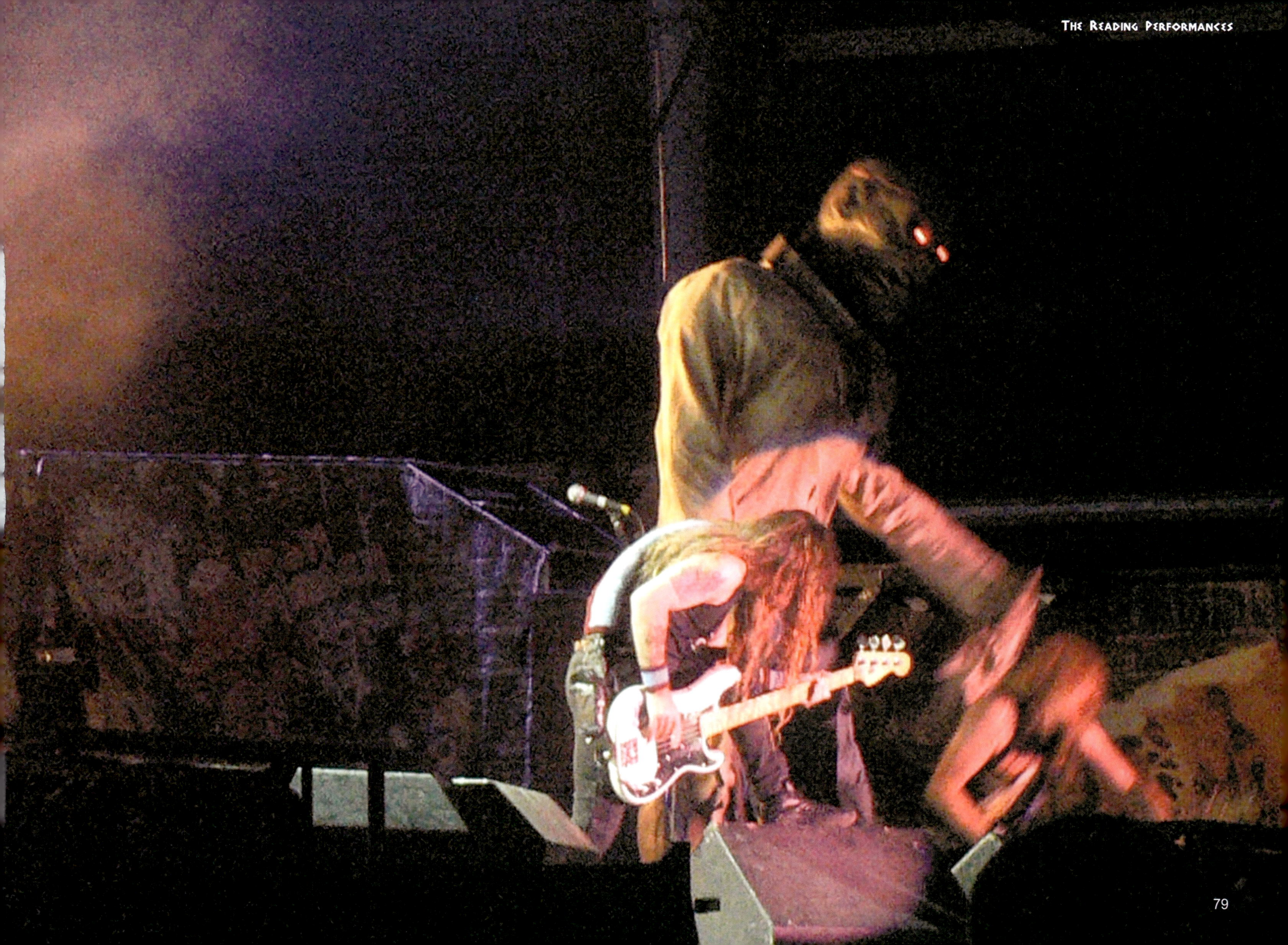

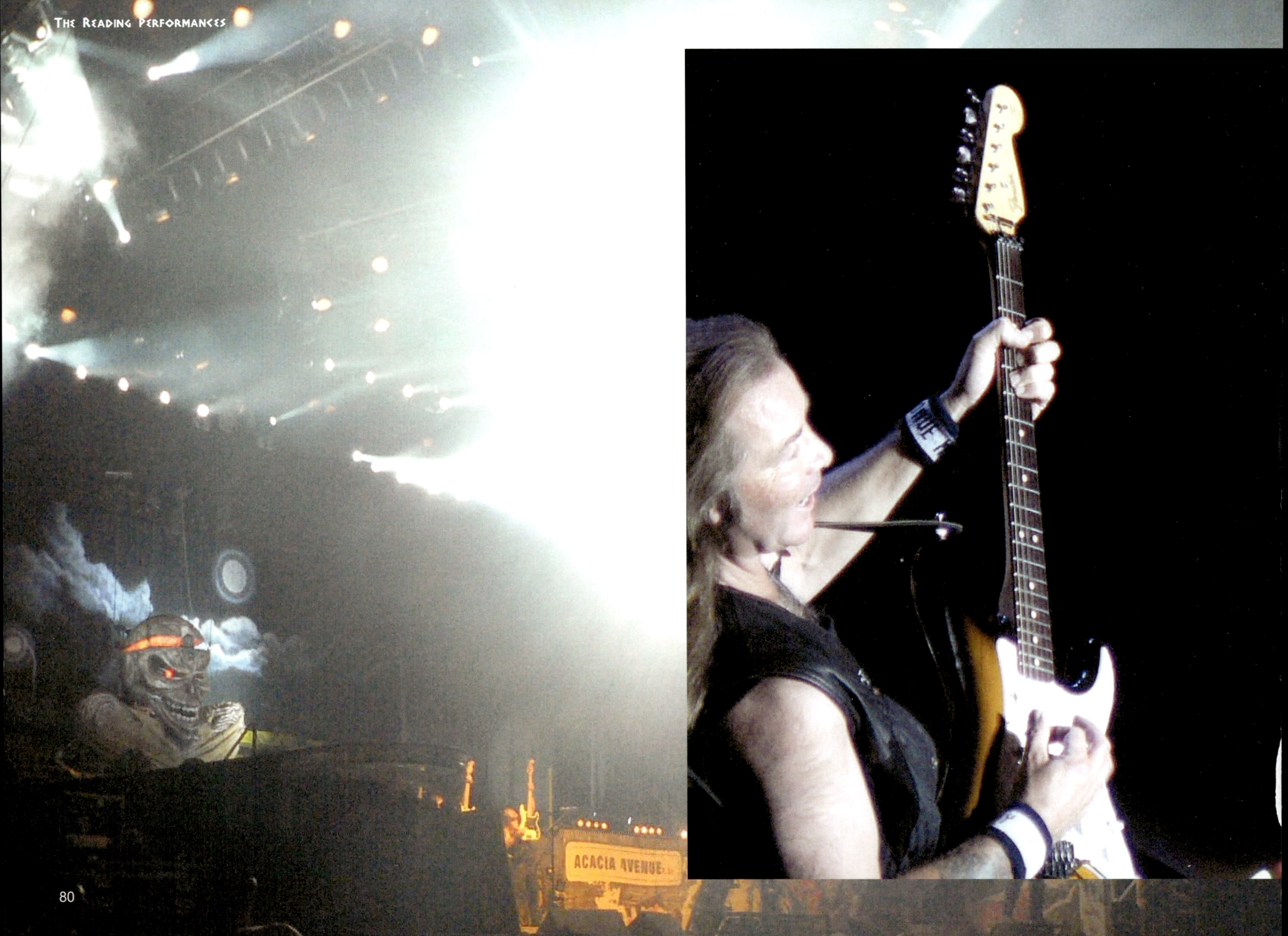
ACACIA AVENUE

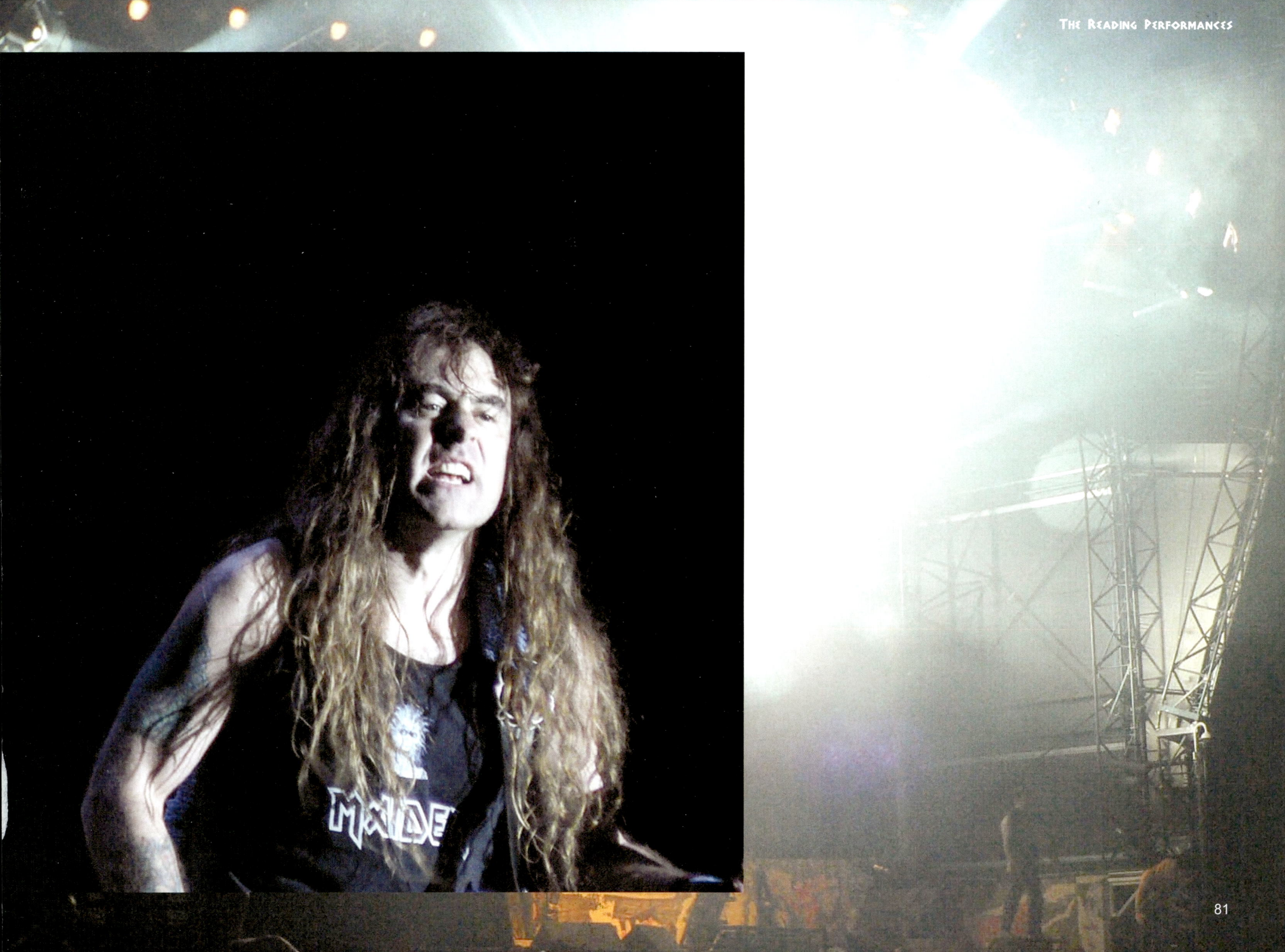

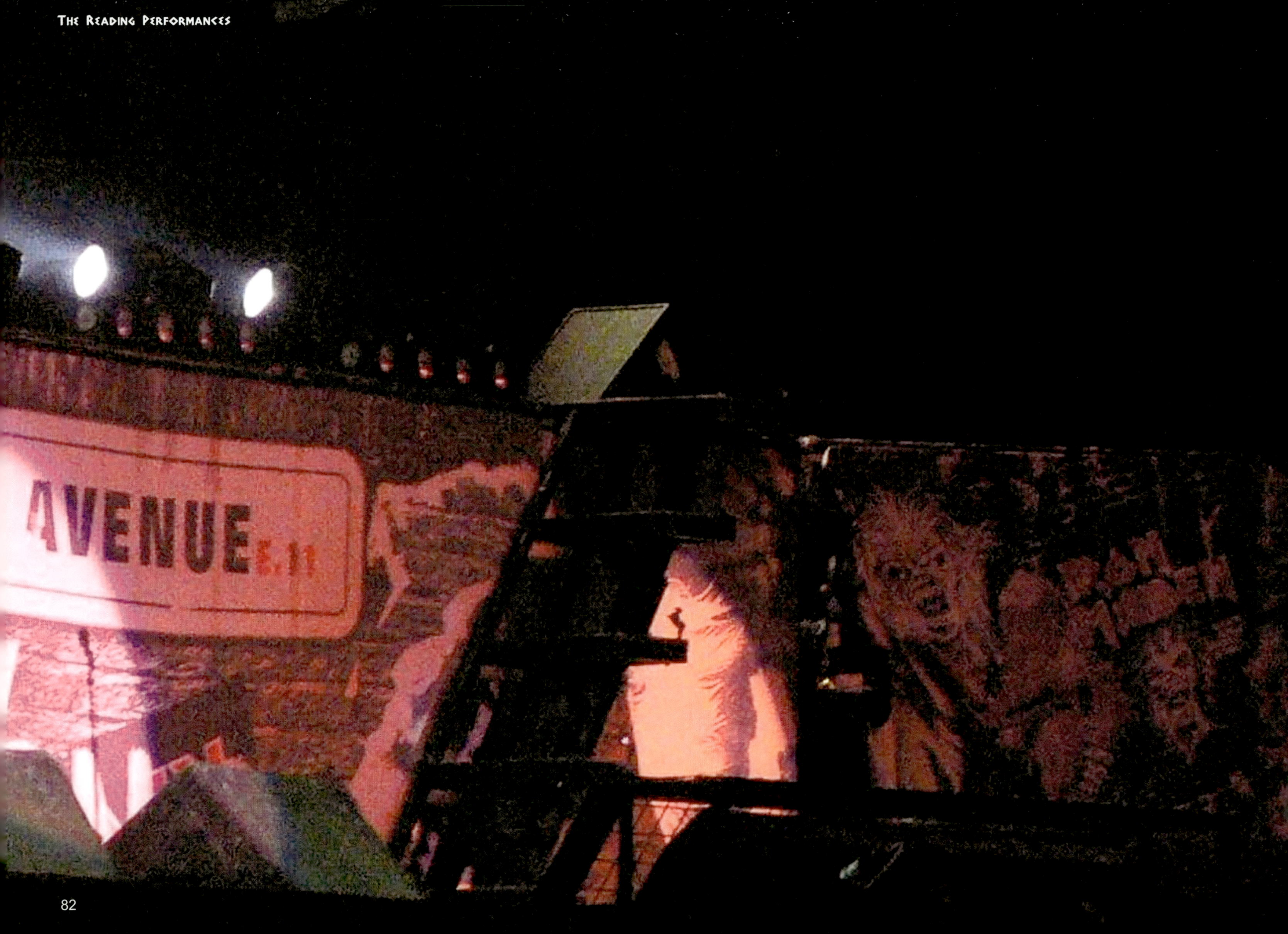
AVENUE

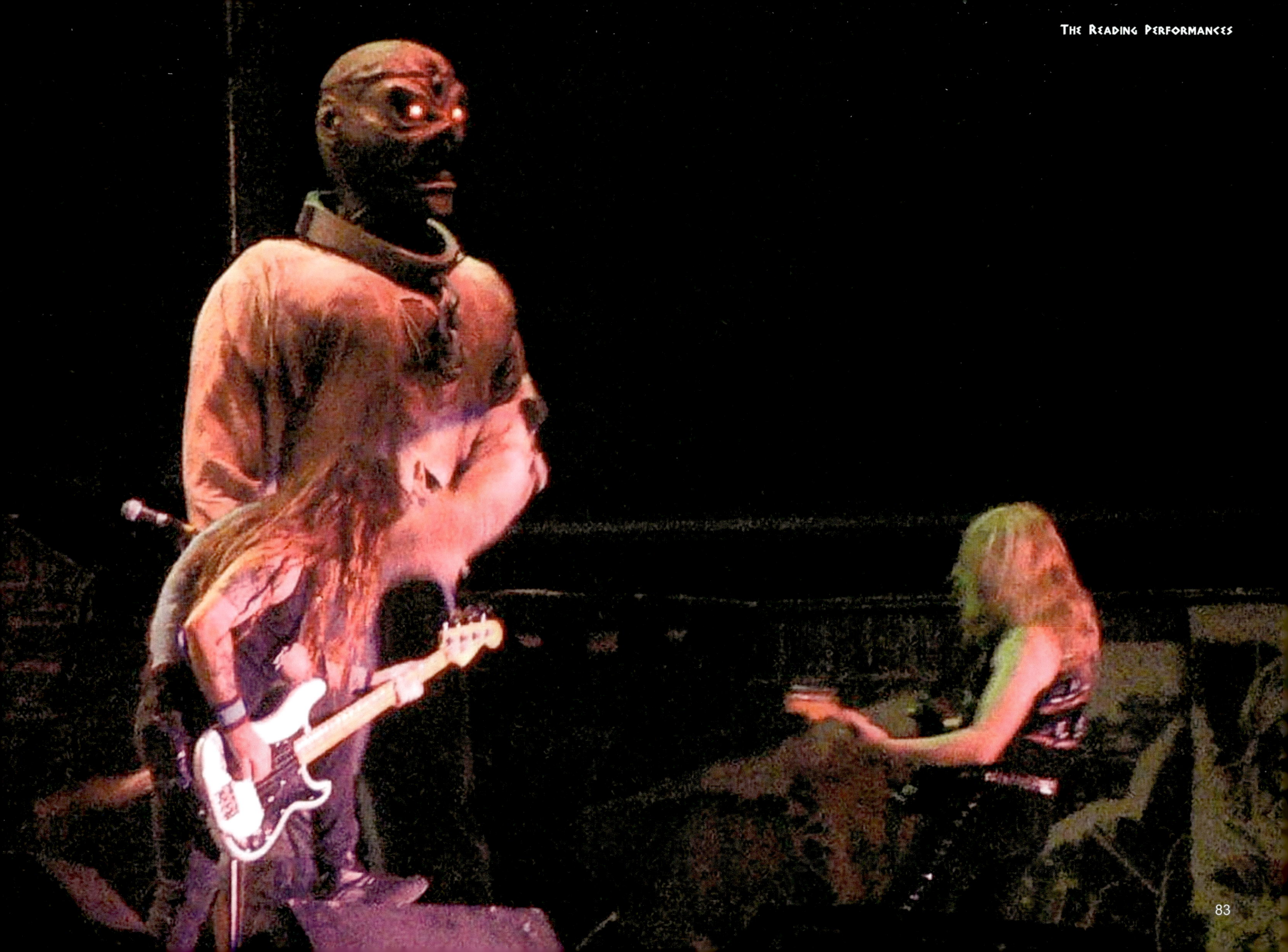

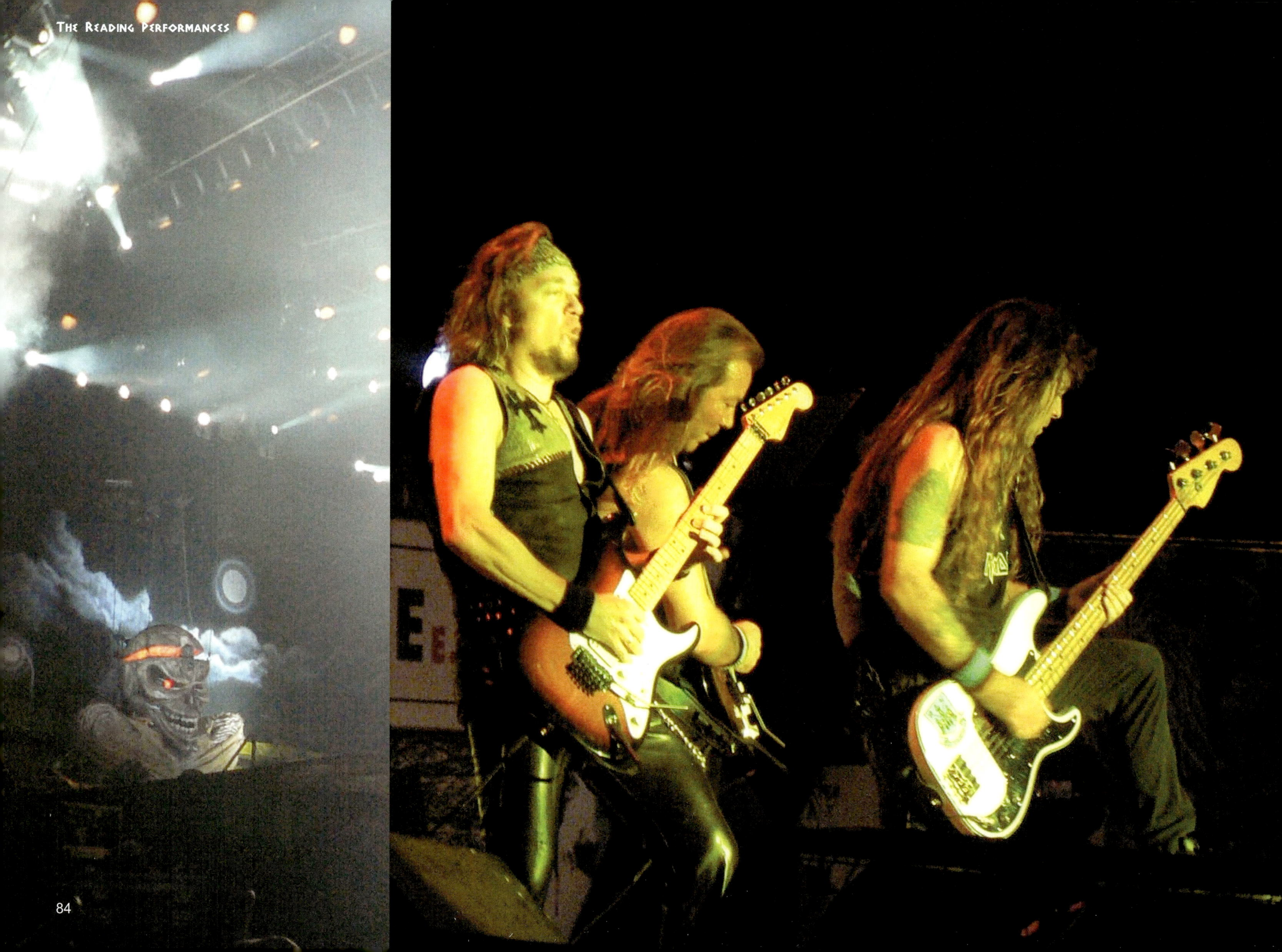

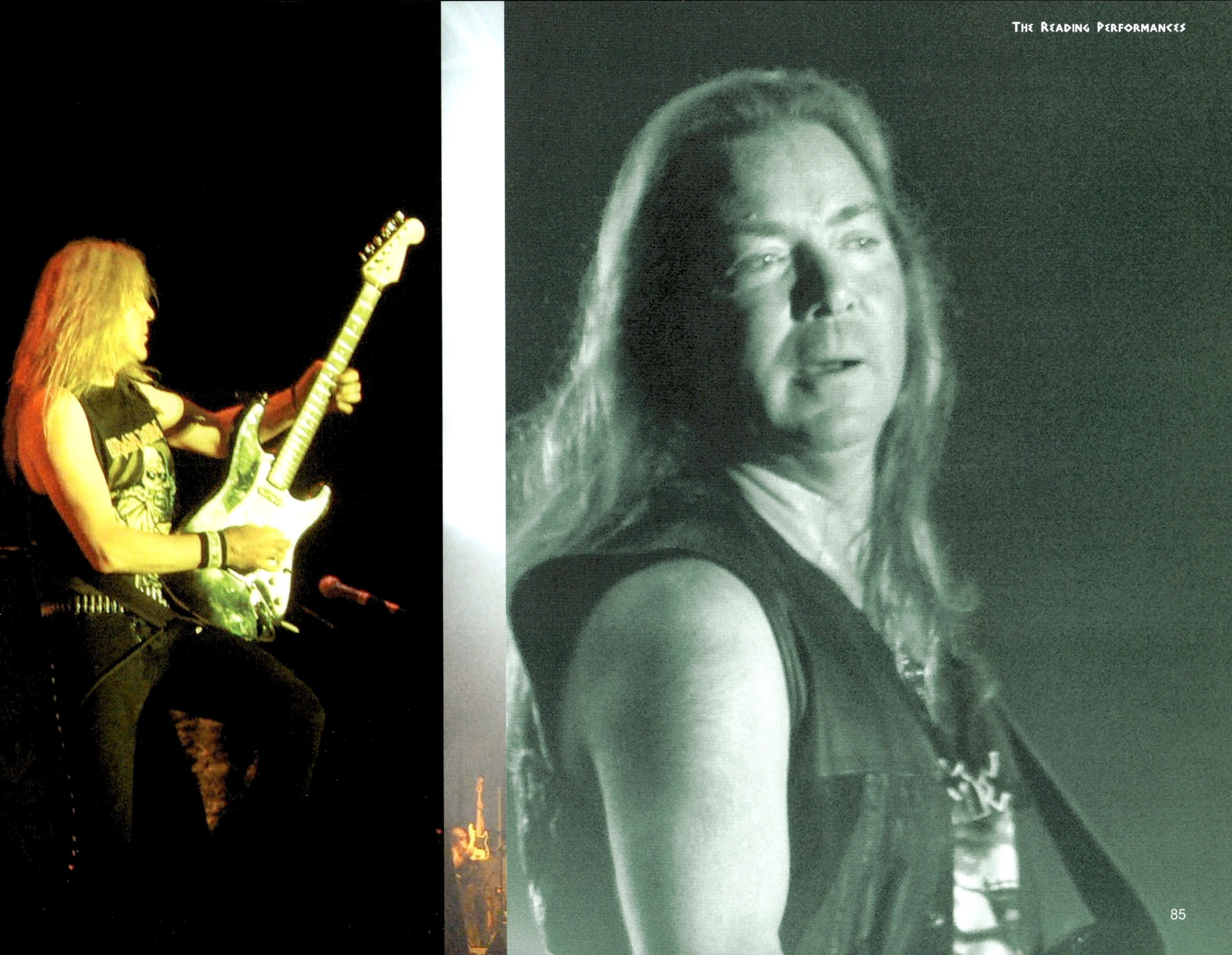

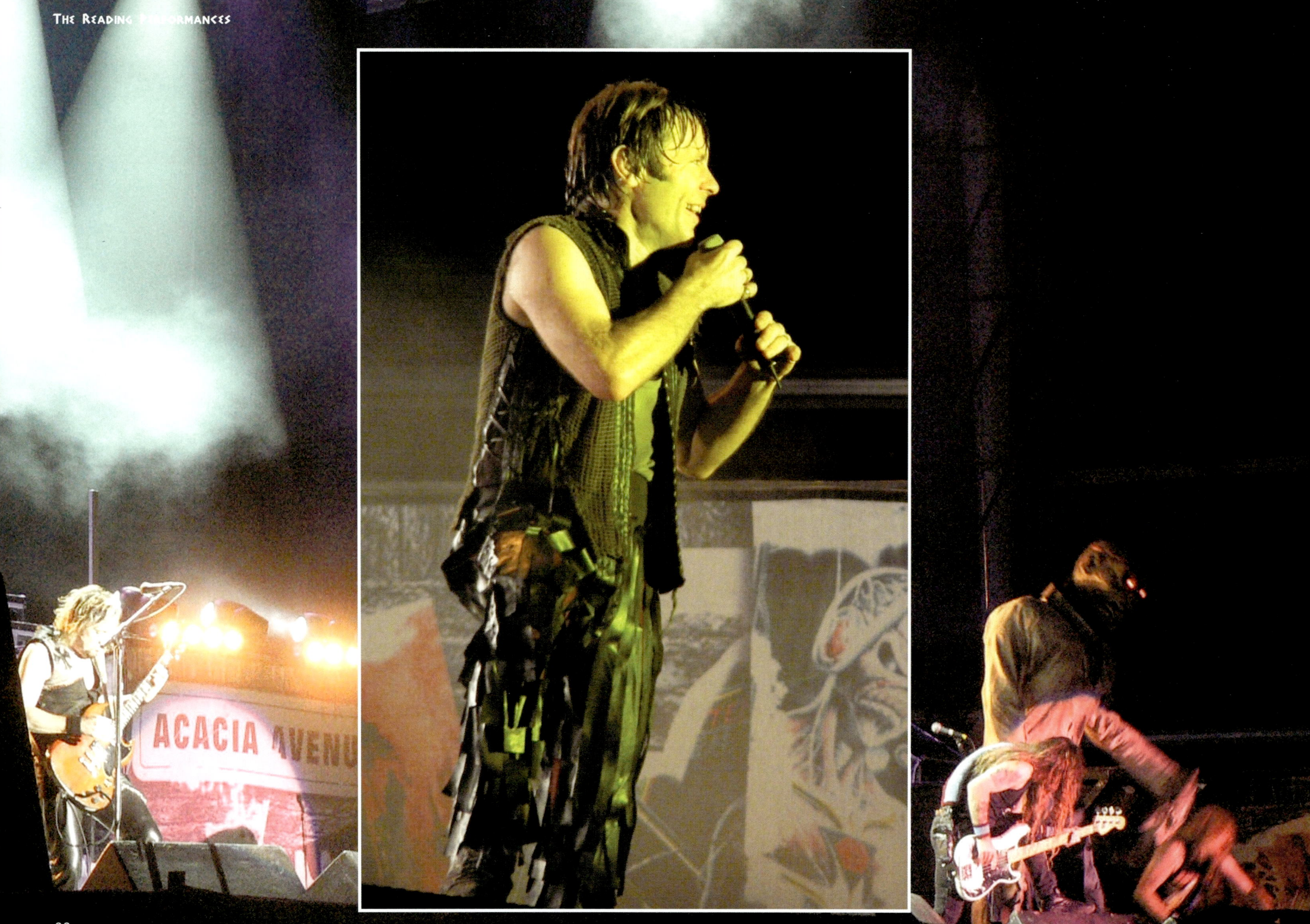
ACACIA AVENU

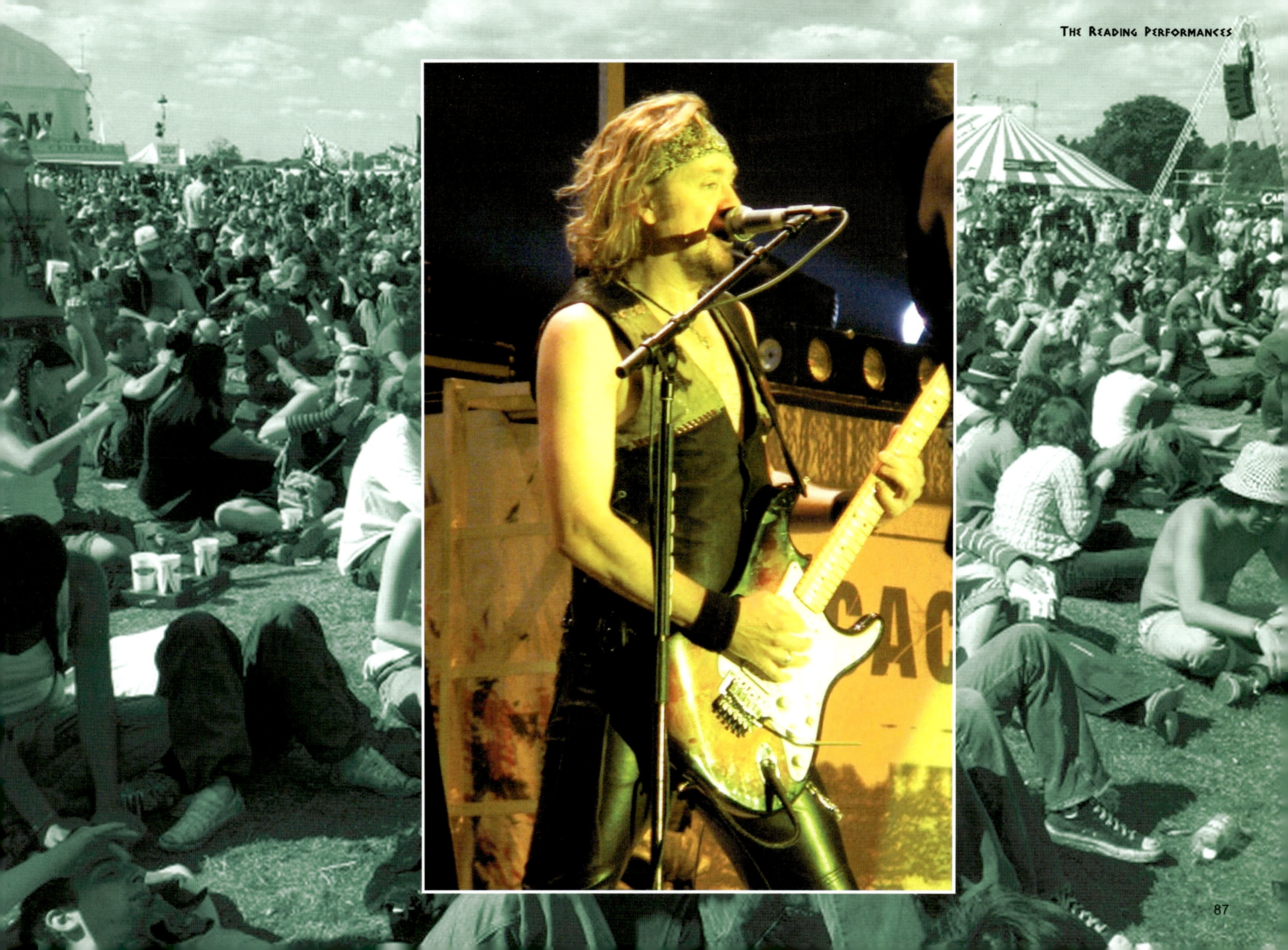

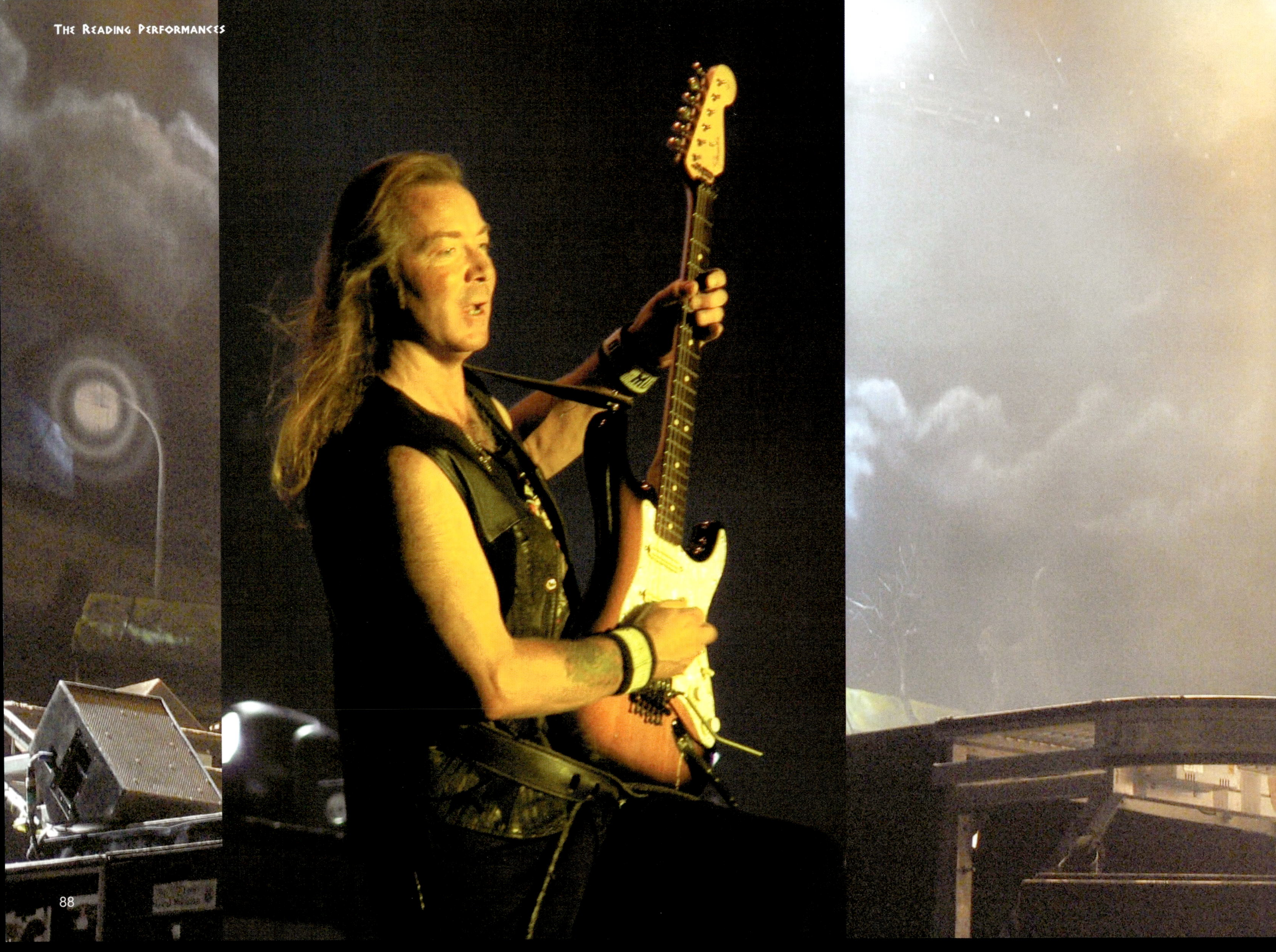

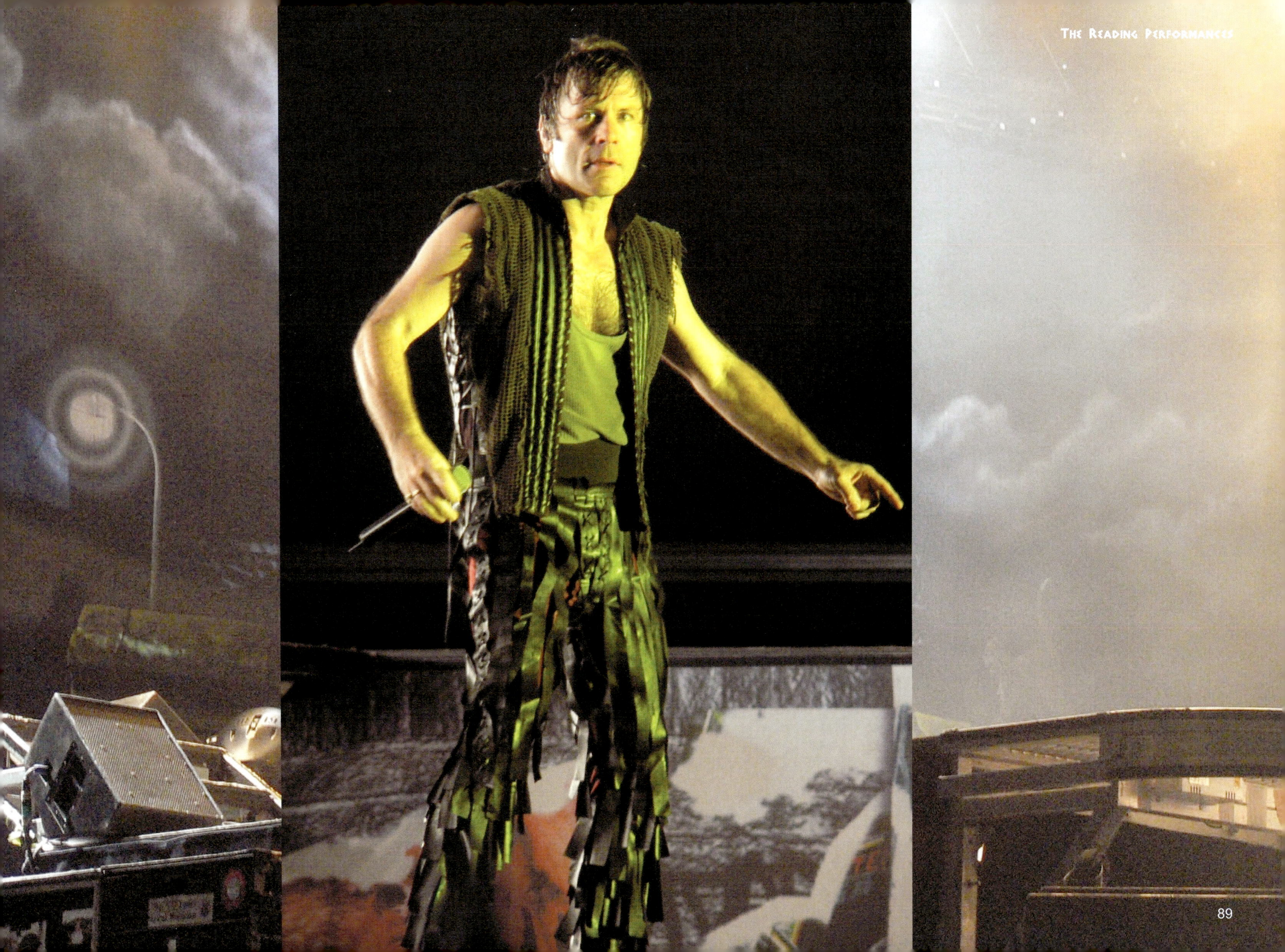

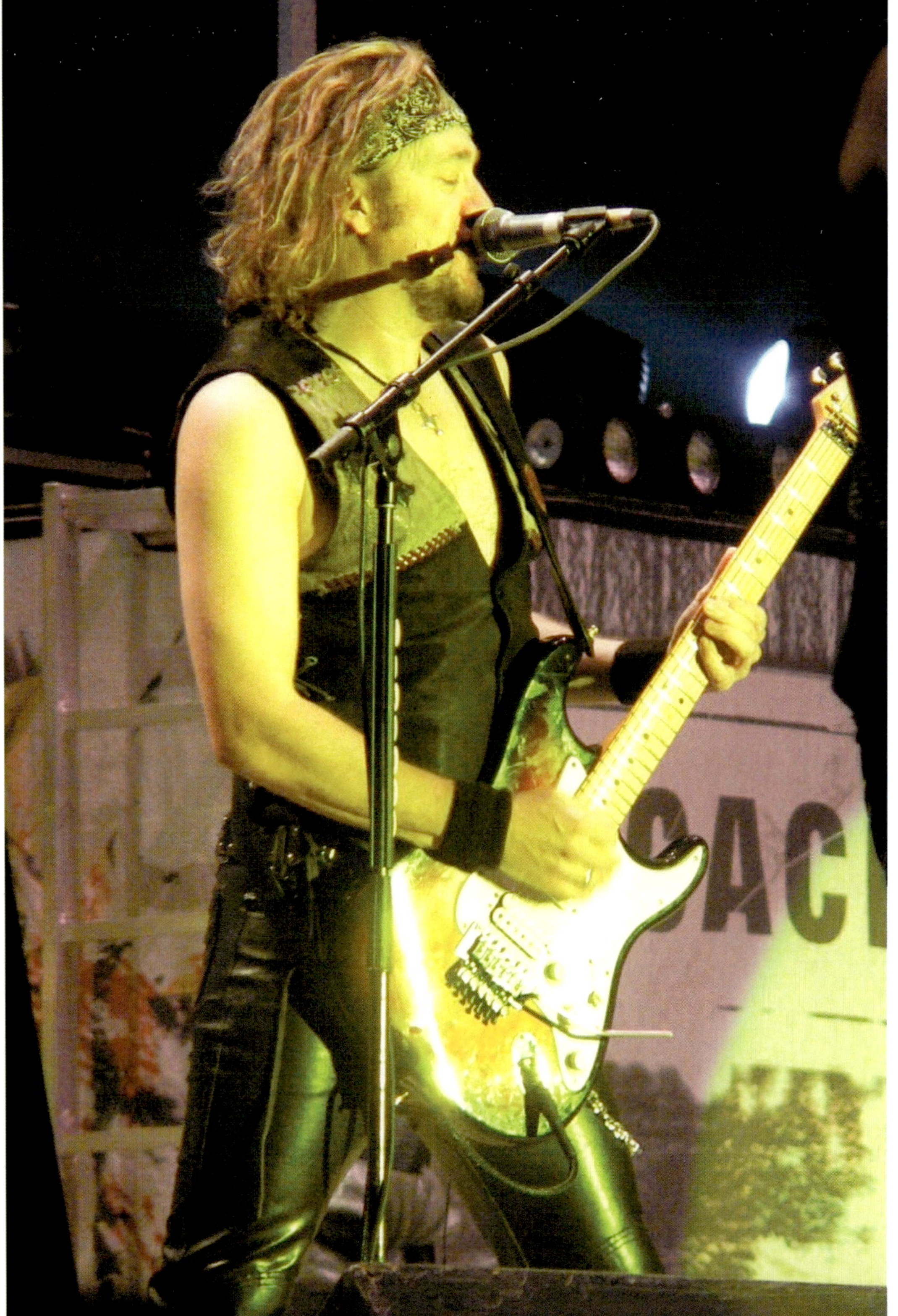

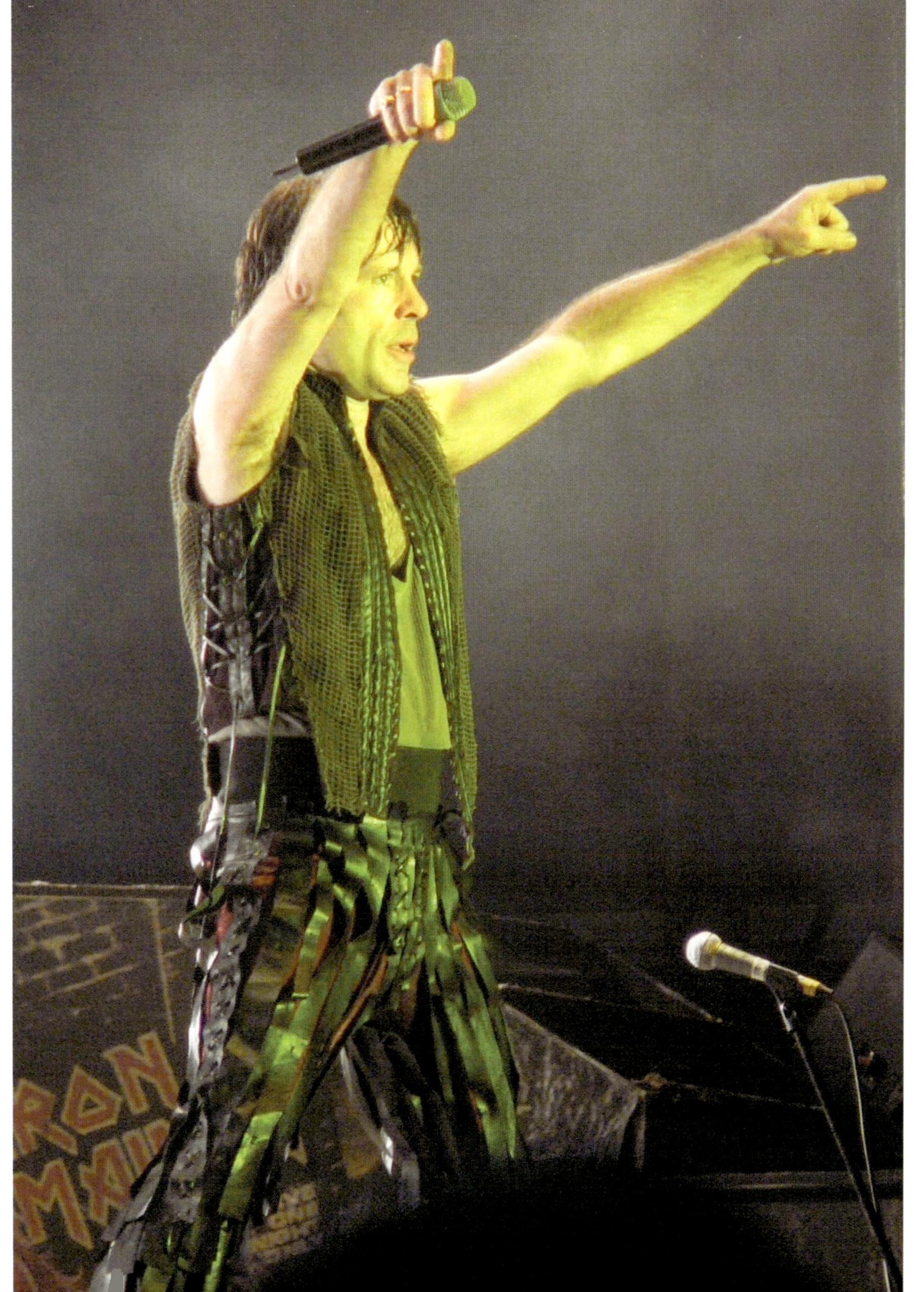

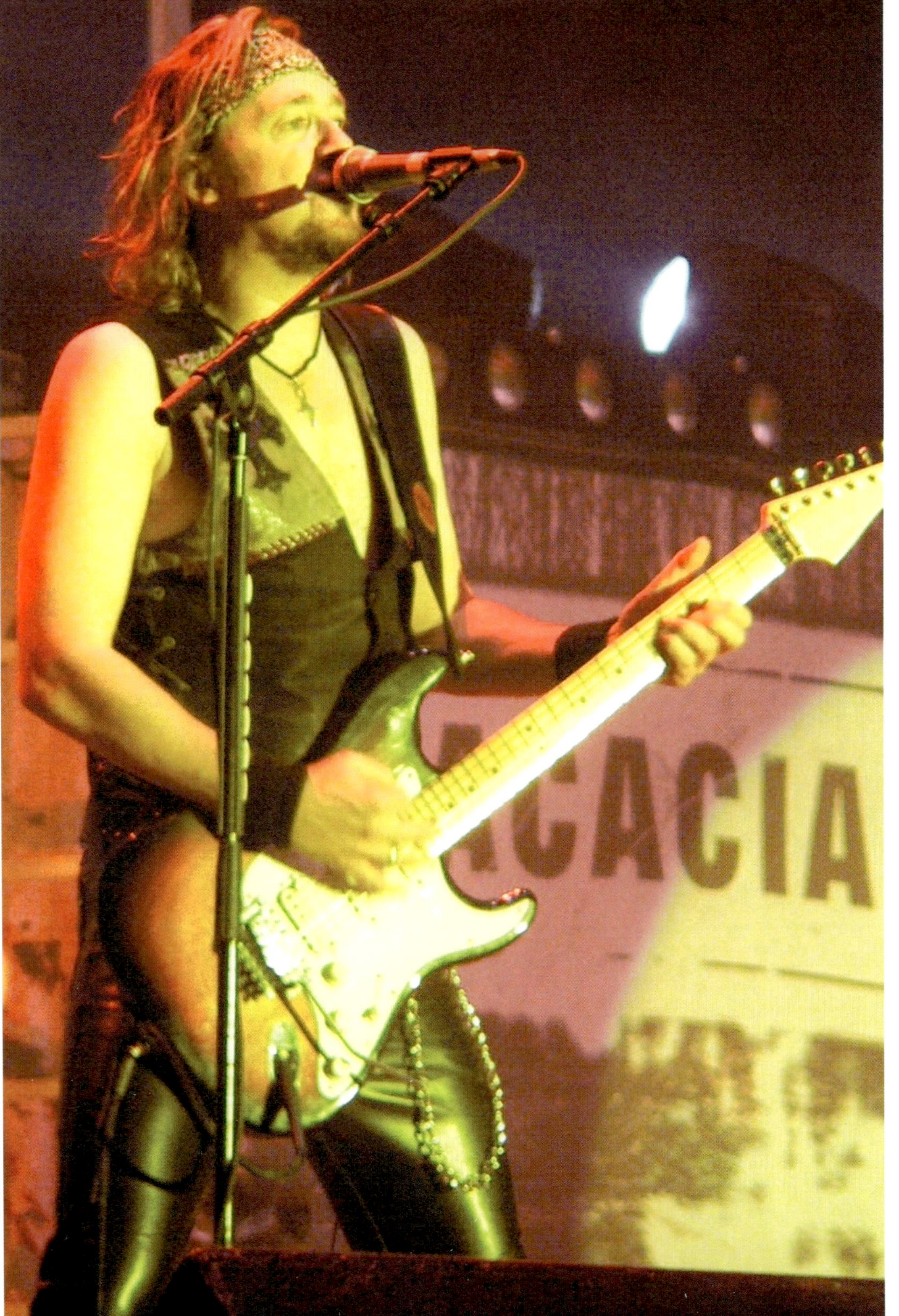
ACACIA

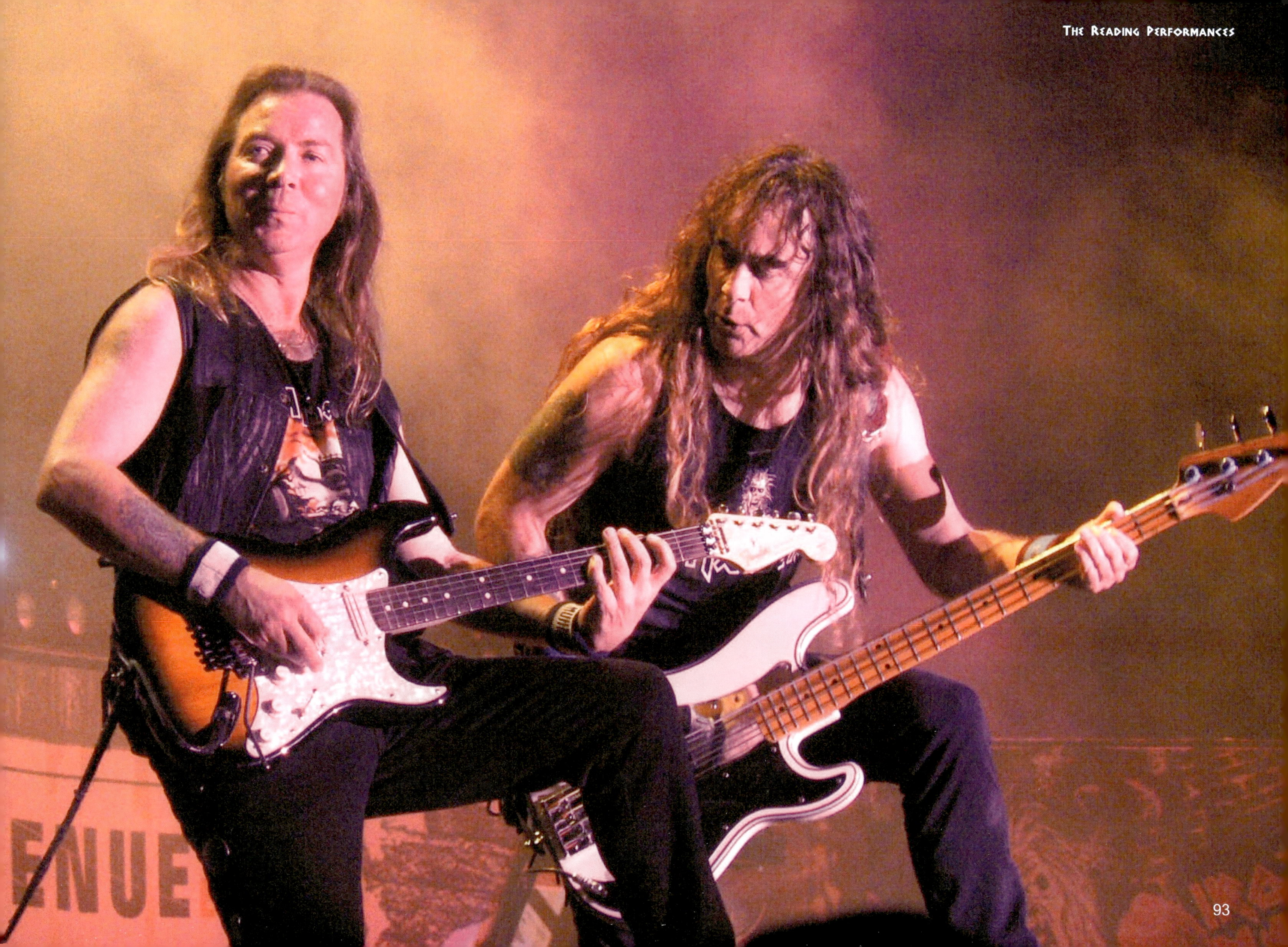
ENUE

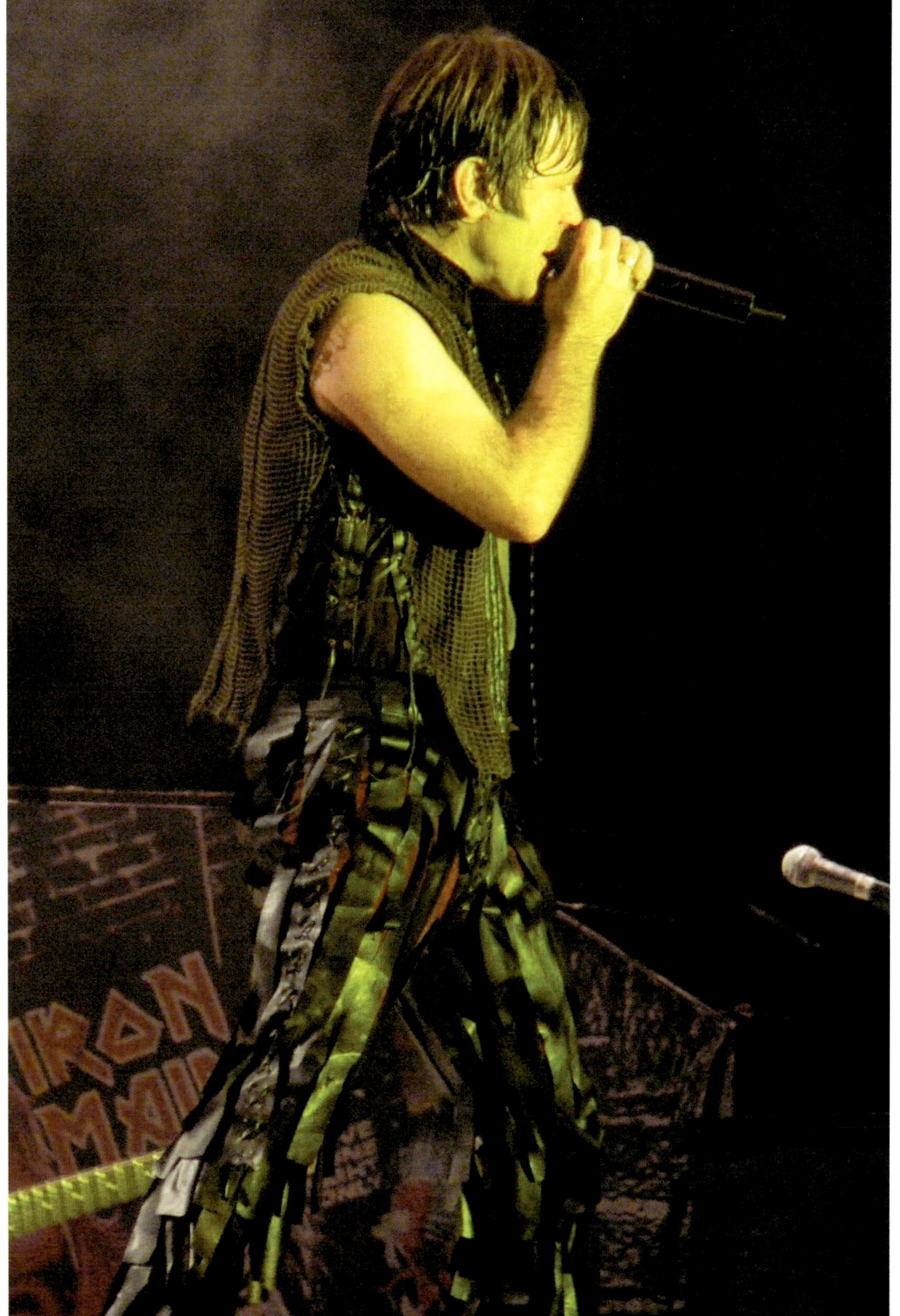

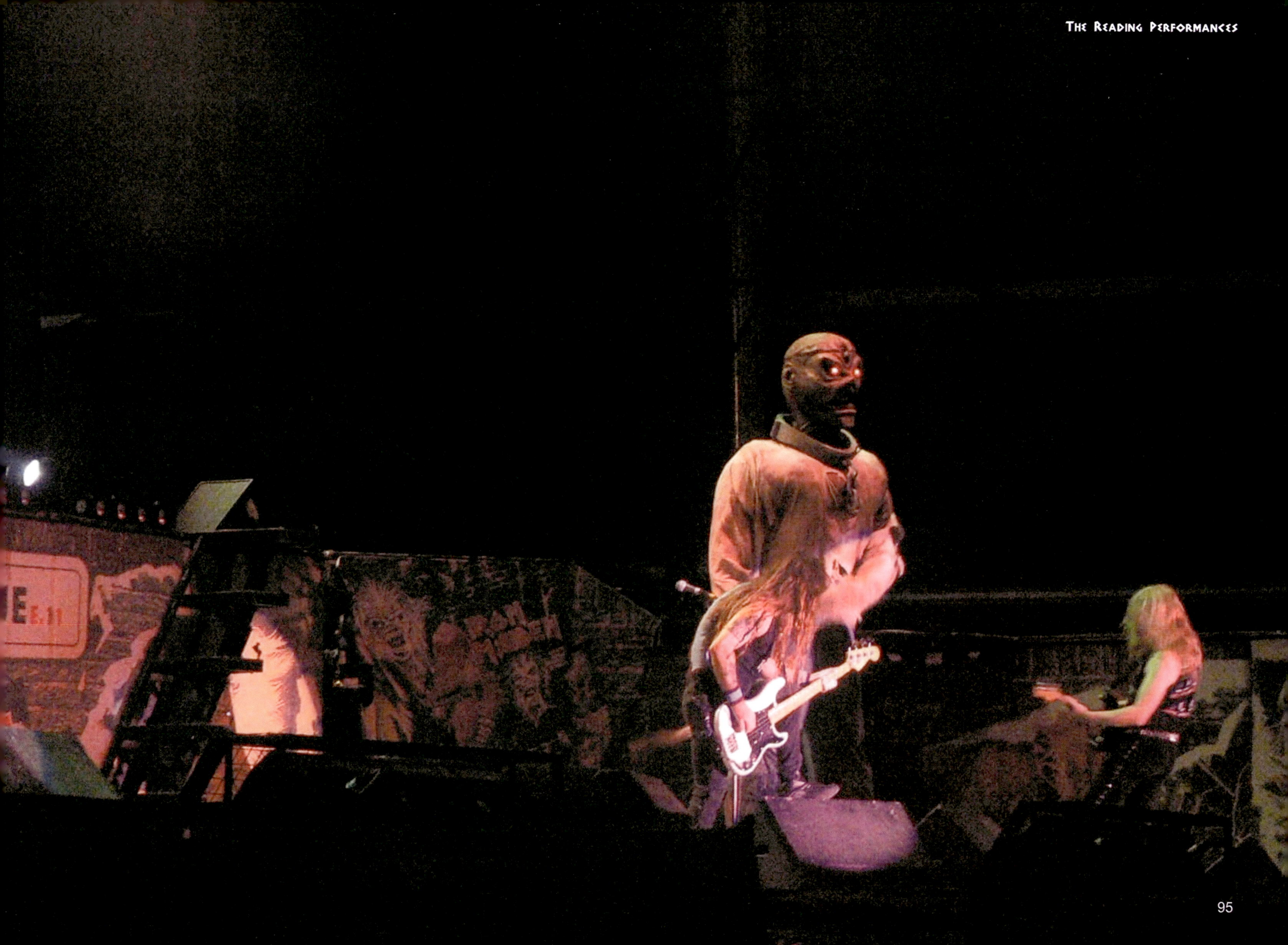

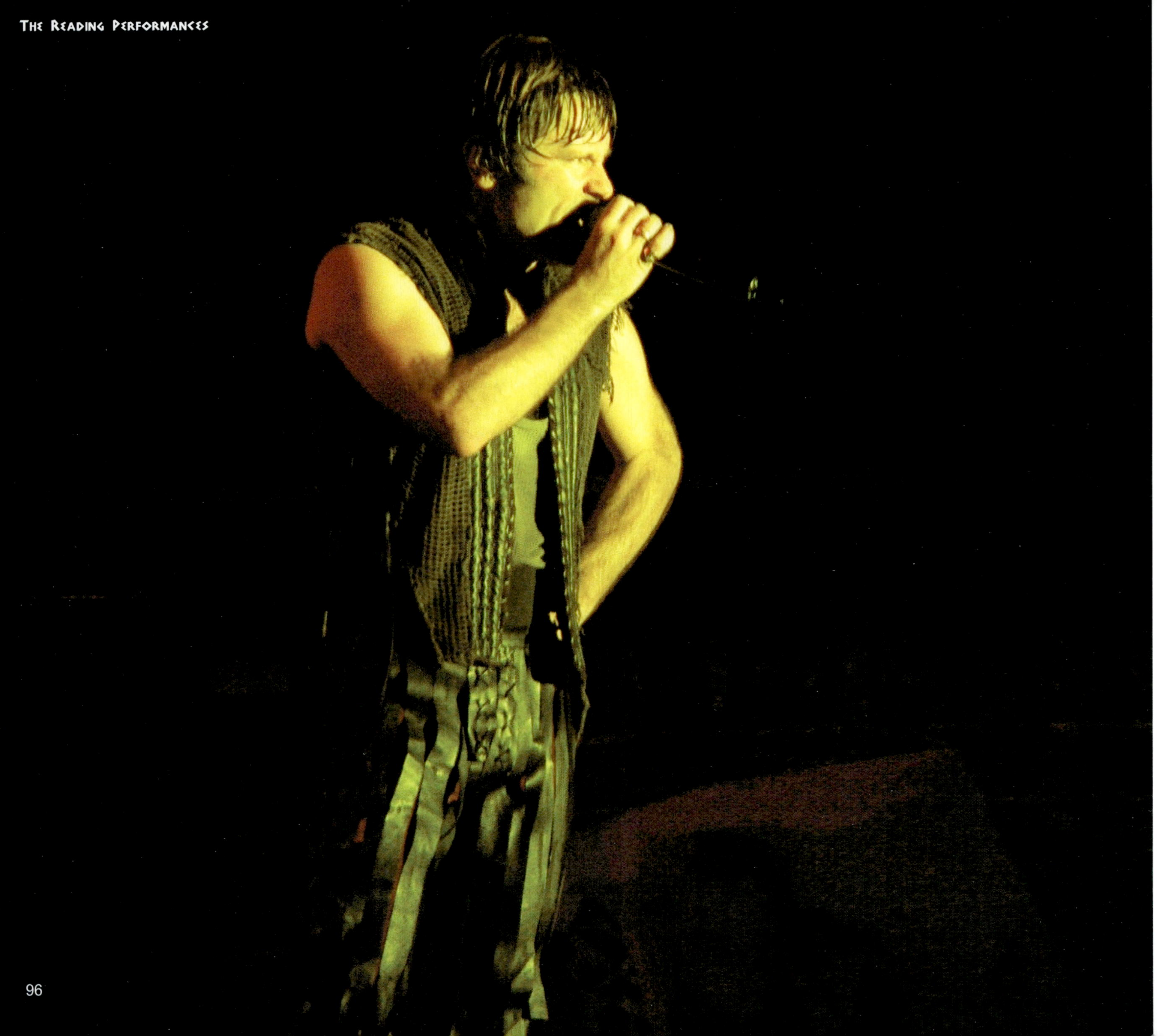

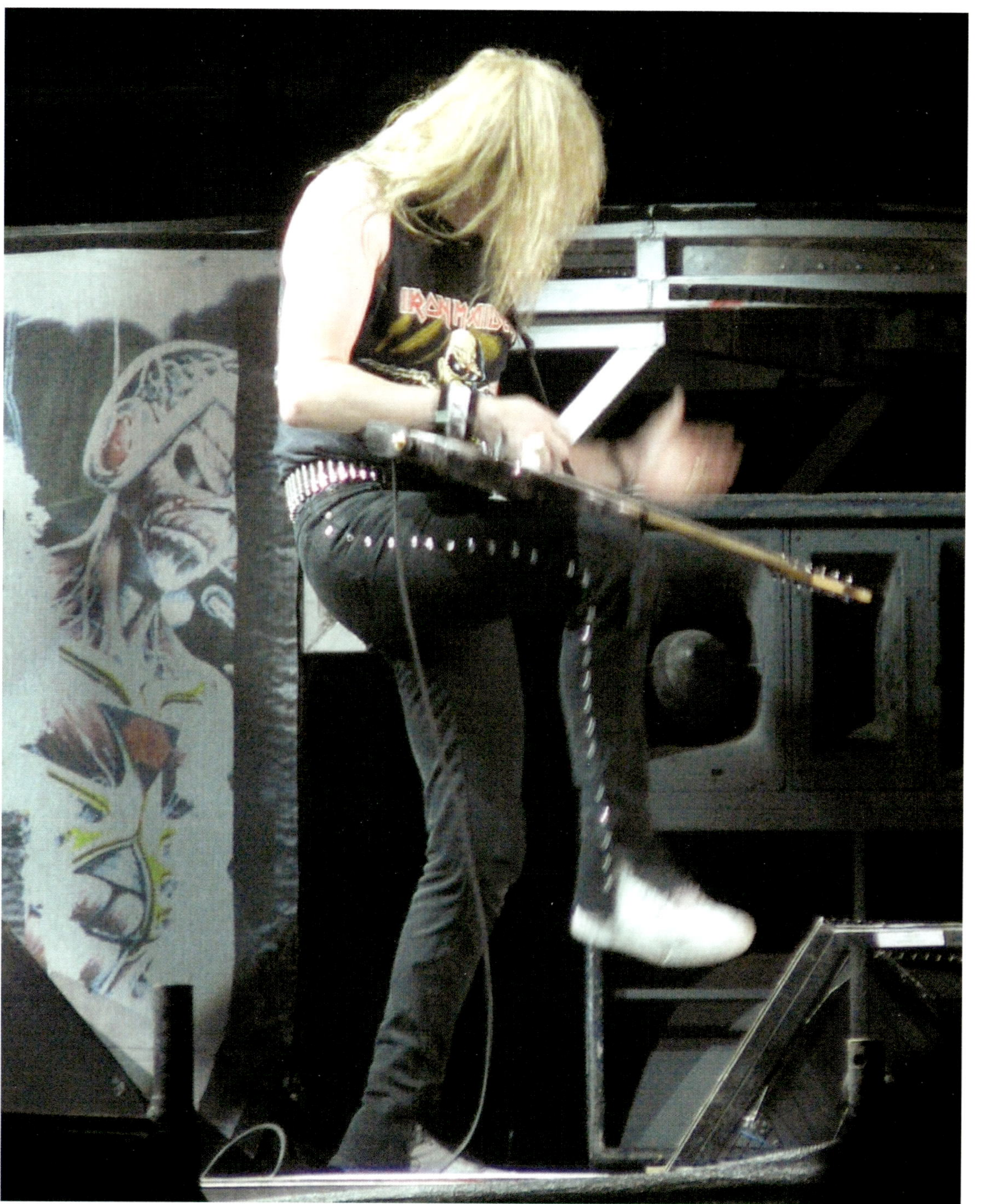

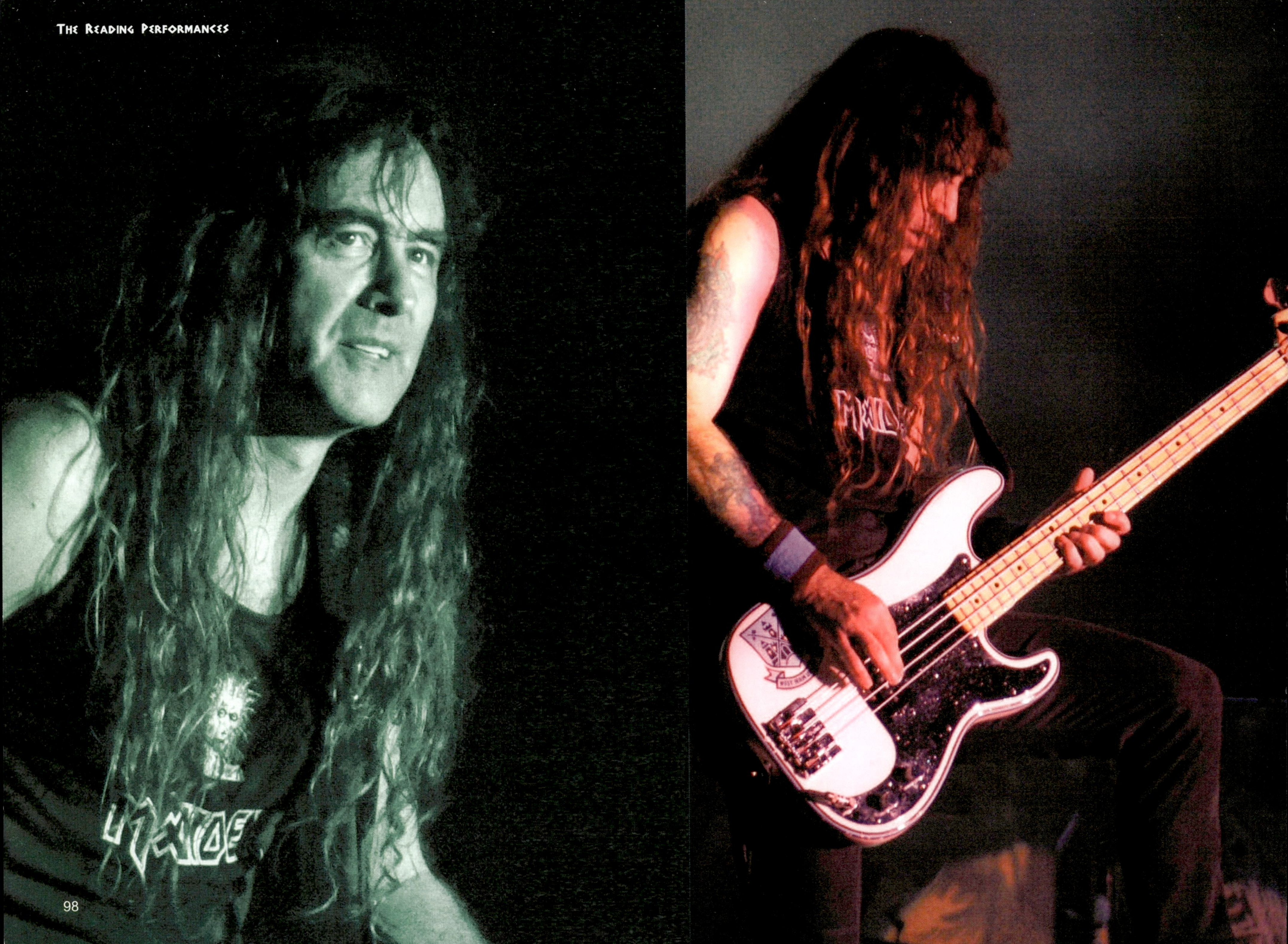

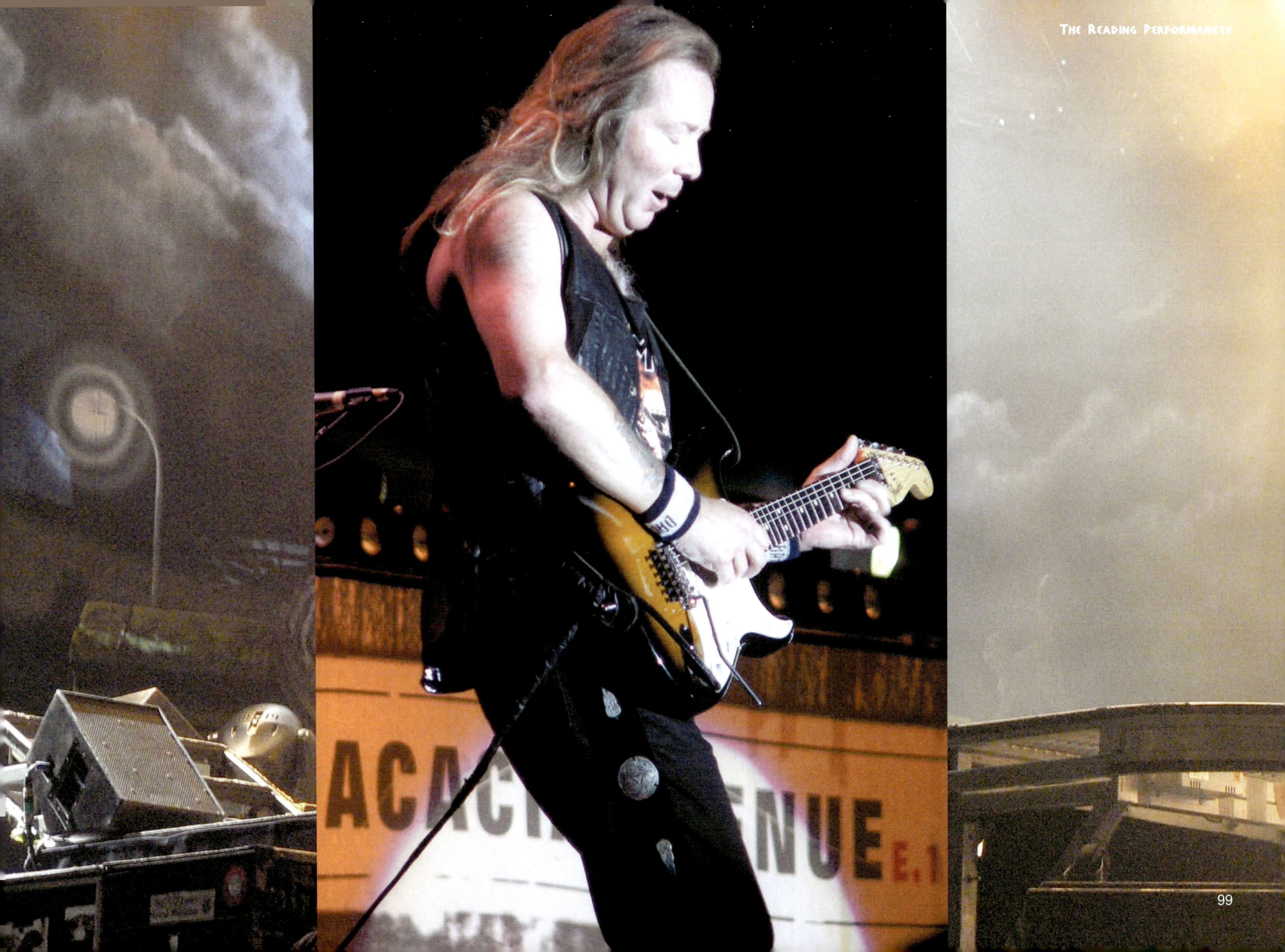

ACACIA AVENUE E.1

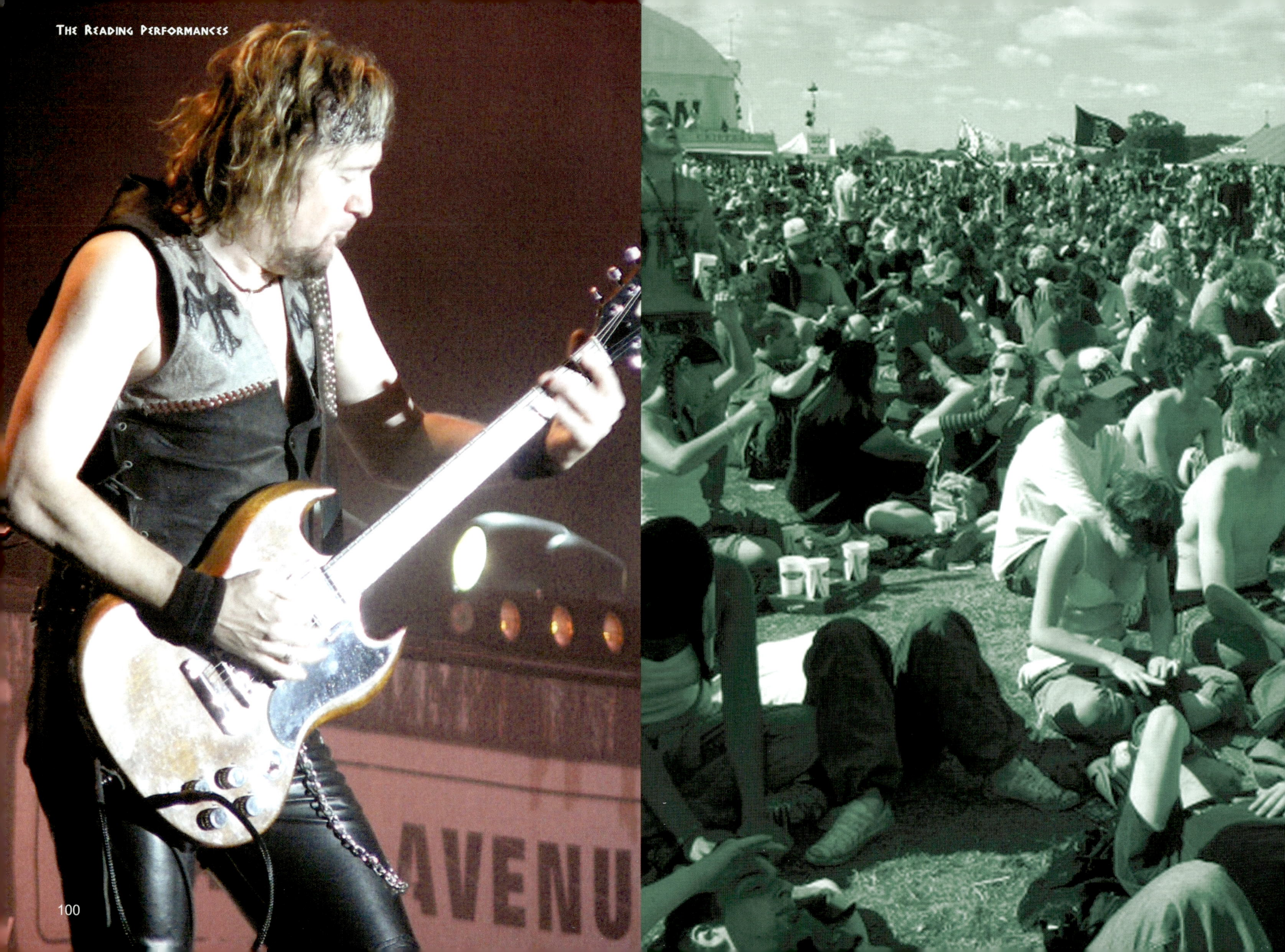

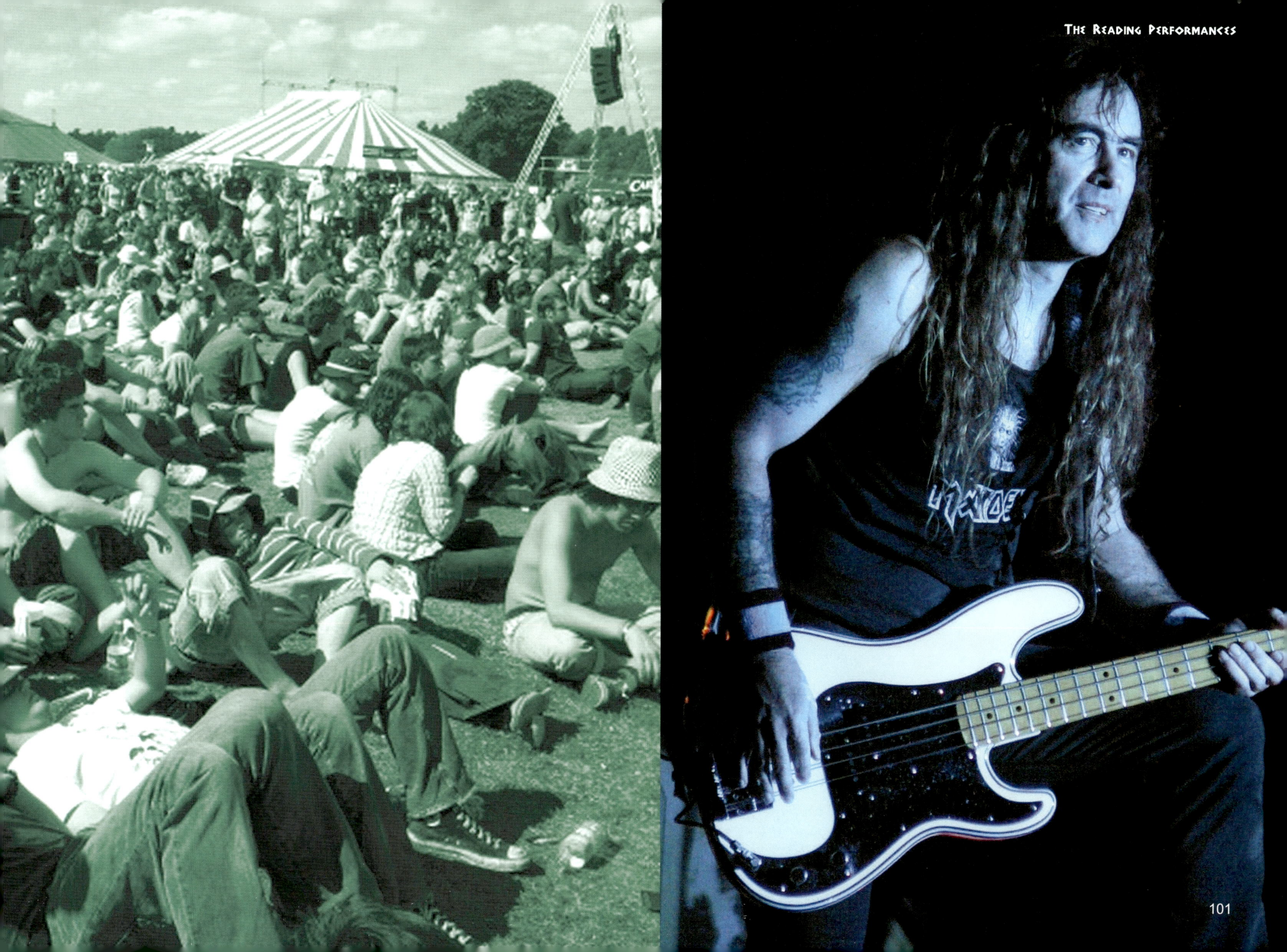

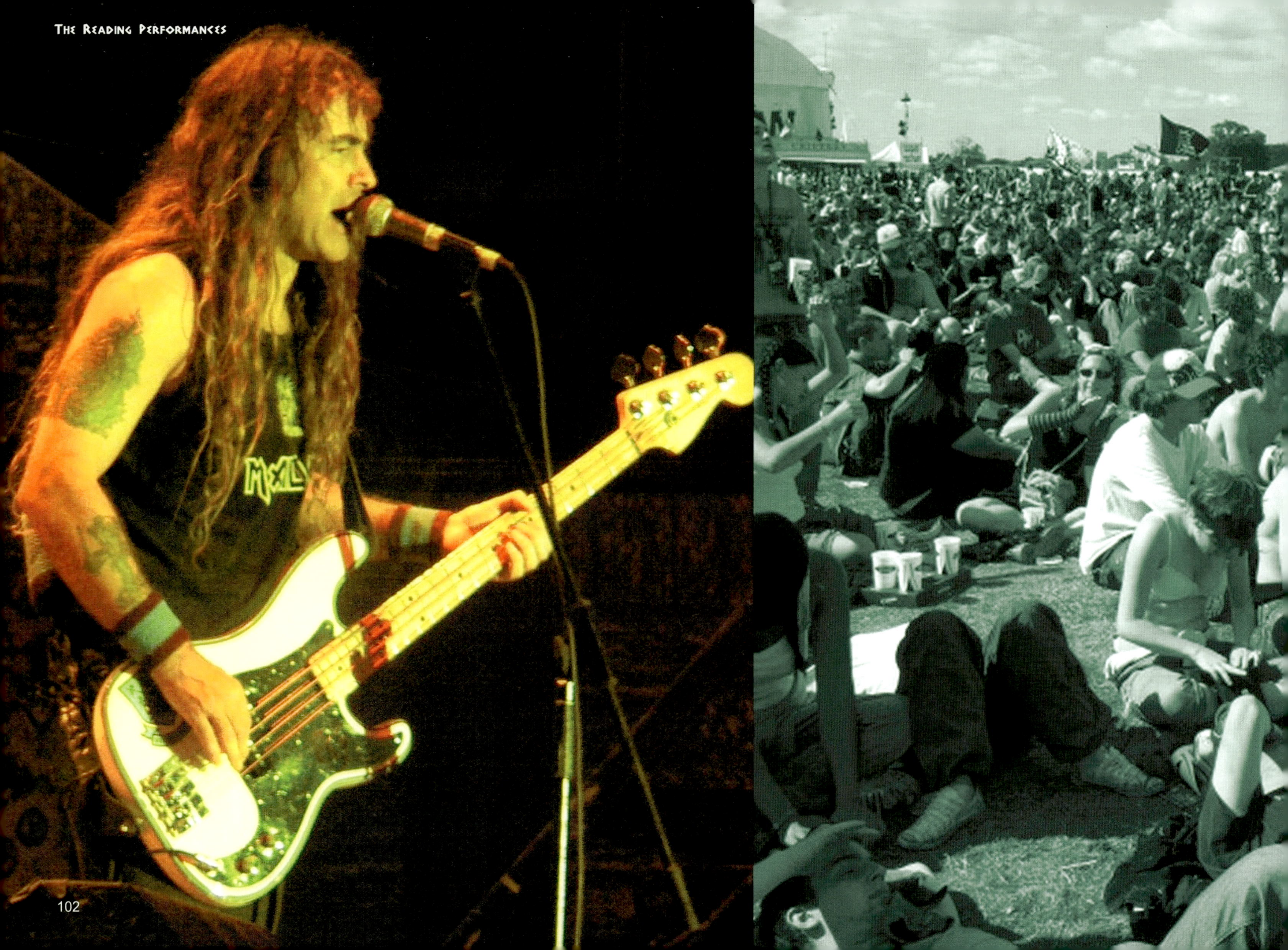

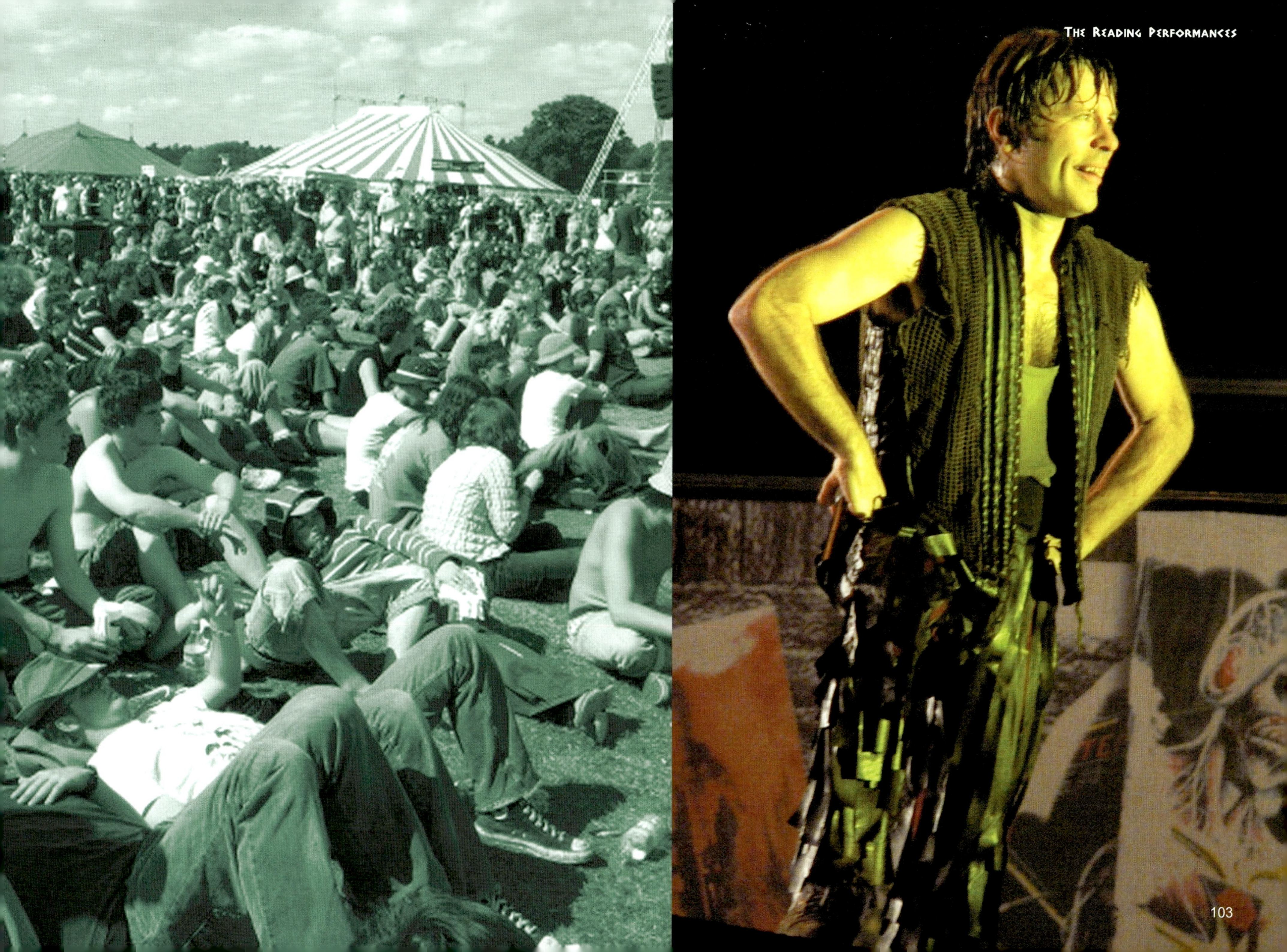

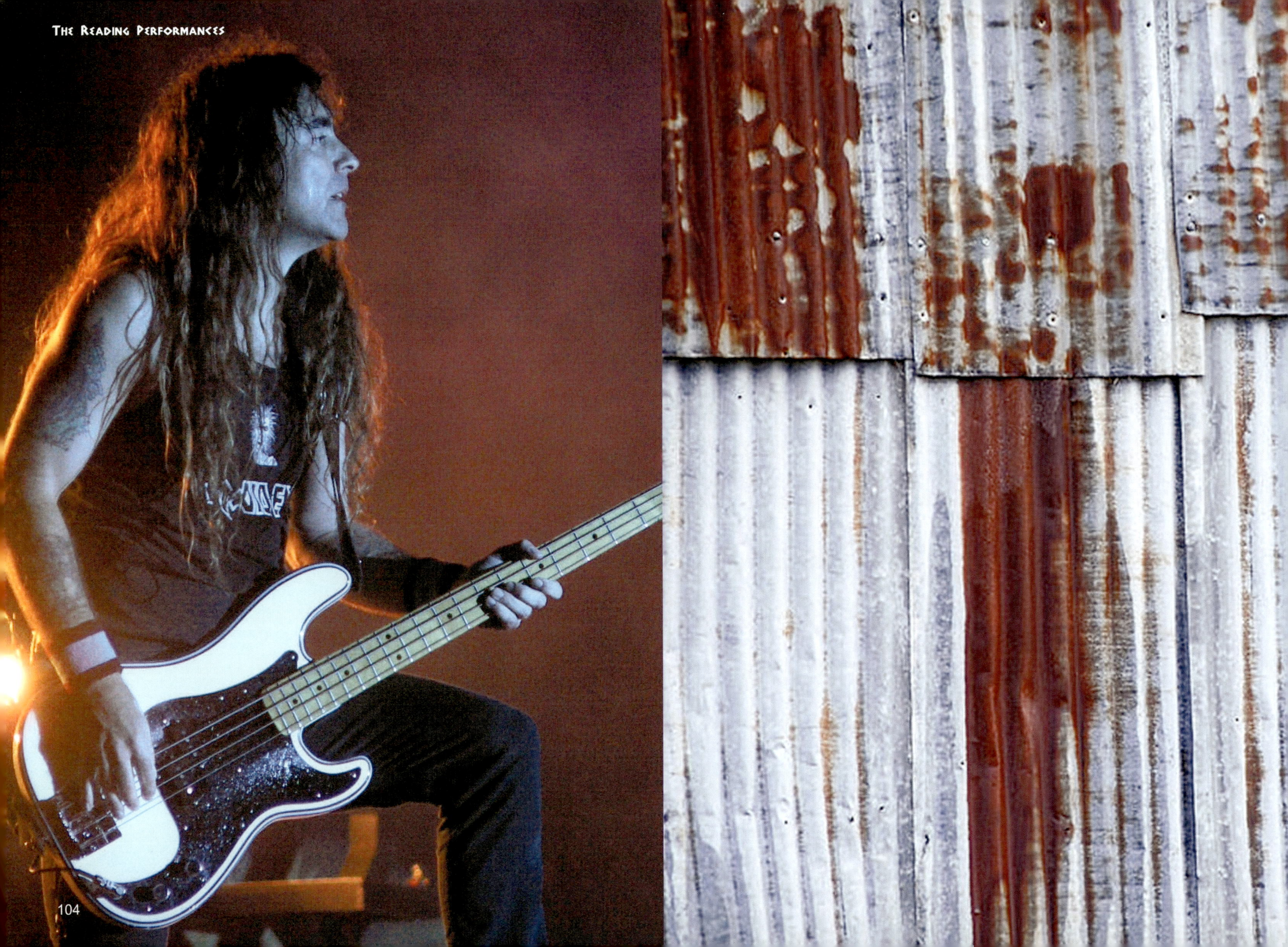

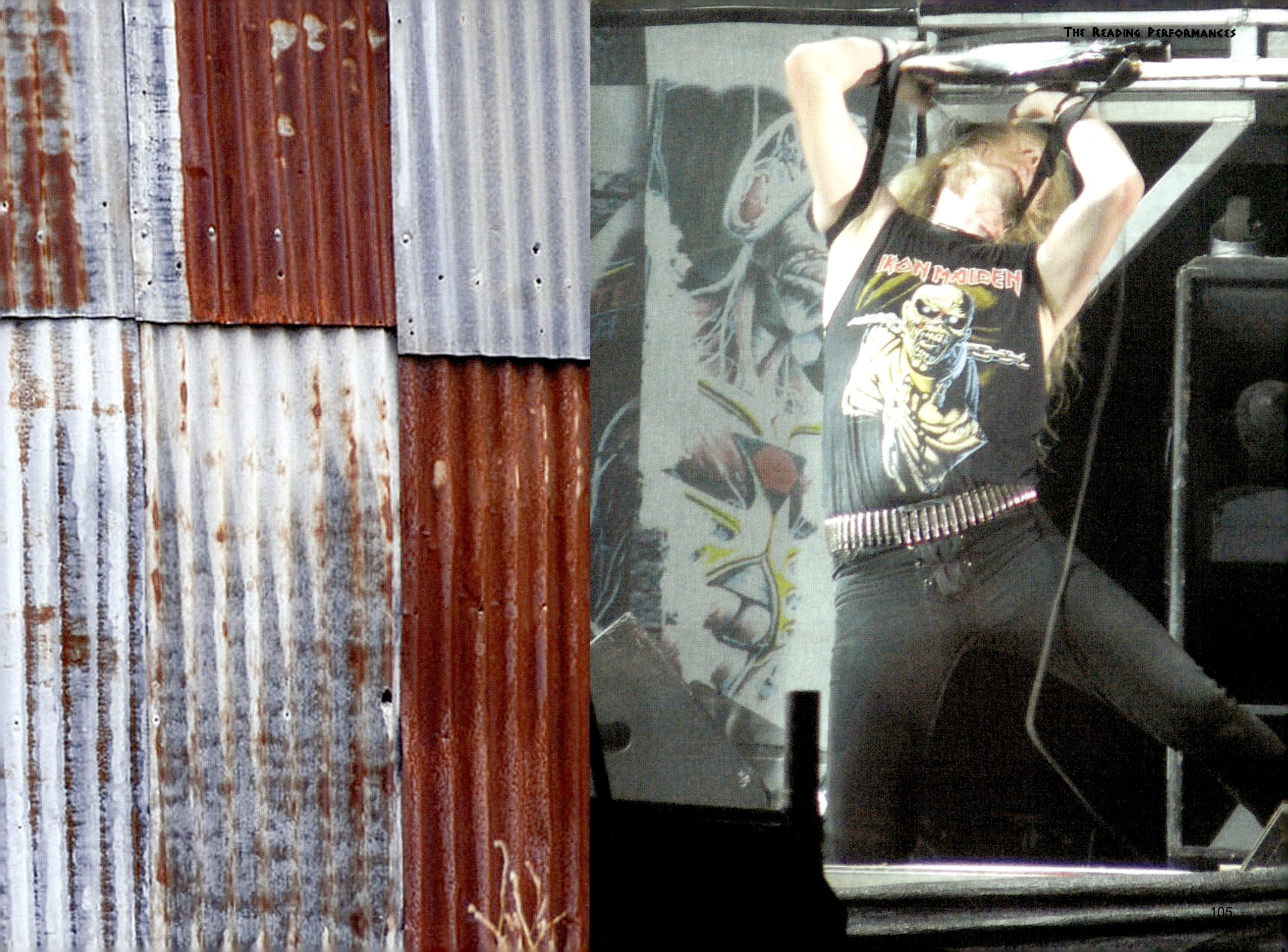

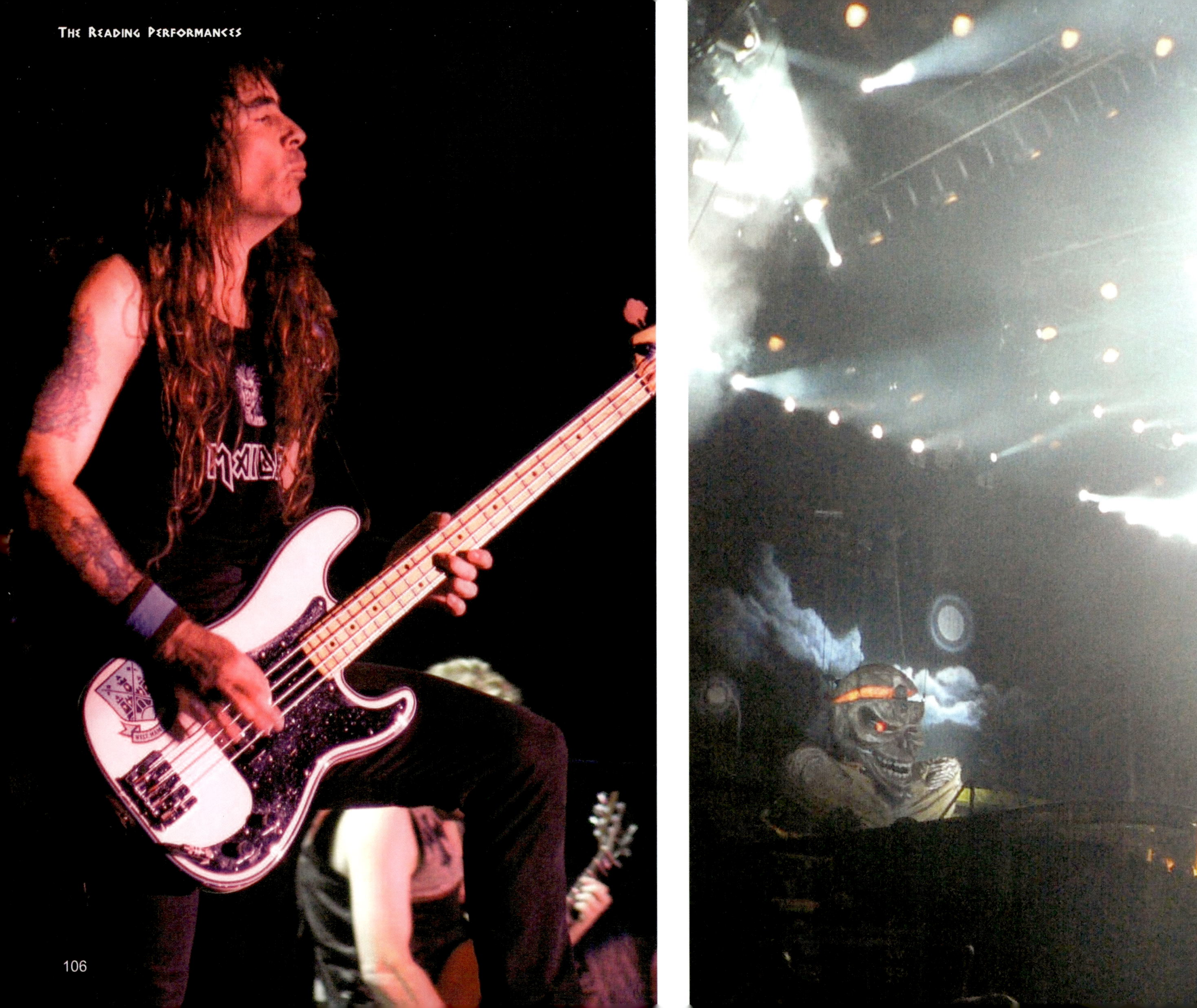

ACACIA

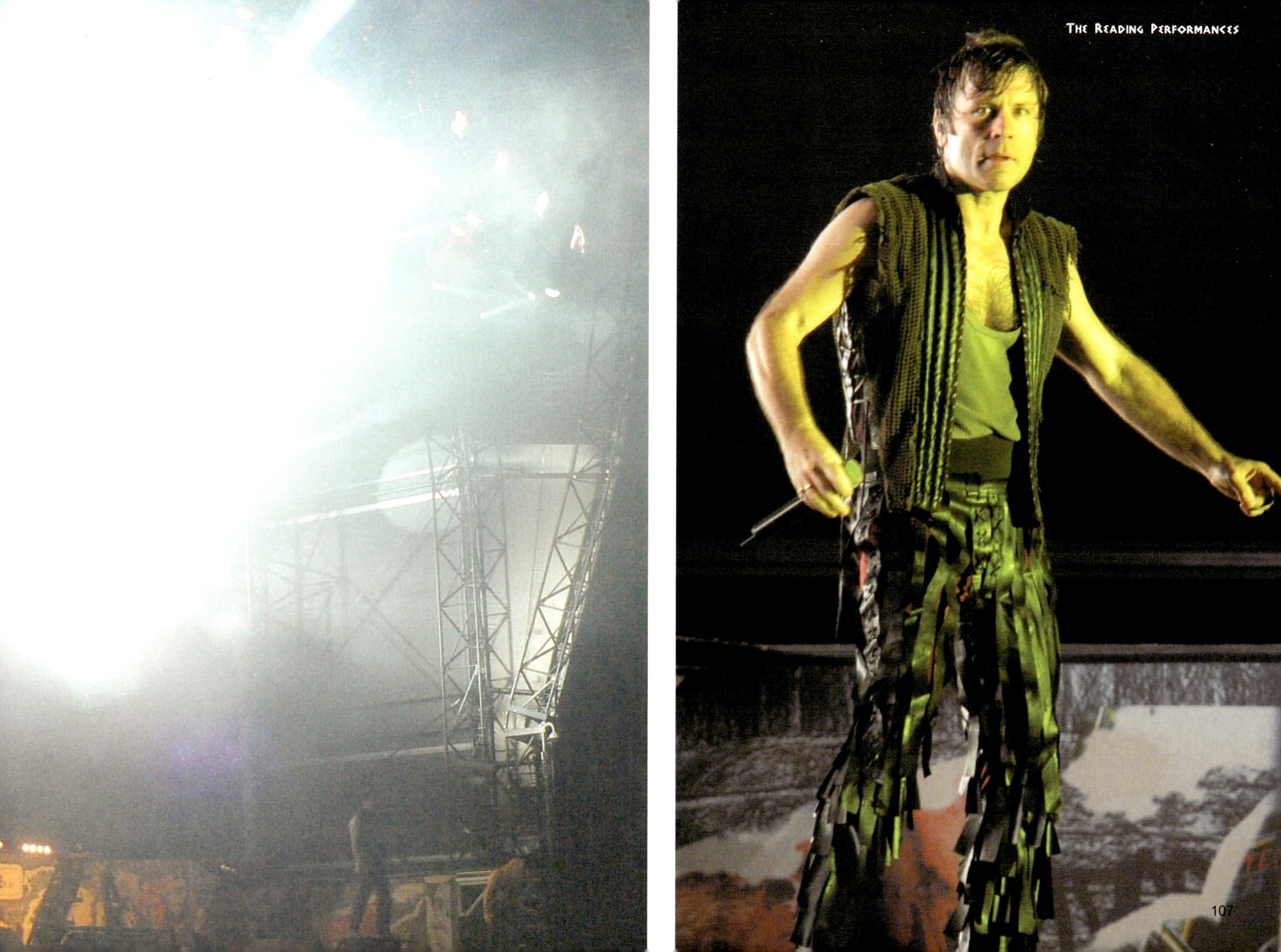

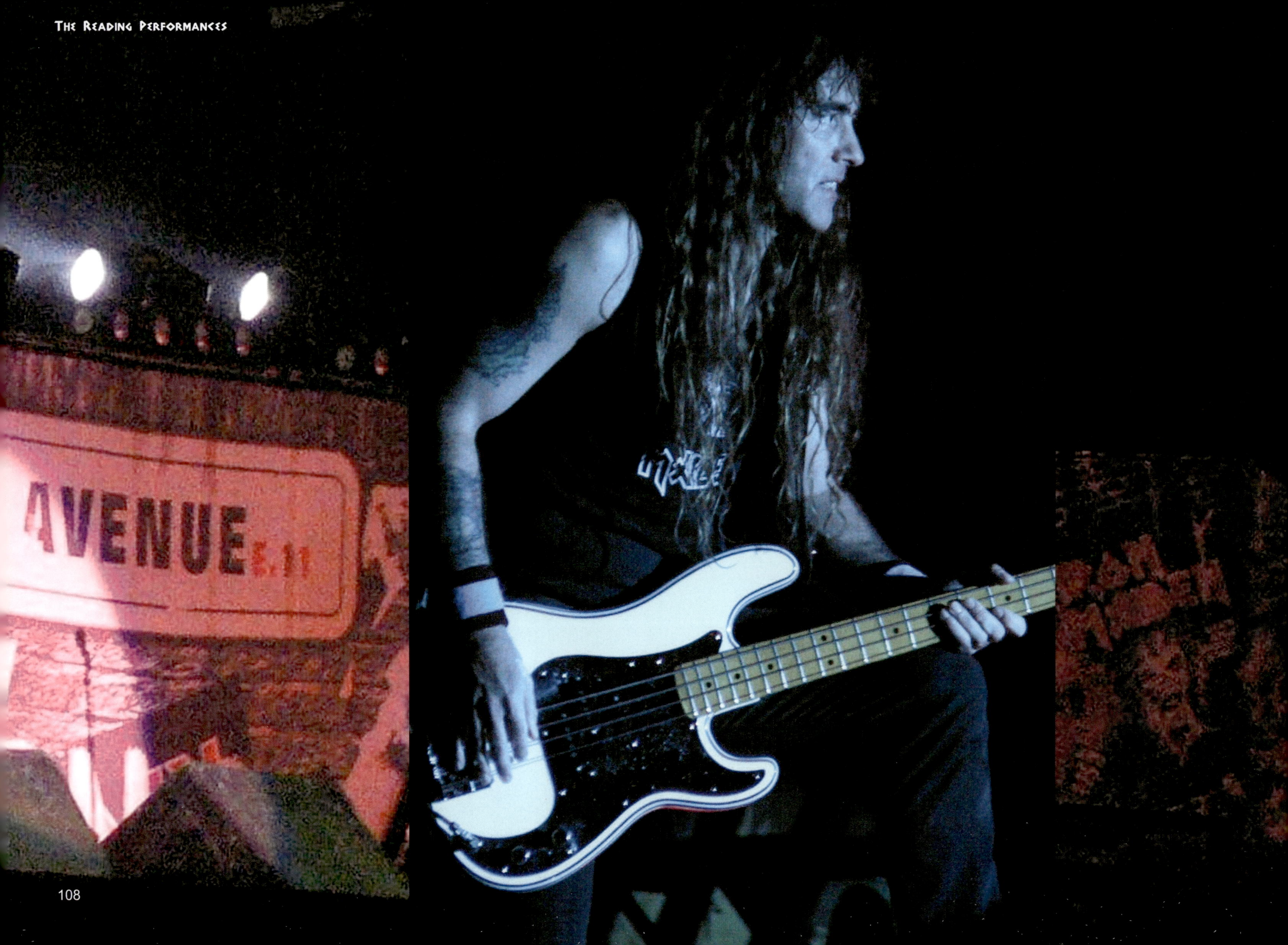
AVENUE E.11

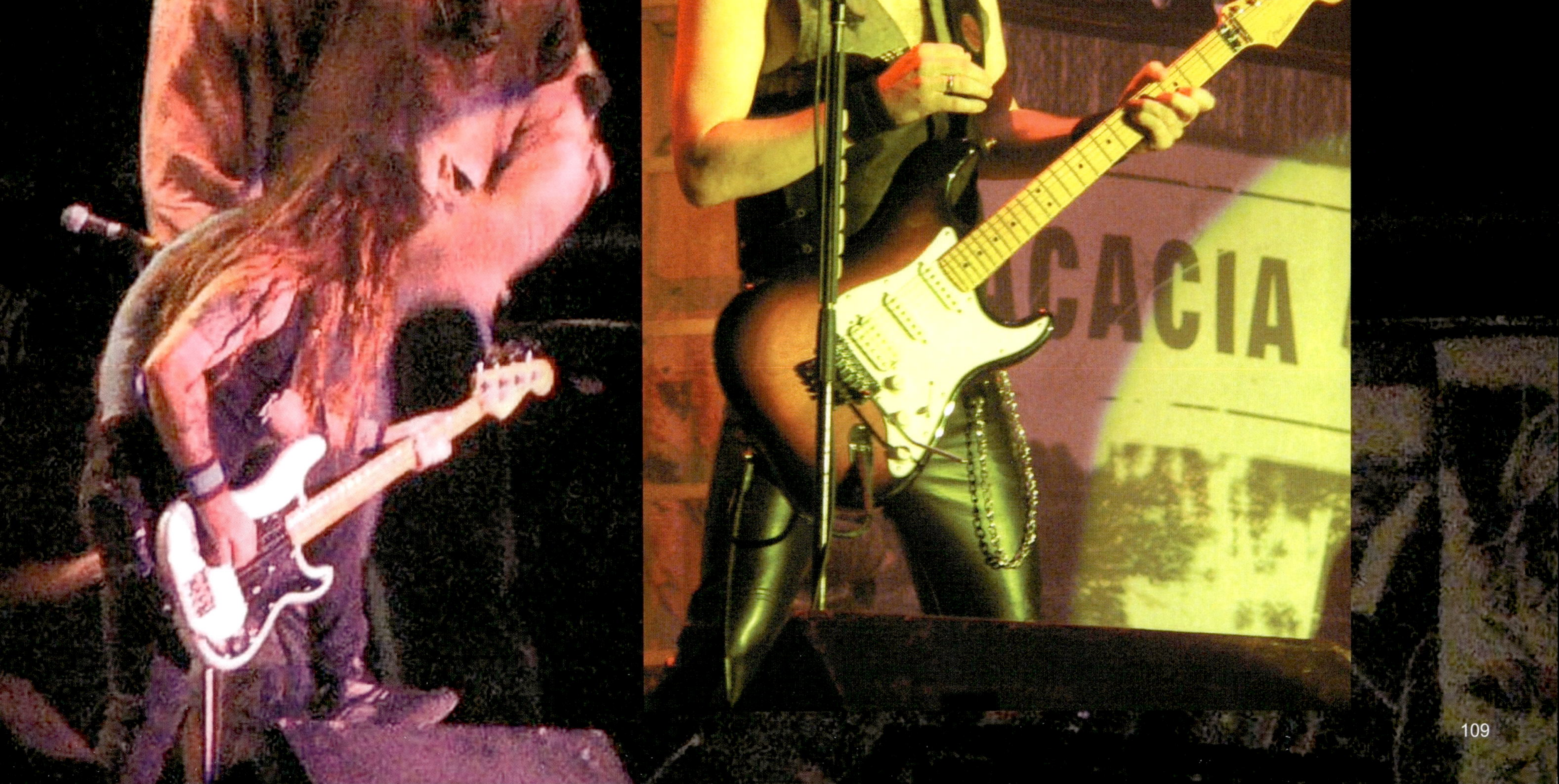
CACIA

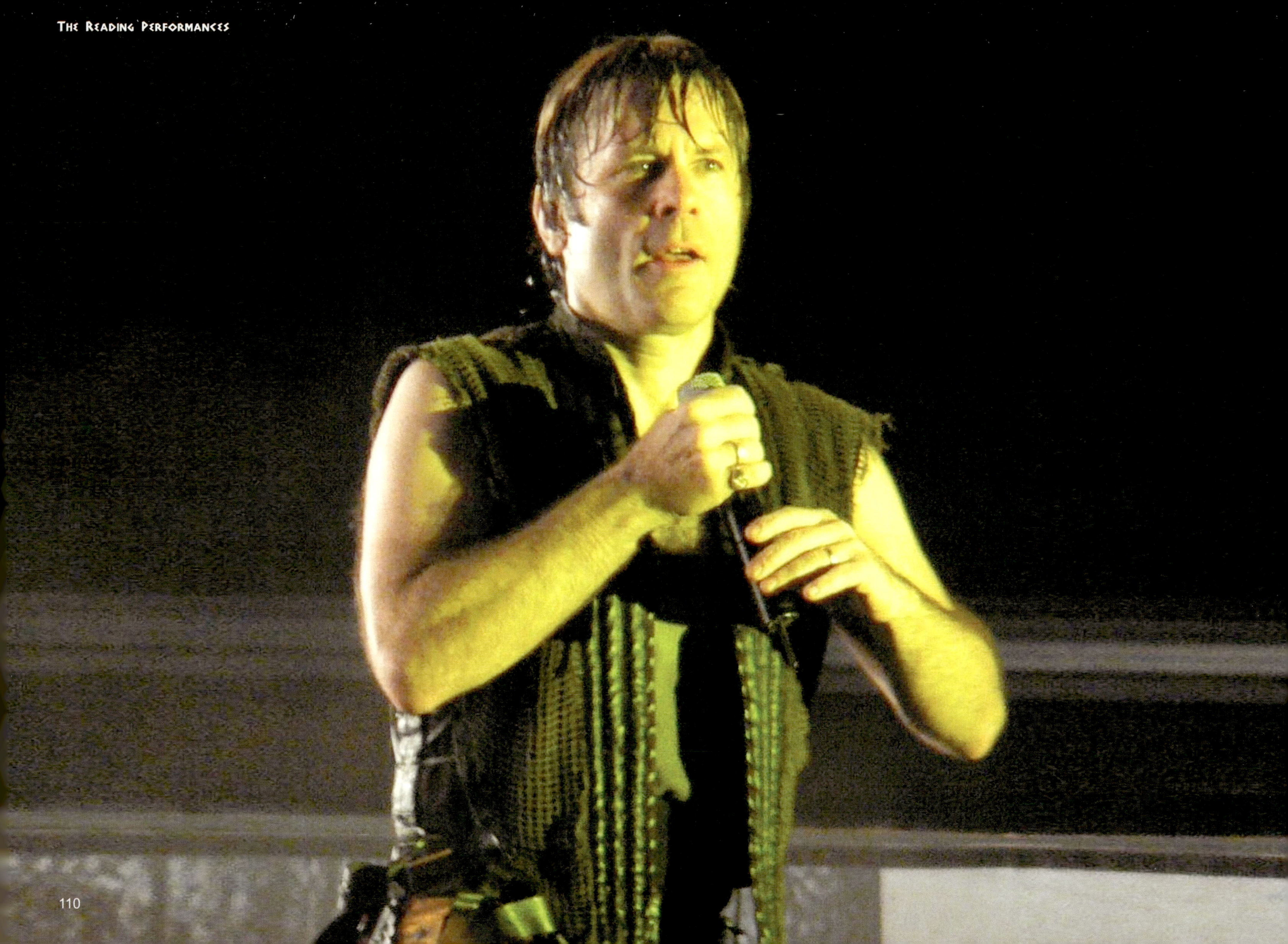

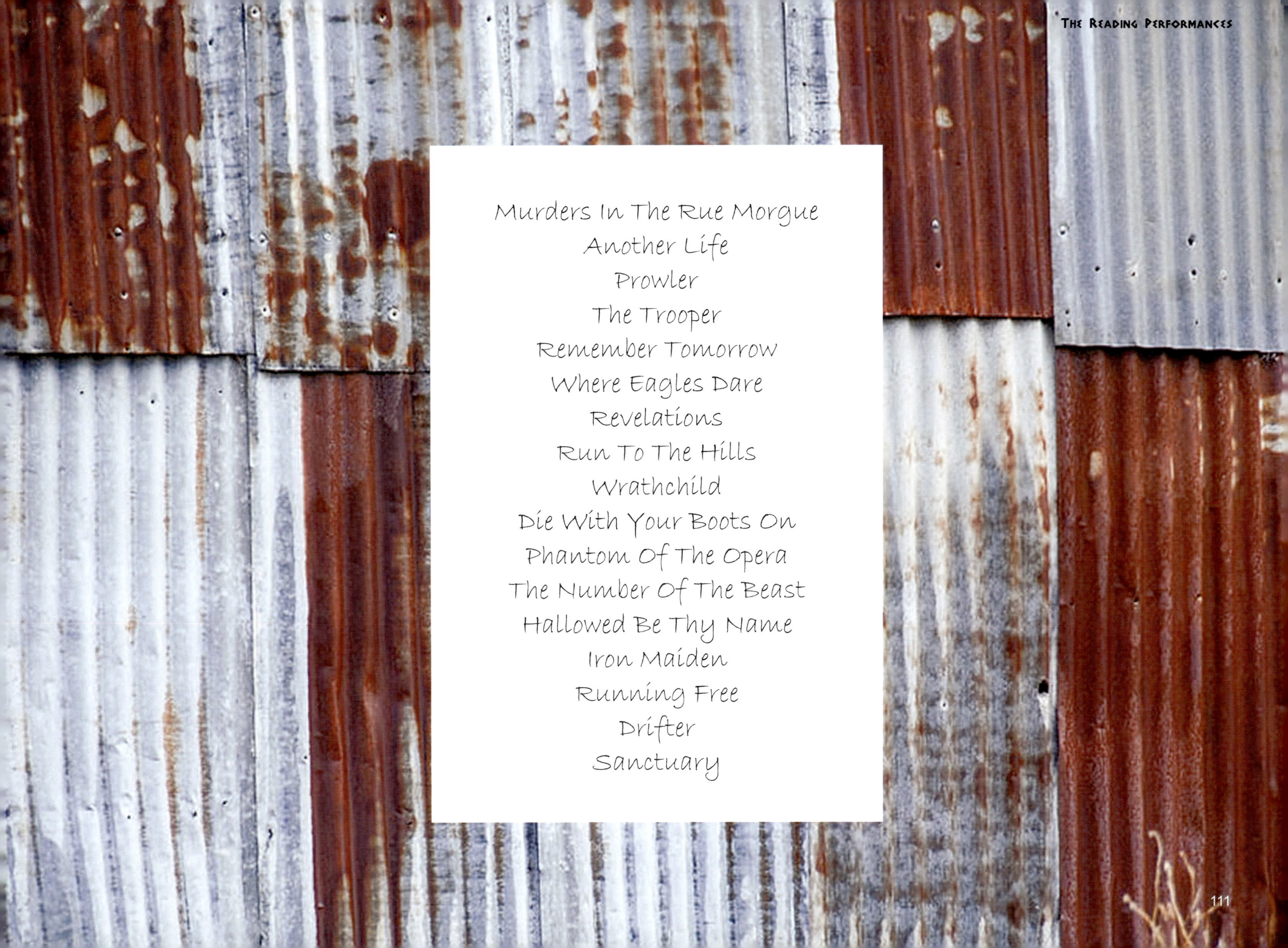
Murders In The Rue Morgue
Another Life
Prowler
The Trooper
Remember Tomorrow
Where Eagles Dare
Revelations
Run To The Hills
Wrathchild
Die With Your Boots On
Phantom Of The Opera
The Number Of The Beast
Hallowed Be Thy Name
Iron Maiden
Running Free
Drifter
Sanctuary

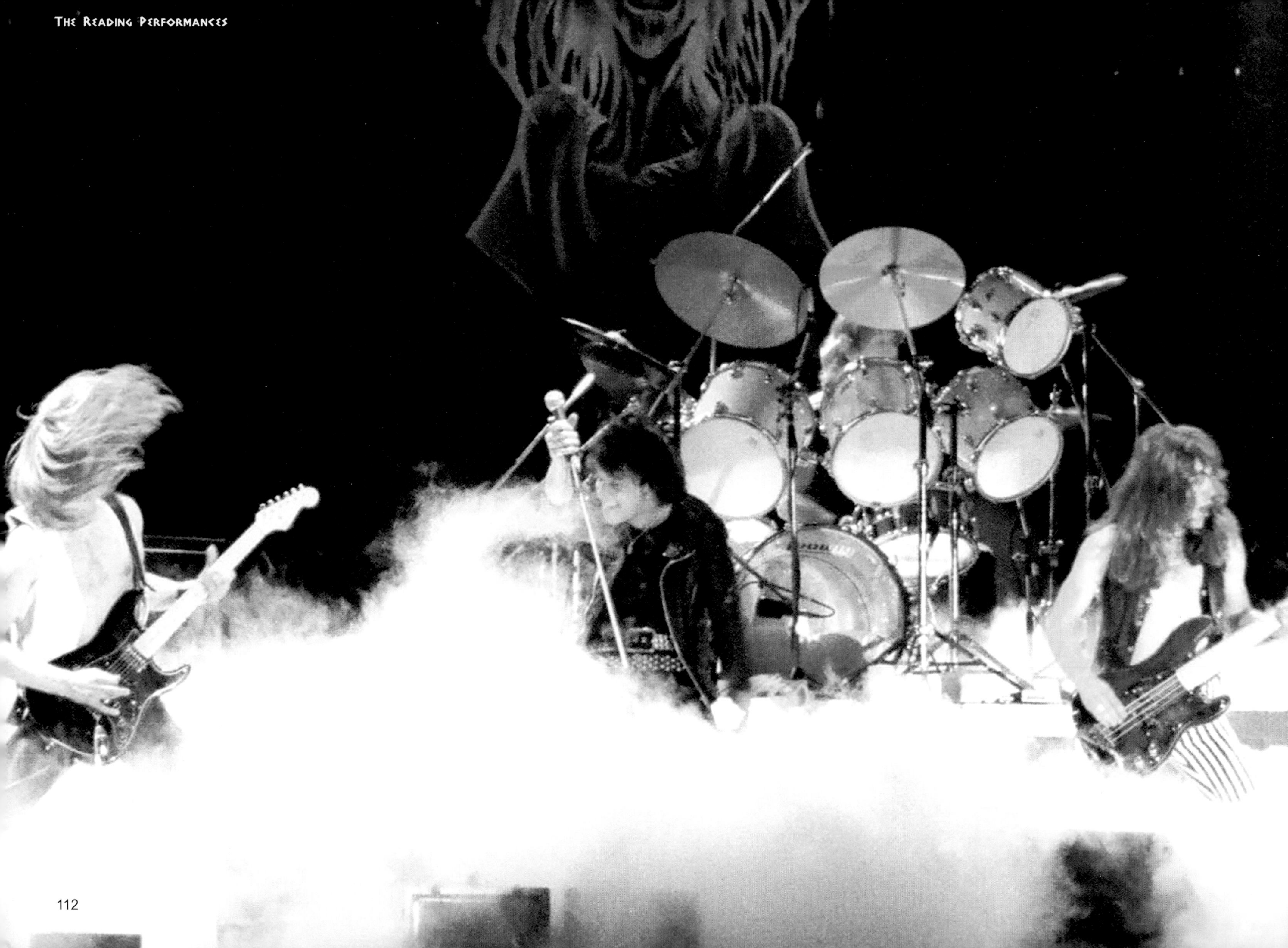

Somewhere In Time

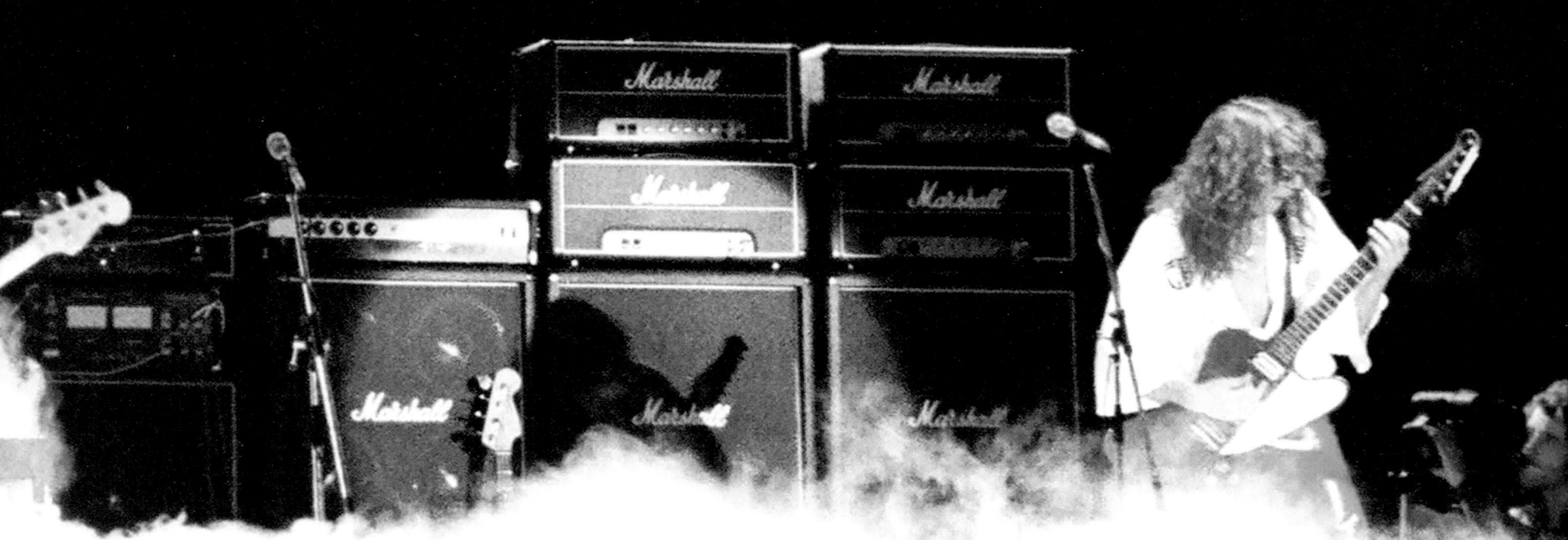

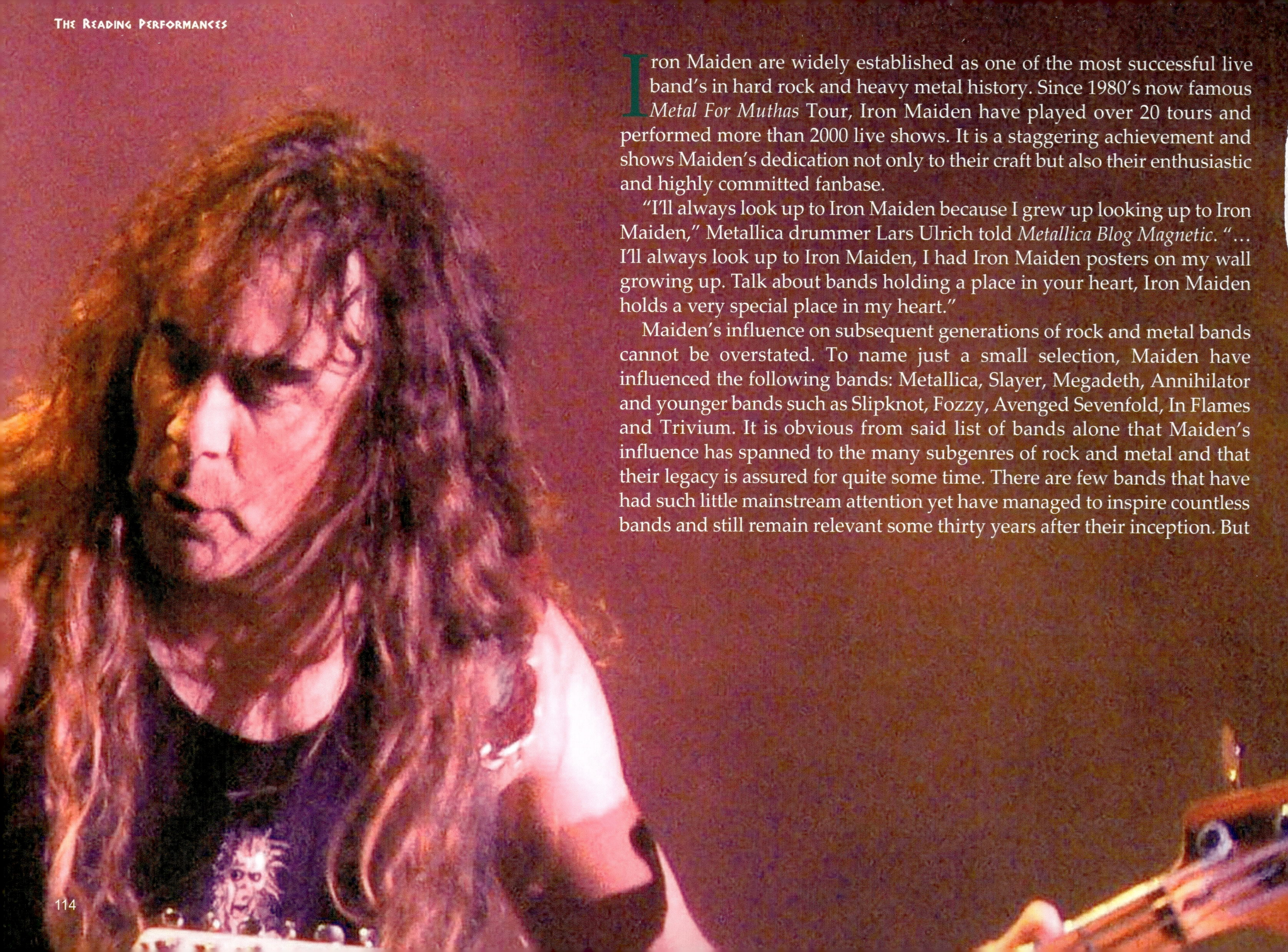

Iron Maiden are widely established as one of the most successful live band's in hard rock and heavy metal history. Since 1980's now famous *Metal For Muthas* Tour, Iron Maiden have played over 20 tours and performed more than 2000 live shows. It is a staggering achievement and shows Maiden's dedication not only to their craft but also their enthusiastic and highly committed fanbase.

"I'll always look up to Iron Maiden because I grew up looking up to Iron Maiden," Metallica drummer Lars Ulrich told *Metallica Blog Magnetic*. "… I'll always look up to Iron Maiden, I had Iron Maiden posters on my wall growing up. Talk about bands holding a place in your heart, Iron Maiden holds a very special place in my heart."

Maiden's influence on subsequent generations of rock and metal bands cannot be overstated. To name just a small selection, Maiden have influenced the following bands: Metallica, Slayer, Megadeth, Annihilator and younger bands such as Slipknot, Fozzy, Avenged Sevenfold, In Flames and Trivium. It is obvious from said list of bands alone that Maiden's influence has spanned to the many subgenres of rock and metal and that their legacy is assured for quite some time. There are few bands that have had such little mainstream attention yet have managed to inspire countless bands and still remain relevant some thirty years after their inception. But

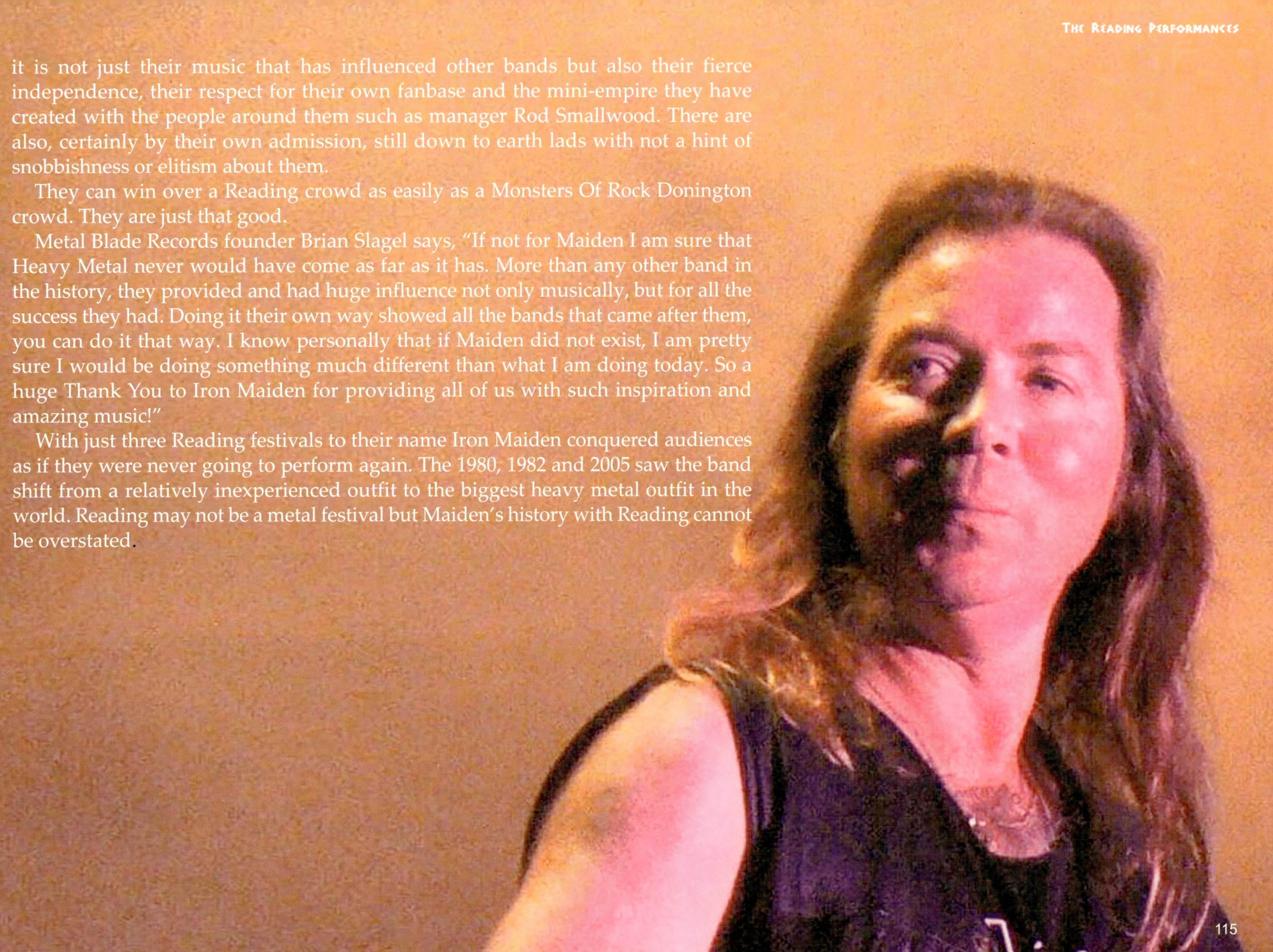

it is not just their music that has influenced other bands but also their fierce independence, their respect for their own fanbase and the mini-empire they have created with the people around them such as manager Rod Smallwood. There are also, certainly by their own admission, still down to earth lads with not a hint of snobbishness or elitism about them.

They can win over a Reading crowd as easily as a Monsters Of Rock Donington crowd. They are just that good.

Metal Blade Records founder Brian Slagel says, "If not for Maiden I am sure that Heavy Metal never would have come as far as it has. More than any other band in the history, they provided and had huge influence not only musically, but for all the success they had. Doing it their own way showed all the bands that came after them, you can do it that way. I know personally that if Maiden did not exist, I am pretty sure I would be doing something much different than what I am doing today. So a huge Thank You to Iron Maiden for providing all of us with such inspiration and amazing music!"

With just three Reading festivals to their name Iron Maiden conquered audiences as if they were never going to perform again. The 1980, 1982 and 2005 saw the band shift from a relatively inexperienced outfit to the biggest heavy metal outfit in the world. Reading may not be a metal festival but Maiden's history with Reading cannot be overstated.

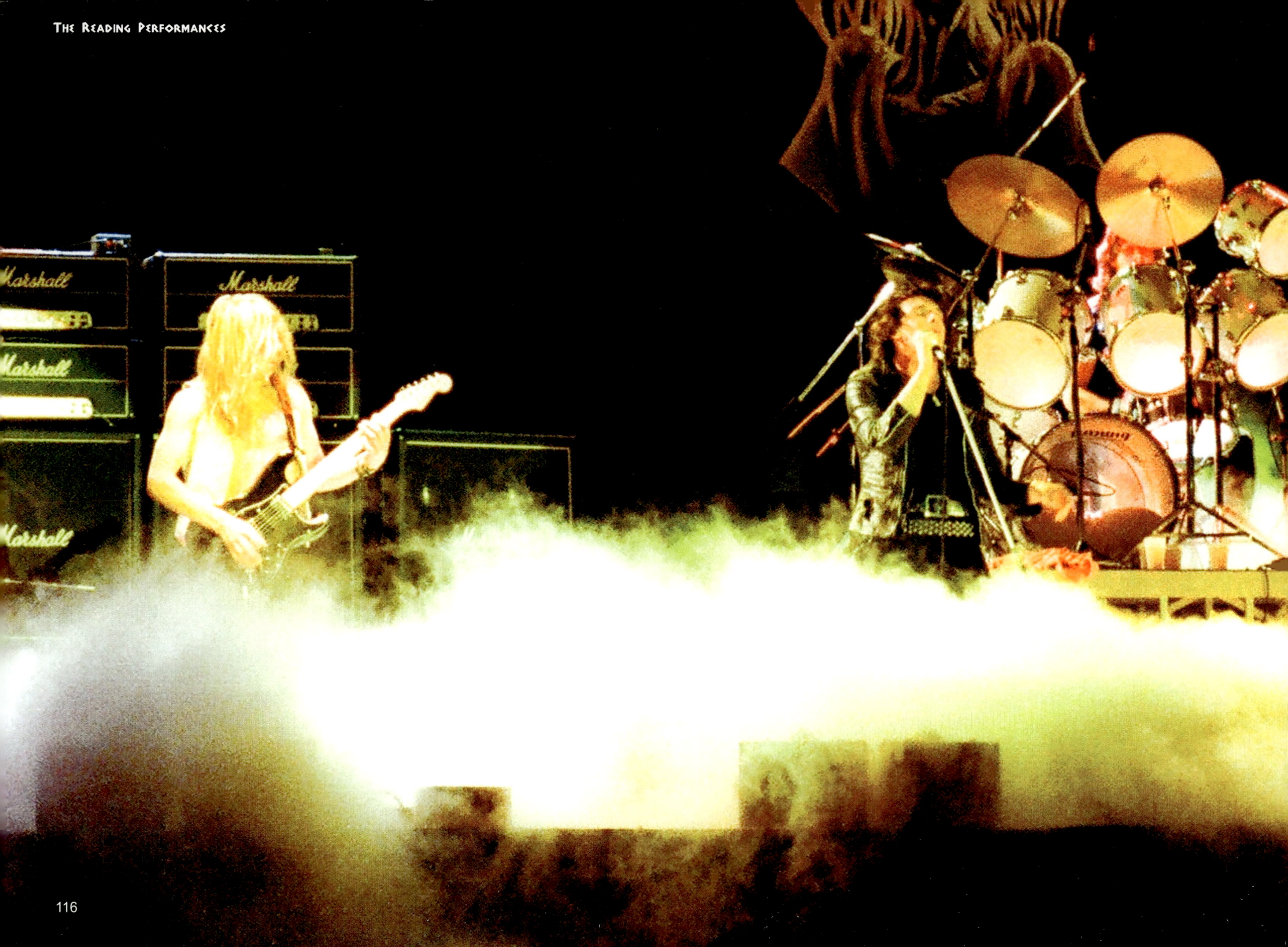

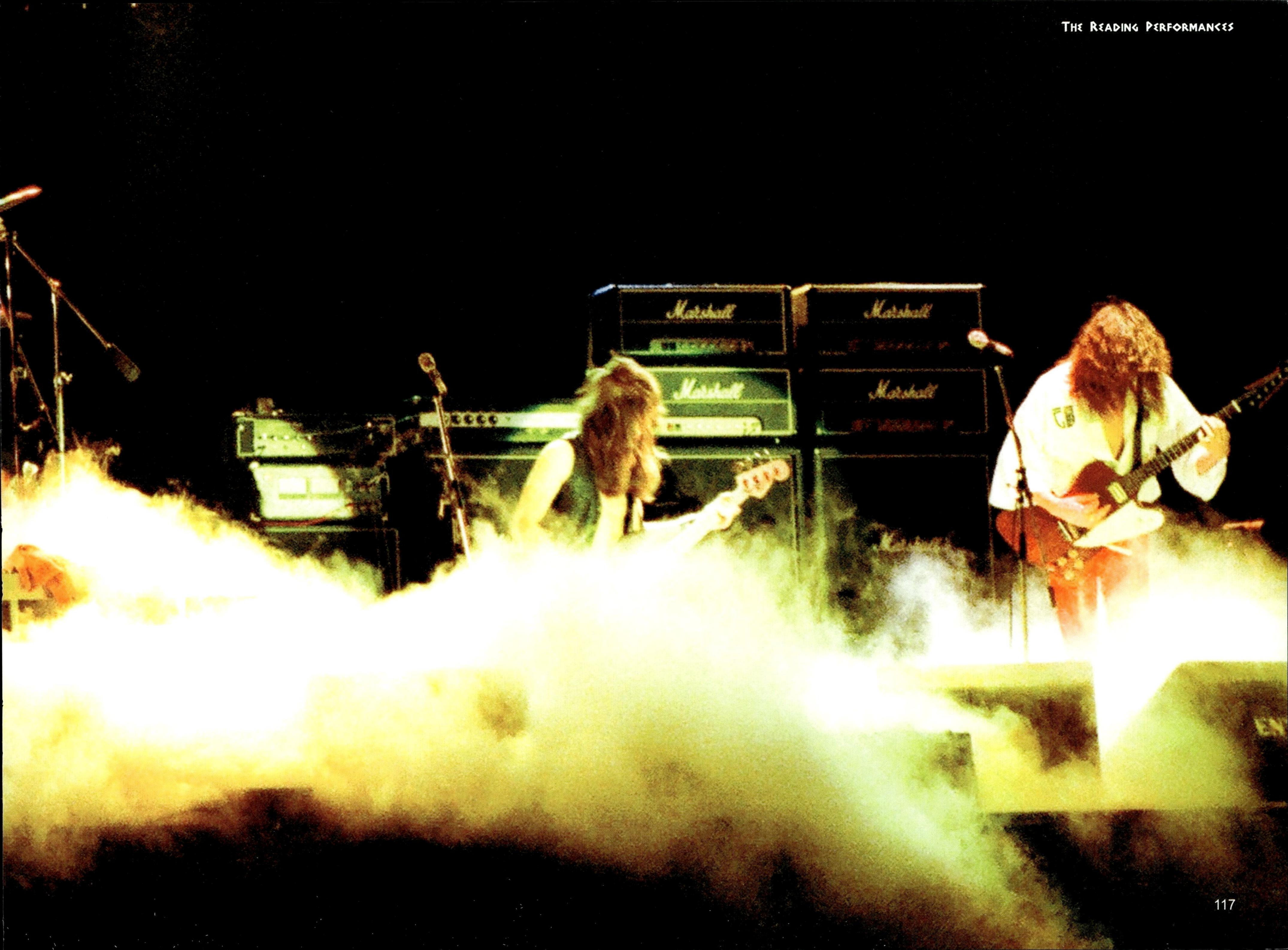
Marshall
Marshall
Marshall
Marshall

THE MEN OF MAIDEN

The nine men of Maiden who performed at the three Reading Festivals, spanning twenty-five years.

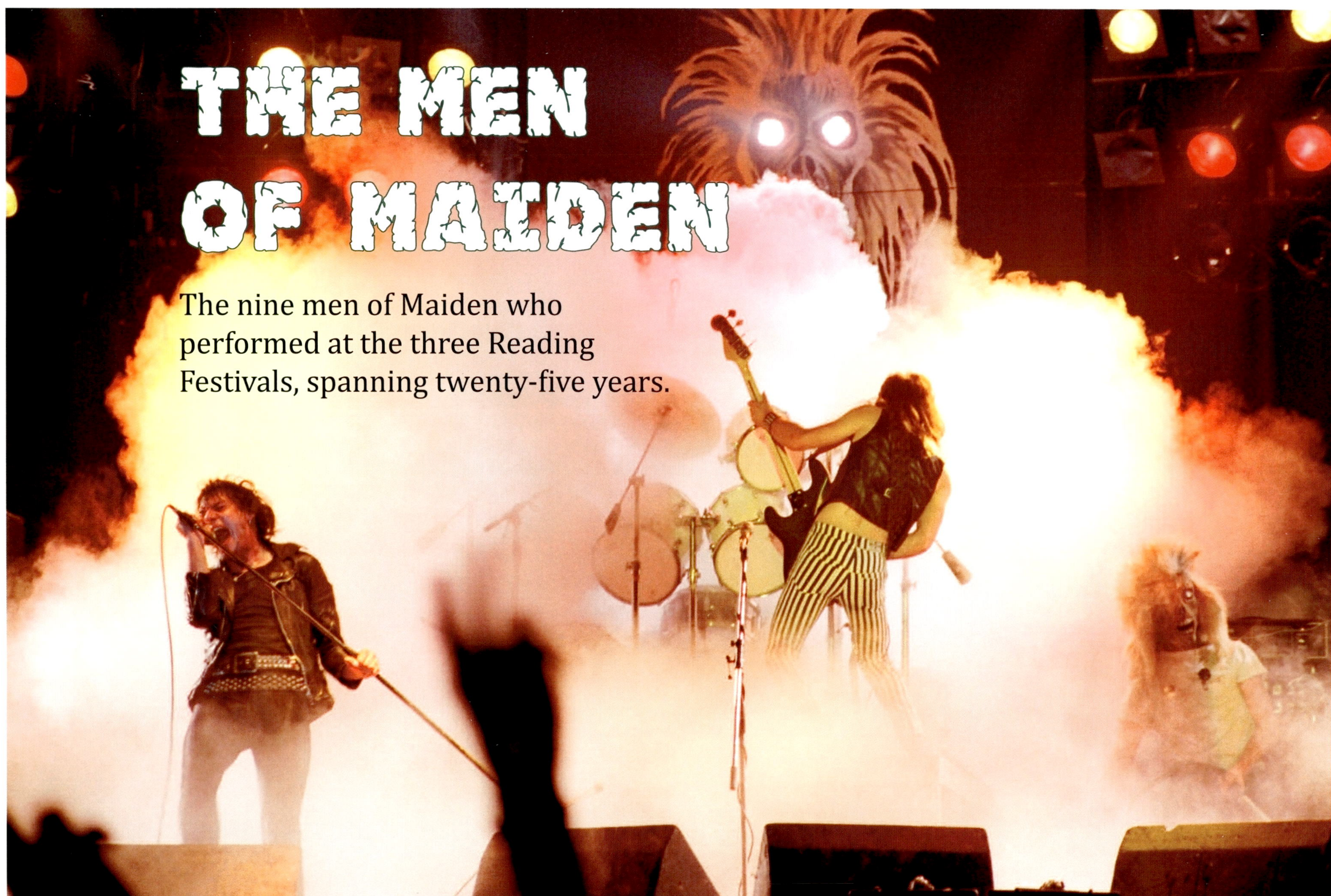

Steve Harris

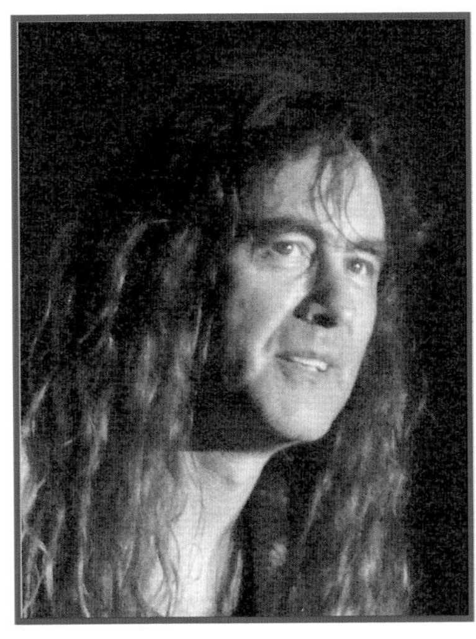

Indisputably Steve Harris is Iron Maiden. Born in Leytonstone, East London on 12 March 1956 Steve formed the band in 1975 and has been the only constant member since Maiden's inception. Along with guitarist Dave Murray he is the only one to have appeared on all of their albums.

As a result of Maiden's phenomenal success as the main songwriter Harris is a very wealthy man: A giant leap forward from the days before Iron Maiden signed their contract with EMI, when he worked as an architectural draughtsman before being made redundant and then took a job as a road sweeper.

As we know Steve has a passion for football and had aspirations to become a professional. When he was younger he was asked to train with his beloved West Ham United. Whether or not he would have made it is anybody's guess but within the world of rock music he is arguably the most talented footballer! A Maiden 11 have played against other rock teams and when they played against a Deep Purple 11 in 1993 fellow avid footballer Ritchie Blackmore had to confess that Harris was the man of the match as his team won comfortably! He also played at West Ham's then ground, Upton Park in 2012 in a charity match alongside ex-players and other celebrities.

Steve released his debut solo album, *British Lion* on 24 September 2012.

Dave Murray

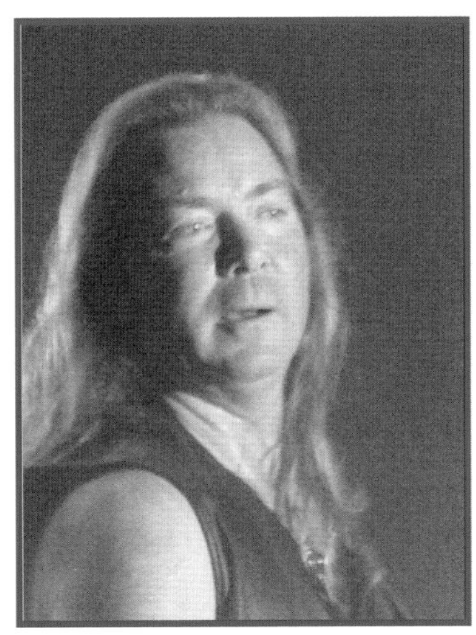

Born 23 December 1956, Dave came to the Maiden party the year after Steve formed it. Despite a brief period where he was sacked following an altercation with then vocalist Dennis Wilcock—he returned six months later and has been a mainstay ever since.

Aged 15, it was hearing Jimi Hendrix's 'Voodoo Chile' that took him away from his then unsavoury existence in a skinhead gang and from that moment on it was full steam ahead with rock music.

At 16 Dave formed his first band, Stone Free, which also included Adrian Smith on vocals. From there, Murray would answer ads in *Melody Maker* and regularly audition for different bands at the weekend, leading to short stints in Electric Gas, an American soft-rock style band and to the other extreme with a crazy punk rock band The Secret.

Like Steve, in the early days he had a full-time job (working as a store keeper for Hackney Council) before the EMI contract was signed. Although he has contributed to the song writing he is less prolific than other band members. To date the only song he is solely credited for is 'Charlotte the Harlot' from the debut album.

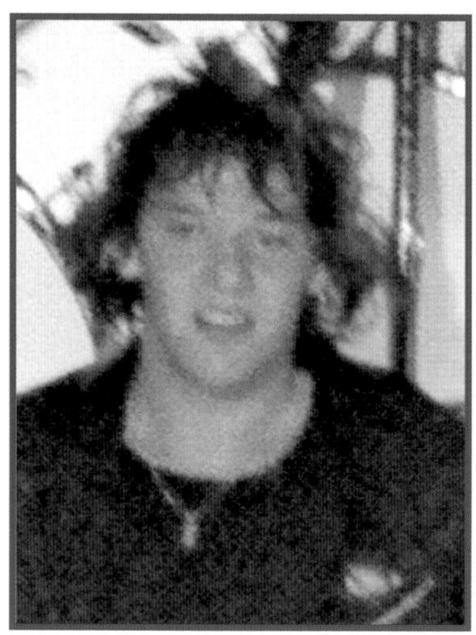

Paul Di'Anno

Following the departure of Dennis Wilcock, Maiden spent much of 1978 rehearsing while searching for a new vocalist. Having being tipped off by drummer friend Doug Sampson about Paul Di'Anno's talent he auditioned in November 1978 and was immediately hired.

Born Paul Andrews on 17 May 1958 he adopted the surname Di'Anno very early in his career.

Many fans who first got into the band during Di'Anno's tenure still have a soft spot for that period and of course his mark is there on the first two studio albums; live releases and compilations. Most notably *BBC Archives* that includes the 1980 Reading performance.

After his departure in 1981 his career has had its ups and downs. He has issued numerous albums over the years, as both a solo artist and as a member of such bands as Gogmagog, Di'Anno's Battlezone and Praying Mantis. Many years were spent with the US-UK band Killers before relocating to Brazil where he teamed up with Brazilian musicians in RockFellas.

However a serious fall from grace occurred in 2011 when he was gaoled for eight counts of benefit fraud. He was released two months into his nine-month sentence. Since then he has made an album with Architects of Chaoz called *The League of Shadows*. In May 2016, he was hospitalised for undisclosed medical issues and was forced to cancel his previously announced June 2016 tour of Brazil. On 29 October 2017 he appeared on stage in a wheelchair with tribute act The Iron Maidens for their encore at the O2 Academy in Islington, London.

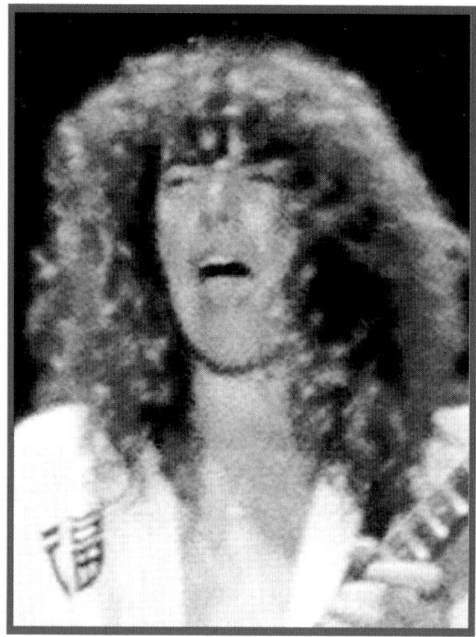

Dennis Stratton

Stratton, like Steve Harris, was a promising schoolboy footballer. He was also briefly on the books at West Ham United until the guitar and rock music took preference. Born 9 October 1952 in Canning Town, East London, he had been in several bands before he joined Maiden. Having formed the band Remus Down Boulevard in 1975 they gained experience playing outside the pub circuit, playing to large crowds, touring in support with Rory Gallagher and Status Quo and recording a *Live at the Marquee* album with producer Jonathan King.

It was as a member of Remus Down Boulevard that he was brought to the attention of Steve Harris and duly invited to join Maiden.

After his departure from Iron Maiden, Stratton played with bands such as Lionheart and after a NWOBHM tour with them in 1990 joined Praying Mantis. Over the next sixteen years with Praying Mantis he recorded nine studio albums and two live ones. Stratton officially left Praying Mantis in 2006, although his final recorded material with them was in 2003. During that period he also had a project with Paul Di'Anno called The Original Iron Men in which both of them sang. They released three albums.

Stratton can still be seen playing in pubs around East London and Essex. Stratton also performs in a reformed Remus Down Boulevard and often tours Europe with various bands playing classic-era Iron Maiden songs.

Clive Burr

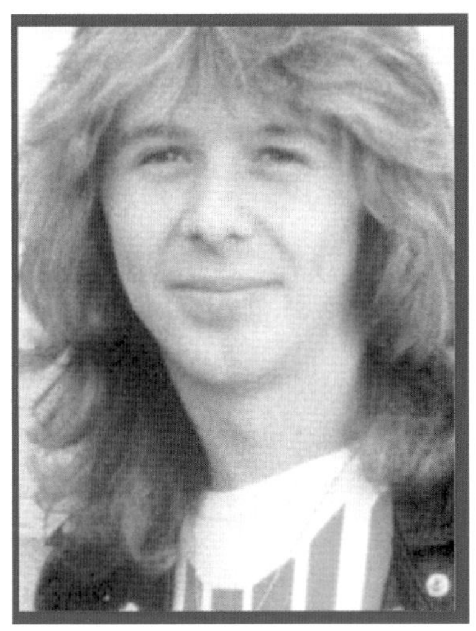

Previously a member of Samson, Burr replaced previous drummer Doug Sampson on 26 December 1979 at the suggestion of Dennis Stratton. Born 8 March 1957 he was eventually fired from the band following their North American tour in 1982, having played on their first three records: *Iron Maiden*, *Killers* and the breakthrough release *The Number of the Beast*.

After "leaving" Iron Maiden, Burr briefly played in the French group Trust and briefly with the American band Alcatrazz. He featured in the short-lived NWOBHM supergroup Gogmagog which also included ex-Iron Maiden vocalist Paul Di'Anno and future Maiden guitarist Janick Gers and ex-Def Leppard guitarist Pete Willis. He also had a band known as Clive Burr's Escape (later known as Stratus), featuring former Praying Mantis members, which disbanded after releasing one album. Burr then joined Dee Snider in his post-Twisted Sister outfit Desperado, which was never fully realized due to a falling out with the band's record company. Burr performed with British bands Elixir and Praying Mantis in the 1990s, but did not become a member of either.

He was diagnosed with multiple sclerosis and used a wheelchair because of his condition. The treatment left him deeply in debt. Iron Maiden staged a series of charity concerts and were involved in the founding of the Clive Burr MS Trust Fund. He was also the patron of Clive Aid, a charity formed in 2004. Clive Aid has continued to raise awareness and funds for various cancer and multiple sclerosis programs around the world through the staging of rock events. He passed away on 12 March 2013.

Adrian Smith

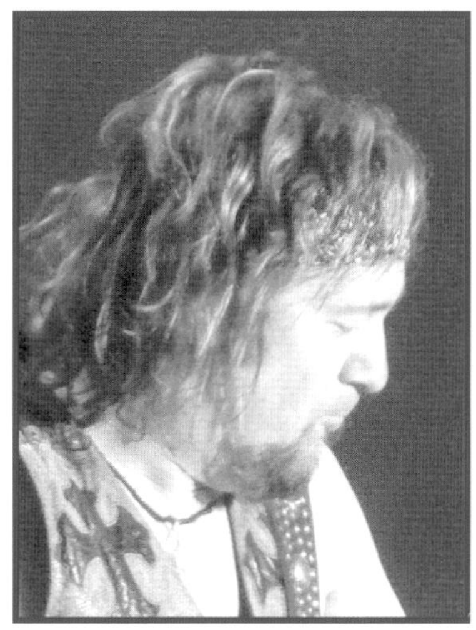

Born 27 February 1957 Adrian, a childhood friend of Dave Murray he was initially invited to join Maiden in 1979 when the band were on the verge of signing with EMI but turned them down to continue with his own band, Urchin. A year later, Urchin split up and Adrian joined Iron Maiden in November 1980.

Adrian agreed to leave Iron Maiden in 1990 as he did not approve of the band's direction at the time. After a nine year absence, during which he formed his own band, Psycho Motel and joined Bruce Dickinson's solo outfit, he rejoined Maiden in 1999.

He has a side project called Primal Rock Rebellion. He is a keen angler, and apparently used to take worms and maggots on tour. Adrian was featured on the front cover of *Angler's Mail* on 25 August 2009.

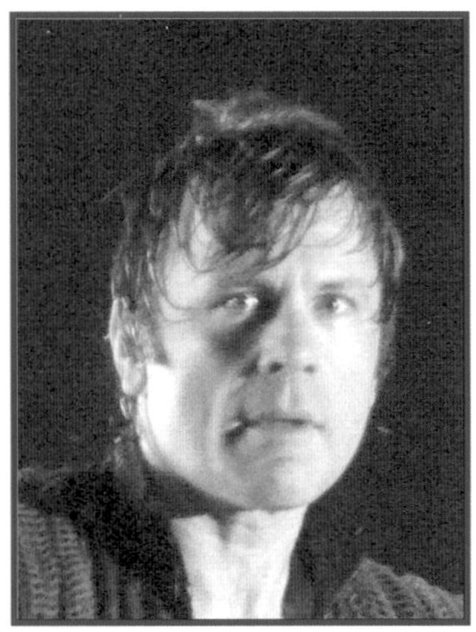

Bruce Dickinson

Although most band members past and present hail from London, Paul Bruce Dickinson was born in Worksop, Nottinghamshire, 7 August 1958.

Bruce received a good education and left school with Advanced Levels in English, History and Economics. He initially joined the Territorial Army for six months, then he applied for a place to read history at Queen Mary College, London. University gave him the opportunity to get involved in the college music scene and he began fronting small pub bands. In 1979, he got his first break when he joined Samson and performed on two studio records.

Having admired Maiden it was a dream come true when he was asked to join in 1981. To the surprise of fans, in 1993, after much deliberation, Bruce decided to leave and focus on a solo career. After six years, and four albums Rod Smallwood convinced him to rejoin in January 1999 and the rest as they say, is history.

Bruce is a man of many talents. Internationally adept at sword fencing he is also a commercial airline pilot, entrepreneur, author and broadcaster. Having grown up as a massive fan of Deep Purple he got the chance to perform with Jon Lord on the keyboard player's studio recording of his *Concerto For Group & Orchestra*. After Lord's death, Bruce also performed at the Jon Lord Tribute concert at the Royal Albert Hall alongside former Purple man Glenn Hughes as well as with Purple on the grand finale. Since his return to Maiden, he has issued one further solo record in 2005, *Tyranny of Souls*.

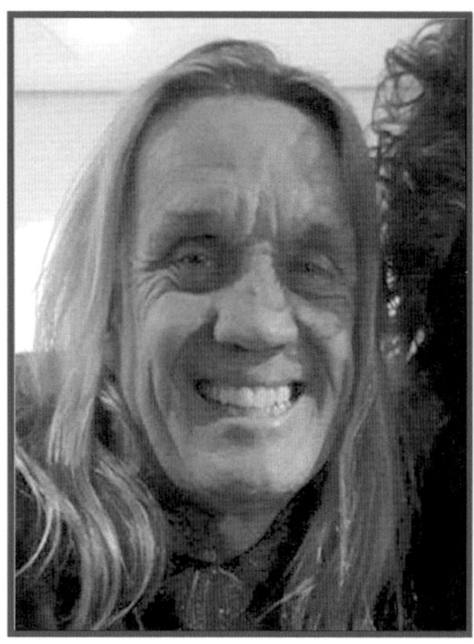

Nicko McBrain

After the departure of Clive Burr, Nicko was immediately invited to join the group and has been the drum stalwart ever since.

Born in Hackney, London, 5 June 1952, Michael Henry "Nicko" McBrain had plenty of experience before joining the Maiden crew. Having played in small pub bands from the age of 14, he was paying for his won keep with session work before he joined a variety of artists, such as Streetwalkers, Pat Travers, and the French band, Trust.

From an early age he was known as "Nicky", a nickname given to him by his parents after his teddy bear, Nicholas. So the story goes, an intoxicated musician friend Billy Day introduced him to CBS Records head Dick Asher as "Neeko". He liked the name but wrote it as Nicko so that it sounded more English.

When he replaced Clive Burr because Burr's departure had not been announced he made his first appearance on German TV disguised as Eddie.

Janick Gers

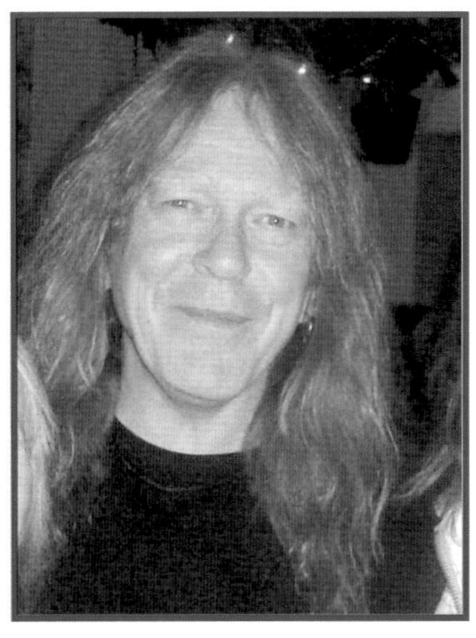

Like Bruce Dickinson, Janick is not a Londoner, but hails from the North East where he still resides. He was born 27 January 1957 in Hartlepool. His first major band was White Spirit. They achieved moderate success and were often support act to larger bands. One of which was Gillan, fronted by the then former Deep Purple vocalist Ian Gillan. This bought Janick to their attention and when in the middle of the tour guitarist Bernie Tormé quit, Janick took over just three days later!

After making two albums with the band, Ian Gillan disbanded it and they guys found themselves instantly unemployed. Janick initially undertook a Humanities degree before joining Gogmagog, alongside Paul Di'Anno and Clive Burr. The project came to nothing and he went on to work with Marillion vocalist Fish before being asked to record a song called 'Bring Your Daughter... to the Slaughter' with Iron Maiden vocalist Bruce Dickinson for the soundtrack to *A Nightmare on Elm Street 5: The Dream Child*. The project expanded into the album *Tattooed Millionaire* and during its recording Janick was asked to join Maiden in place of the departing Adrian Smith.

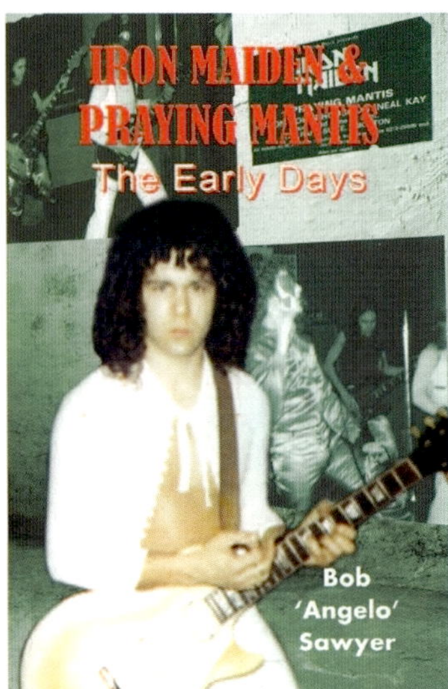

Also from Wymer Publishing

The Early Days: Iron Maiden and Praying Mantis
by Bob 'Angelo' Sawyer

ISBN: 978-1-908724-84-7

Publication date: 19th October 2018

The uncharted depths of the early years of Iron Maiden and Praying Mantis
through the memories of one-time Maiden guitarist Bob Sawyer.
Bob's own diaries and archives have enabled him to recall in great detail
some of the early part of the careers of both these bands of which he was a part of. Included is:

·   Beginnings — Starting out and other encounters

·   Pre-Maiden — Bands leading up to Maiden

·   Maiden — My time in Maiden including gig recollections

·   On the road with Praying Mantis — covering 'The Metal for Muthas' tour and other gigs

·   The 'Major Offensive' — Mantis supporting Maiden on the first headline tour — all gigs described day by day

·   The Aftermath...

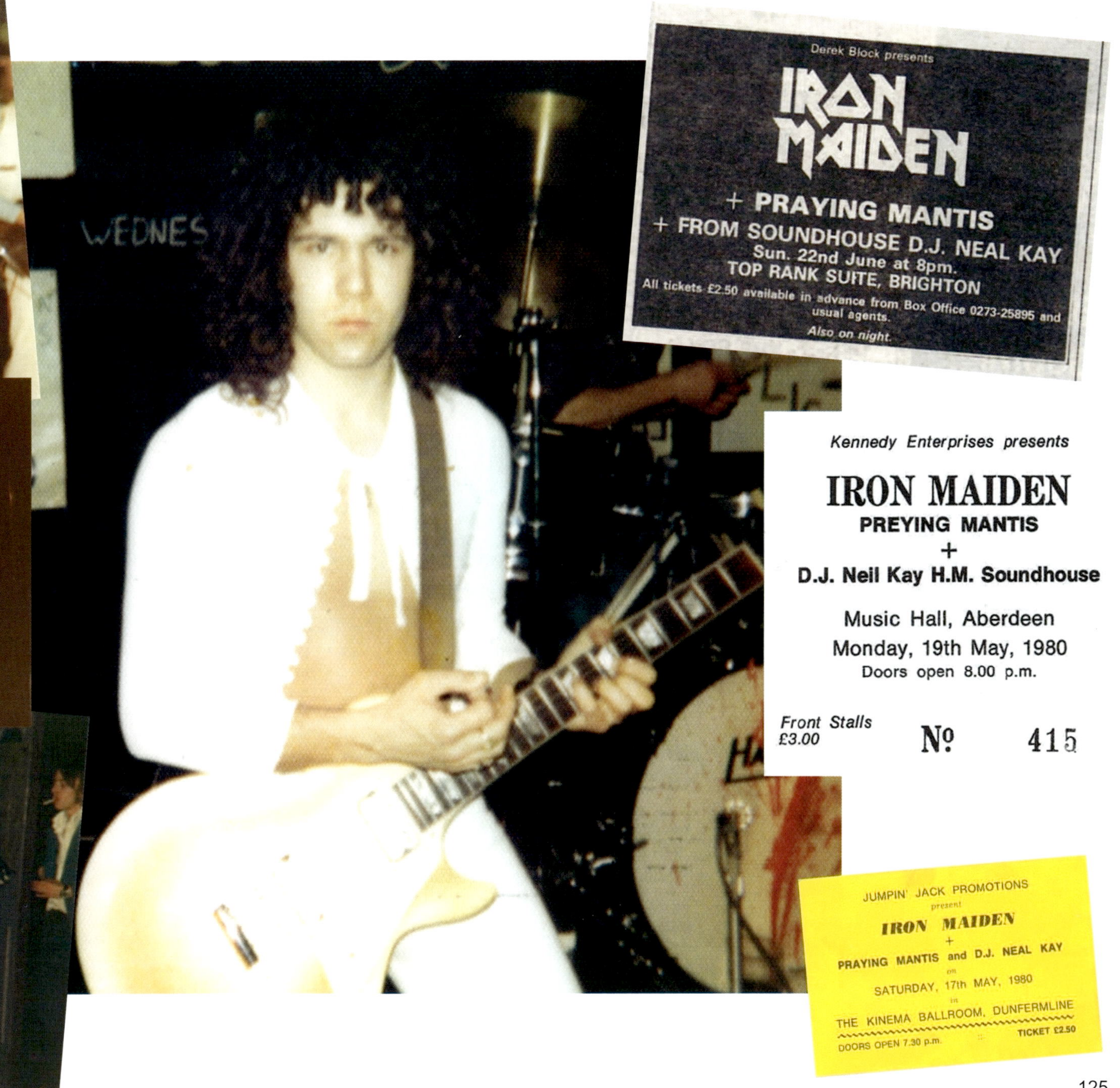
WEDNES
Derek Block presents
IRON MAIDEN
+ PRAYING MANTIS
+ FROM SOUNDHOUSE D.J. NEAL KAY
Sun. 22nd June at 8pm.
TOP RANK SUITE, BRIGHTON
All tickets £2.50 available in advance from Box Office 0273-25895 and usual agents.
Also on night.
Kennedy Enterprises presents
IRON MAIDEN
PREYING MANTIS
+
D.J. Neil Kay H.M. Soundhouse
Music Hall, Aberdeen
Monday, 19th May, 1980
Doors open 8.00 p.m.
Front Stalls
£3.00
Nº 415
JUMPIN' JACK PROMOTIONS
present
IRON MAIDEN
+
PRAYING MANTIS and D.J. NEAL KAY
on
SATURDAY, 17th MAY, 1980
in
THE KINEMA BALLROOM, DUNFERMLINE
DOORS OPEN 7.30 p.m.
TICKET £2.50

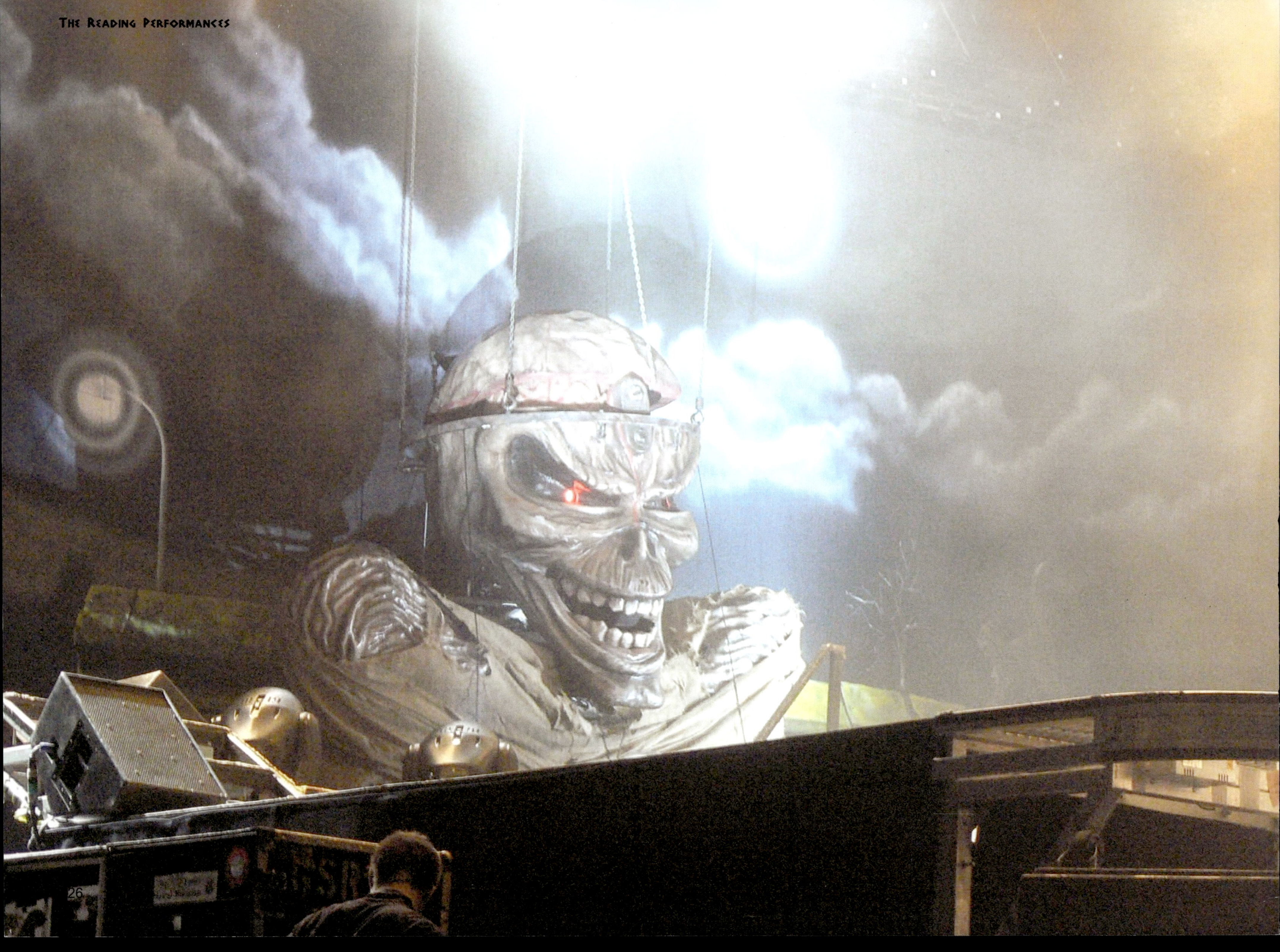

CREDITS

Rev Barker at www.ukrockfestivals.com, Dave Ling, Nicola Lock at Mixam and Rene Nethitt.

Book design and layout by The Andys.

All the live photos of Iron Maiden (and Samson 1980) from the three Reading shows have been licensed from the copyright holder Alan Perry and must not be reproduced without prior permission.
All other photos courtesy of Trinity Mirror and www.ukrockfestivals.com.